MicroSim

PSpice

for Windows

2nd Edition

Volume I
DC, AC, and Devices and Circuits

A Circuit Simulation Primer

Roy W. Goody

Mission College, Santa Clara, CA

Prentice Hall

Upper Saddle River, New Jersey   **Columbus, Ohio**

Library of Congress Cataloging-in-Publication Data

Goody, Roy W.

      MicroSim PSpice for Windows / Roy W. Goody. — 2nd ed.
           p.   cm.
      Previous ed. published under title: PSpice for Windows.
      Includes index.
      Contents: v. 1. A circuit simulation primer
      ISBN 0-13-655796-1
      1. PSpice for Windows. 2. Electric circuits—Computer simulation.
   3. Electronic circuits—computer simulation. I. Goody, Roy W.
   PSpice for Windows. II. Title
   TK454.G66 1998   97-7764
   621.3815'01'135369—dc21   CIP

Cover photo: M. Angelo, Westlight
Editor: Linda Ludewig
Production Editor: Christine M. Harrington
Design Coordinator: Karrie M. Converse
Cover Designer: Rod Harris
Production Manager: Laura Messerly
Marketing Manager: Debbie Yarnell

This book was printed and bound by Courier/Kendallville, Inc. The cover was printed by Phoenix Color Corp.

 © 1998 by Prentice-Hall, Inc.
Simon & Schuster/A Viacom Company
Upper Saddle River, New Jersey 07458

Earlier edition entitled *PSpice for Windows: A Circuit Simulation Primer,* © 1995 by Prentice-Hall, Inc.

Printed in the United States of America

10 9 8 7 6 5 4 3

ISBN: 0-13-655796-1

Prentice-Hall International (UK) Limited, *London*
Prentice-Hall of Australia Pty. Limited, *Sydney*
Prentice-Hall of Canada, Inc., *Toronto*
Prentice-Hall Hispanoamericana, S. A., *Mexico*
Prentice-Hall of India Private Limited, *New Delhi*
Prentice-Hall of Japan, Inc., *Tokyo*
Simon & Schuster Asia Pte. Ltd., *Singapore*
Editora Prentice-Hall do Brasil, Ltda., *Rio de Janeiro*

Contents

PSpice for Windows

Part IV — The Field-Effect Transistor

Part V — Special Solid-State Studies

Part VI — Special Processes

Part VII — Analog Communications

Appendices

Index

Preface

*The only way to predict the future
is to have power to shape the future.*

ERIC HOFFER

With this second edition, we know the shape of the future more clearly and more brightly then ever before. When the new millennium dawns in just a few short seasons, the power of *simulation* will transform the way we design our products, acquire needed skills, and entertain our minds. Some of the first to be transformed are the design, development, testing, and troubleshooting of electronic circuits.

This text is designed to ease your way into this amazing new world.

OVERVIEW

If you are a technician, technology, or engineering student or employee, and are looking for a comprehensive introductory text on circuit simulation based on the most popular software currently available, then this text—*PSpice for Windows*—was designed with you in mind.

PSpice for Windows is offered in two volumes. This text, Volume I, emphasizes Devices & Circuits, but begins with an introduction to DC/AC. Volume II continues our studies into operational amplifiers, and digital and advanced filter design, and assumes that the basic PSpice techniques of volume I have been mastered.

The major features of *PSpice for Windows* are as follows:

- It is based on the popular PSpice software from MicroSim Corporation.

- It will operate on any computer that runs Windows 95, 3.1, or NT and has 8M or more of extended memory.

PSpice for Windows

- It combines both circuit simulation and electronic theory.

- Most of the experimental activities can be done "hands-on" using conventional equipment, as well as PSpice.

- It is designed to supplement or replace a laboratory or theory text in a conventional devices and circuits course.

- It is comprehensive, covering nearly every available feature of PSpice.

- It requires no previous knowledge of circuit simulation or devices and circuits theory.

- It is aimed at the technology student, but it is entirely appropriate for technicians or engineers.

THE SECOND EDITION

In format and content, this second edition is very similar to the first. Although new chapters have been added and improvements have been made in content, graphics, and layout, its major difference lies in the use of PSpice version 7.1. If you are presently using the first edition, you will find it very easy to adjust to the changes.

In fact, the timely release of new editions based on updated versions of PSpice is a major feature of this text series. Because all text and graphics is done on the computer, manuscripts are submitted to the publisher in camera-ready format—greatly reducing publication costs and allowing a faster-than-normal edition update.

Therefore, the promise and commitment of the author and publisher is to assure you the continuous availability of a state-of-the-art PSpice experience.

MICROSIM *DESIGNLAB*

PSpice version 7.1 (known as *DesignLab*) represents a major step forward in circuit design. DesignLab provides a fully integrated environment to *capture* analog/digital and gate array circuits directly on the monitor, *simulate* the circuit action, *analyze* the results in graphical form, and prepare the design for PC board development—everything from start to finish!

It is incredibly powerful, easy to learn, and simple to use. Quite simply, the *DesignLab* software package is one of the best learning tools to come along in many years.

PSpice for Windows

THE EVALUATION VERSION

Fortunately, for those of us in education, MicroSim Corporation has made *evaluation* software available at no cost—with copying of the software "welcome and encouraged.". Evaluation version 7.1 on CD-ROM comes with the *Instructor's Guide* to this text. The evaluation software is also available directly from MicroSim or from their web site—from which floppy disks can be created.

Newer versions of the PSpice software are constantly being released and the chances are good that they will work with this manual. In general, you should use the latest version that is available; if any adjustments are necessary, they should be minor. *However, to be perfectly safe, you may wish to stay with version 7.1 until the next edition of PSpice for Windows is released.*

All the activities in this book are based on the evaluation version. Its only major limitation is the number of symbols and components that can be placed on the schematic, and that all circuits must fit on a single schematic page. Fortunately, we can adjust easily to these limitations, and for the most part they will be completely invisible. For those who may wish to go beyond the evaluation version, MicroSim Corporation also gives very generous academic discounts on their full-fledged software packages.

SYSTEM REQUIREMENTS

- PSpice version 7.1 (used with this second edition) requires 8Mb of RAM (16Mb recommended), a 486 or Pentium computer, and Windows 3.1, 95, or NT, and it is most easily installed via CD-ROM (but can be installed from MicroSim's website, or by way of floppy disks created from the website). Version 7.1 is the last release that will support Windows 3.1.

- Version 6.0 (used by the first edition) requires only 4MEG of RAM, can be run easily on a 386 computer, can be used with Windows 3.1 (but <u>not</u> Windows 95), and is contained on only 3 floppy disks.

If the equipment required for version 7.1 presents a problem, you may wish to temporarily stay with the 6.0-based first edition.

HOW TO USE THE TEXT

The first nine chapters (Part I) cover simple DC/AC theory. Because the most basic PSpice techniques are presented in Part I, *all students should at least peruse the nine DC/AC chapters.*

The rest of the text (parts II through VII) covers topics commonly found in a Devices & Circuits course. Material from these sections can be more selectively chosen to match the emphasis of the class. The *special processes* of part VI can greatly enrich the class content because they offer advanced techniques that are not normally part of a hands-on laboratory experience.

A SUGGESTION

Although circuit simulation is the major design and development tool of the future, we recommend that the reader also receive hands-on experience by prototyping actual circuits and troubleshooting with conventional instruments.

One computer-saving approach is to divide a class into two or more groups and rotate between PSpice and hands-on techniques. It is especially instructive to perform the same activity using both PSpice and hands-on techniques, and to compare the two approaches. *In this regard, most of the experimental activities outlined in this text can be performed using either PSpice or hands-on techniques.*

Another suggestion is to perform the nine DC/AC chapters in the DC/AC classes. Then, upon entering the solid-state (devices and circuits) course, you have a running start into the solid-state chapters.

PREREQUISITES

Besides the ability to perform simple mathematical operations, the only prerequisite needed is a cursory knowledge of Windows 95 or 3.1. If you have no previous experience with Windows, we have found that a brief half-hour summary will provide sufficient background to begin the activities. A brief tutorial on Windows 3.1 and 95 is presented in Appendix E.

FURTHER STUDY

If you ordered the complete set of manuals that comes with *MicroSim DesignLab*, you would be confronted with more than one thousand pages of data, instructions, and reference material.

Clearly, all the information contained within those thousand pages can not appropriately be placed into this introductory text series. Instead, we have included only the most vital, important, and commonly-used features of PSpice. For a comprehensive description of all the features of PSpice, refer to the complete set of manuals from MicroSim. (They are also available on the evaluation CD-ROM from MicroSim.)

PSpice for Windows

CREDITS

A very special thanks to copy editor Marianne L'abbate for her profound knowledge of the English language, her ability to root out the most entrenched errors, and her willingness to make many useful suggestions concerning organization and substance.

I also wish to express my sincere gratitude to production editor Christine Harrington and administrative editor Linda Ludewig of Prentice Hall Publishing. Under their careful guidance, the project steadily moved forward and was released right on time.

Of course, MicroSim Corporation deserves special credit for making the evaluation disk available at no cost. Their foresight makes it possible for colleges and universities to teach circuit simulation at the professional level without breaking their ever-shrinking budgets.

Thank you for adopting *PSpice for Windows*; good luck and good success.

Roy W. Goody
Mission College

Introduction

Dreaming is an act of pure imagination
E. F. HEDGE

We all have awakened suddenly from a dream, only to be surprised that the images we experienced so clearly were not real at all—they were *simulated* within the brain. So perfect is the simulation under PSpice that you may occasionally find the need to "wake up" and be reminded that the circuits and components you are working with also do not actually exist.

Because all components exist only as mathematical abstractions, we can mold them into any configuration, perform any test, and display any results that our mathematics and dreams will allow us.

Without a doubt, the kind of dreaming we will do under PSpice will indeed be an act of pure imagination.

THE CIRCUIT ANALYSIS PROCESS

Under *The DesignLab* software package umbrella are three major interactive programs: *Schematics*, *PSpice*, and *Probe*.

To design, modify, or analyze a circuit, we call on these programs during a four-step process:

1. Draw the circuit under *Schematics*.

2. Select the mode of analysis, also under *Schematics*.

3. Simulate the circuit under *PSpice*.

4. Display the results under *Probe*.

THE PSPICE FILES

During the circuit simulation process, the PSpice software creates and accesses a number of files. Because an understanding of these files will enhance your appreciation of PSpice simulation, we describe these major files next.

Circuit Files

The first file created is the *Schematics file* (.sch), generated when a schematic circuit is saved. When the schematics file is analyzed, three new files are generated: the *circuit file* (.cir), the *netlist file* (.net), and the *alias file* (.als). The circuit file (the master file) contains the *simulation directives* and references to the *netlist, alias*, and *model* files. The netlist file contains a Kirchhoff-like set of equations that lists *parts* and how they are connected. The alias file provides a mapping between the Schematics part and pin names and the simulator device and node names, and the model file lists the characteristics of each component.

Library Files

Each *part* listed in the circuit (master) file has a *model* definition and a corresponding *symbol* definition. The model definition is found in the *model library file* (such as *diode.lib*), and is a set of ASCII parameters that determine the part's electrical behavior. The corresponding symbol definition is found in the *symbol library file* (such as *diode.slb*), and specifies the part's geometric shape on the *Schematics* screen. Most of the part definitions used in a circuit come from standard libraries (model and symbol) that are shipped with PSpice. However, if desired, the user can create custom part definitions.

Output and Data Files

When PSpice is run, each simulation directive in the circuit (master) file specifies the information to be sent to the *output* and *data* files. The output file (*.out*) is an ASCII file that holds the audit trail for the simulation and contains a wide variety of information, including the original netlist, all output variables, and various tables. The data file (*.dat*) is sent to *Probe*, which uses the binary information to generate plots and graphs within the probe window.

MOUSE CONVENTIONS

Under Windows, most commands can be entered using either the mouse or the keyboard. In this text, we concentrate on using the mouse, although keyboard action can occasionally speed up a process. We assume the use of a standard mouse with left and right buttons. (The center button, if there is one, is ignored.)

The mouse follows an *object-action* sequence. First, you select an object and then you perform an action.

- A single click left *selects an item.*

- A double click left *performs an action.*

Throughout this text, we will adopt the following convention:

- **CLICKL** or **BOLD PRINT** *(click left once)* to select an item.
- **DCLICKL** *(double click left)* to perform an action.
- **CLICKR** *(click right once)* to abort a mode.
- **DCLICKR** *(double click right)* to repeat an action.
- **CLICKLH** *(click left, hold down, and move mouse)* to drag a selected item. Release left button when placed.
- **DRAG** *(no clicks, move mouse)* to move an item.

GETTING STARTED

The evaluation version 7.1 on CD-ROM comes with the Instructor's Guide to this text. You may also contact MicroSim Corporation and ask for a copy, order a copy from MicroSim's website, or download the software from the website. The website will also allow you to make a floppy disk set.

MicroSim Corporation **20 Fairbanks** **Irvine, CA 92618**	
GENERAL:	**phone: (714) 770-3022** **fax: (714) 455-0554** **autofax: (714) 454-3296** **WWW: http://www.microsim.com** **FTP: ftp://ftp.microsim.com**
SALES:	**phone: (800) 245-3022** **E-mail: sales@microsim.com**
TECH SUPPORT:	**phone: (714) 837-0790** **E-mail:** **tech.support@microsim.com**

Be aware that the busy folks at MicroSim are constantly releasing new versions of PSpice, and chances are good that the new versions would work with this manual. However, to be perfectly safe, we recommend the use of version 7.1.

INSTALLING THE SOFTWARE

There are three methods of installing PSpice software: CD-ROM, download from website, using floppy disks (originally made from the website).

CD-ROM

Windows 95

1. Place CD ROM in drive.

2. Wait for the MicroSim *AutoPlay* screen to appear.

3. Follow the directions. (We recommend that you use all default selections.)

    If the AutoPlay function is not enabled:

1. Select Run from the Start Menu.

2. Enter D:\SETUP.EXE.

3. Follow the directions. (Use all default selections, and *Full* option.)

Windows NT

1. Place CD ROM in drive.

2. Select Run from the File menu of the Program Manager.

3. Enter D:\SETUP.EXE.

4. Follow the directions. (Use all default selections, and *Full* option.)

Windows 3.1

1. Place CD ROM in drive.

2. Enter the File Manager and **CLICKL** on drive D.

3. **DCLICKL** on SETUP.EXE.

4. Follow the directions. (Use all default selections, and *Full* option.)

DOWNLOAD FROM WEBSITE / CREATE FLOPPIES

1. Go to MicroSim's website: **http://www.microsim.com**

2. CLICKL on **Download**.

3. CLICKL on *Evaluation requirements, installation* to bring up the <u>About the MicroSim DesignLab Evaluation Version</u> page. Either print or make a copy of the <u>How to Install the Windows Evaluation Versions</u> section.

4. Follow steps 1-5 of the install instructions. Be aware that all files are self-extracting ZIP files. (If your intent is to create the 13-disk floppy set, be sure to download the 13-pieces version.)

ENTERING SCHEMATICS

Windows 95

1. **CLICKL** on *Start*, **Drag** to *Programs*, **Drag** to *MicroSim71* (or other), **Schematics**. The Schematics window appears.

2. Turn to Chapter 1; you are ready to go!

Windows 3.1

1. Bring up the Program Manager window and the *MicroSim Eval* group (**CLICKL** on appropriate icons, as necessary). **DCLICKL** on the *Schematics* icon to bring up the *Schematics* window.

2. Turn to Chapter 1; you are ready to go!

EVALUATION VERSION LIMITATIONS

If you were able to download the *Evaluation requirements, installation* page from MicroSim's Website, refer to the "Limitations" section. Otherwise, refer to the abbreviated limitations listed below:

- Maximum of 50 symbols on a single A-size schematic page.
- Maximum of 30 components can be placed on a PCB layout.
- Maximum of 64 nodes, 10 transistors, 2 op amps, or 65 digital primitive devices, or a combination thereof.
- Optimizer limited to one goal, parameter, and constraint.

Special Note

Many times throughout this text you will be asked to bring up the *output file*. Inability to do so typically is caused by an incompatibility between the MicroSoft IntelliPoint mouse drive (pointer.exe) and Windows 95/NT.

To correct the problem, bring up file WIN.INI in directory WINDOWS and look for either of the following:

[WINDOWS]
LOAD=C:\mouse\pointer.exe
        OR
[WINDOWS]
LOAD=C:\MSINPUT\pointer.exe

Delete the LOAD command as follows and reset your computer:

[WINDOWS]
LOAD=

If this does not fix the problem, try any of the following:

- If you are using *Logitech's* Smart mouse driver, obtain a later version.

- Do not use *AfterDark* version 3.0.

- Reload the latest versions of Windows 95 Service Pack and OLE upgrade. Obtain from:

    http://www.microsoft.com

- Contact MicroSim's tech support.

PART I
DC/AC Circuits

In the nine chapters of Part I, we concentrate on the fundamentals of PSpice. For this reason, the test circuits are relatively simple and are limited to the DC/AC category. In these early chapters you will find that every step in the simulation process is presented in detail and nothing is left to your imagination.

In Part II, when we begin solid-state studies (the primary emphasis of this text), we assume that the major PSpice techniques of Part I have been mastered, and we can concentrate on more advanced circuit concepts and PSpice features.

We assume that the reader has a general familiarity with Windows. If necessary, see Appendix E for a short tutorial on Windows 3.1 and 95.

All windows and dialog boxes that appear in this text are based on Windows 95 and PSpice 7.1. Anyone using different versions may note minor differences, *but this should present no problems*.

CHAPTER 1

Introduction to Schematics
Ohm's Law

OBJECTIVES

- To draw a simple DC circuit using the *Schematics* program.
- To analyze the circuit using the *PSpice* program.
- To display the resulting voltages and currents.
- To demonstrate Ohm's law.

DISCUSSION

In this first chapter, we introduce *Schematics* and *PSpice*, the software components that create and analyze circuits. The emphasis is on *Schematics*, the powerful program that lets us build (capture) circuits by drawing them within a window on the monitor. It is the function of *PSpice* to analyze the circuit created by *Schematics* and to generate voltage and current solutions.

To study Ohm's law, we turn to the DC circuit of Figure 1.1. As shown, all circuits consist of s*ymbols*, *attributes*, and *connections*.

- A *symbol* is a graphical representation of an electronic part. Each symbol is associated with a *part name* and stored in a symbol library. For example, a resistor uses a zigzag line for its symbol and *R* for its part name, and is stored in the symbol library *analog.slb*.

- *Attributes* are unique labels for parts. Unlike the generic part name, attributes are different for each instance of the same part. Attributes consist of two sections: a *name* and its associated *value*. For example, as shown by Figure 1.1, part *VDC* displays by default the value portion of its *Package Reference Designator* attribute (V1), and the value portion of its *Magnitude* attribute (+10V).

• *Connections* are made primarily by wire segments and bus strips.

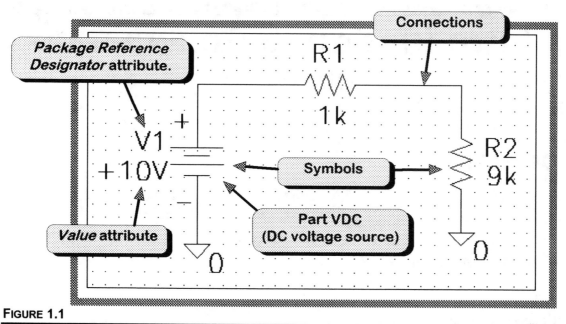

FIGURE 1.1

Simple DC Circuit

A question. When a *part* is placed, which attribute names and values appear by default? The rule is simple: those generally required are displayed by default; the others are hidden in order to avoid clutter. Most attributes can be removed or displayed at the discretion of the designer.

BIAS POINT SOLUTION

Most circuits have both steady and changing voltage and current components. Under PSpice, the steady state (DC) component is known as the *bias point* (or *operating point*) solution and (if present) is always calculated first.

Because the circuit of Figure 1.1 uses only steady state (DC) voltages, it has only a bias point solution. (During a bias point solution, if capacitors are present, they are opened; if inductors are present, they are shorted.)

SIMULATION PRACTICE

The Schematics Window

1. As a starting point, open the *Schematics* window of Figure 1.2. (Reminder: Figure 1.2 is based on Windows 95.)

> To enter Schematics:
>
> **Windows 3.1**: Bring up the *Program Manager* window and the *MicroSim Eval* group. **DCLICKL** on the *Schematics* icon.
>
> **Windows 95**: **CLICKL** on *Start*, **Drag** to *Programs*, **Drag** to *MicroSim Eval 7.1* (or equivalent), **CLICKL** on *Schematics*.

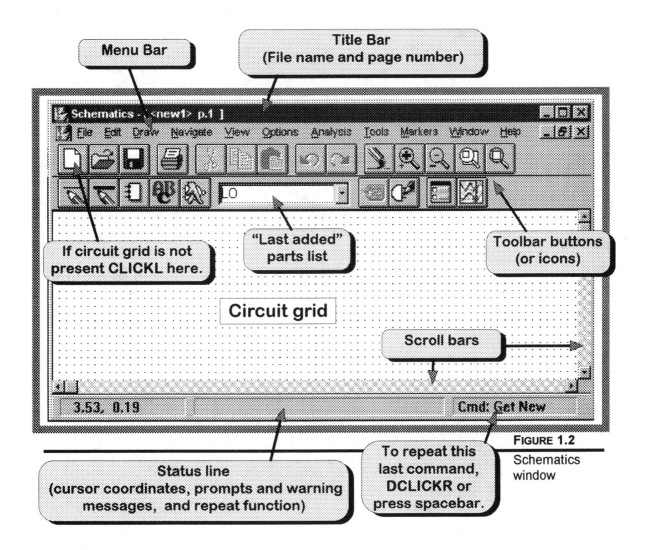

FIGURE 1.2
Schematics
window

2.   Looking at the schematics window on your computer, and referring to Figure 1.2, we observe the following:

- The grid of dots that forms the work space to draw our circuits.

- The *title bar* at the top of the window, which gives the file name and page number.   The file name *<new>* tells us that this is a brand new schematic. Later, *new* will be replaced with a specific file name.   Because the evaluation version is limited to one page, the page number is always 1.

- The *scroll bars* at the right and bottom, which provide a means of positioning the circuit.

- The *Status line* at the bottom, which gives the cursor coordinates, repeat function, prompts and warning messages. Move the cursor over the grid and note the changing cursor coordinates. The repeat function (*Cmd*) "remembers" the last operation, which can be repeated upon **DCLICKR** or spacebar.

- The *main menu* bar at the top of the screen (from *File* to *Help*). Using the mouse, **CLICKL** on each main menu item and note the pull-down menu for each. On the right side of each pull-down menu are listed keyboard alternatives to many of the operations.   When a menu item is selected, its description appears in the middle of the status line. (**CLICKL** anywhere on the workspace to remove any menu.)

- The *toolbar* that gives us the opportunity to perform many activities in a single step. Using the mouse, move the cursor over each of the toolbar buttons and again note the description of each in the status line.

Save File

<u>Note on Schematics operations</u>

For many operations, we have the choice of using the *toolbar*, the *menu bar*, or the *keyboard*.   For example, to save a schematics file we can **CLICKL** on the *Saves the active schematic* toolbar button, **File, Save** from the menu bar, or Ctrl./S from the keyboard.

In this book we will generally favor the *toolbar*, reverting to the *menu bar* or *keyboard* only when necessary or preferable. Each reader should use whatever mix of methods seems most natural.

Step 1: Draw the circuit

3.   The first component we will place on the schematic is the voltage source of Figure 1.3. We begin with **CLICKL** on the *"Selects a Part to Draw"* toolbar button (or **Draw**, **Get New Part**) to open up the *Part Browser Basic* dialog box of Figure 1.4.   (Should the *Part Browser Advanced* box come up, **CLICKL** on *Basic*.)

Select Part

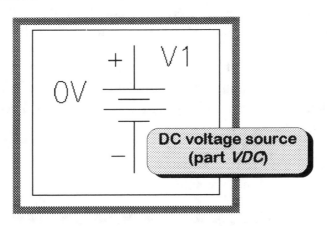

FIGURE 1.3

Voltage source placed

CLICKLH and DRAG on title bar to move window.

Part Browser Basic

Part Name

If you know the part name, enter it here. (Upper- or lowercase okay)

Description

As you enter characters, the system zeros in on the part.

Otherwise, we must search for the part name and CLICKL.

+5V
-5V
2N1595
2N5444
54152A
555D
7400
7401
7402

Close
Place
Place & Close
Help
Libraries
Advanced>>

Full list

See Appendix F for the use of these advanced search techniques.

FIGURE 1.4

Part Browser Basic window

Since we know the part name for the DC voltage source (*VDC*), there is no need to search through the list of parts. Therefore, enter *VDC* in the *Part Name* box, **Place**, **DRAG** component to desired location, **CLICKL** to place component, followed by **CLICKR** to abort the mode.

> When entering values within any PSpice dialog box, we follow the same rules as for any Windows dialog box. Most entries are case insensitive, and can be any mix of upper- and lowercase.

Observe that the value portions of the *Package Reference Designator* attribute (V1) and *Value Attribute* (0V) do appear on the schematic by default, but the *Part Name* (VDC) does not.

4.   Note that when placed, the voltage source is automatically *selected* (highlighted red). Review *Schematics Note 1.1* to learn how and why components are selected.

Schematics Note 1.1
How and why do I <u>select</u> a circuit component?

A component that is selected is red in color. To select (and highlight red) any circuit component, **CLICKL** on the component. Only a selected component can be operated upon.

To select more than one item at a time, perform either of the following:

• Hold the *Shift* key down and **CLICKL** on any number of items.
• **CLICKLH** and use the cursor to draw a box about the items.

To deselect a component, **CLICKL** anywhere else on the schematic window.

Select Part

5.   The next step is to place both resistors on the schematic, as shown in Figure 1.5. (Since we used *Place*, rather than *Place & Close*, the *Part Browser Basic* dialog box of Figure 1.4 is still open. If it is not, **CLICKL** on the *Selects a part to draw* toolbar button.)

As before, enter *R* (or *r*) in the *Part Name* box, **Place**, **DRAG** resistor to R1's location and **CLICKL** (to place R1 and create R2), **DRAG** second resistor to R2's location and **CLICKL**, followed by **CLICKR** (to place R2 and abort operation).

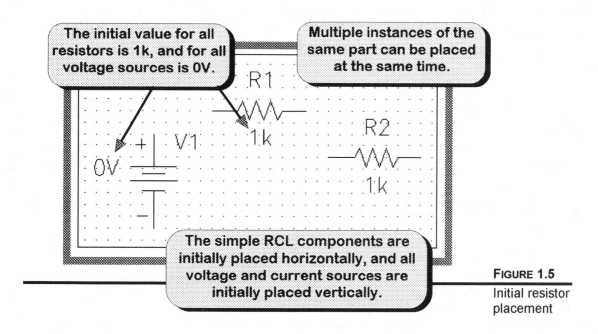

FIGURE 1.5

Initial resistor placement

6. To rotate R2: **Edit**, **Rotate** (or Ctrl/R if dialog box is in the way). (Remember, R2 is highlighted red and therefore already selected.)

7. The chances are R2 is now in the wrong location. Reposition R2 (as shown in Figure 1.6) by following the directions of *Schematics Note 1.2*.

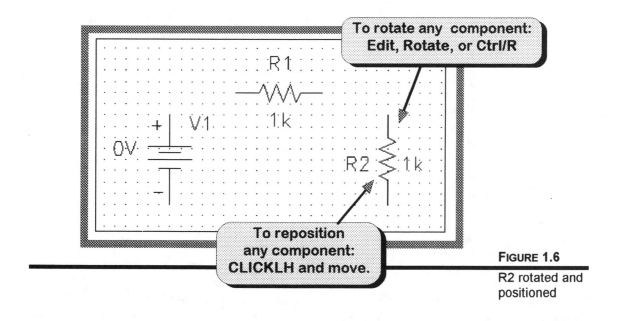

FIGURE 1.6

R2 rotated and positioned

Schematics Note 1.2
How do I reposition components?

To reposition a component, **CLICKL** on the component's <u>symbol</u> to select (highlight red), followed by **CLICKLH**, and move to desired location.

When multiple items are selected, all items move when any one of them is moved. (A good way to select multiple items is to position the cursor, **CLICKLH**, and draw a box around the items.)

8. The next step is to place grounds at the bottom of V1 and R2, as shown in Figure 1.7. However, this time we do not know the part name and must search for it.

If *Part Browser Basic* dialog box is not open...

Select Part

Using the scroll bar within the *Part Browser Basic* dialog box, scan through the alphabetical *full list* of parts and find "AGND" (analog ground). To place the part: **AGND**, **Place & Close** (since this is the last part we will add for now), **DRAG** ground symbol to bottom of V1, **CLICKL** (to place first ground and create second ground), **DRAG** second ground to bottom of R2, **CLICKL** (to place second ground), **CLICKR** (to abort mode).

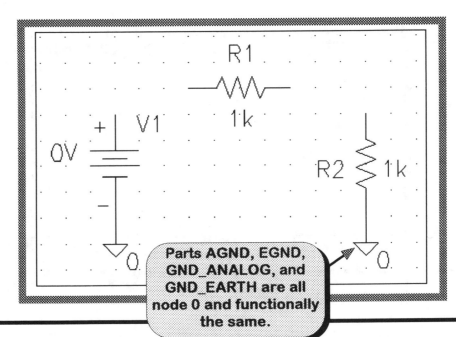

FIGURE 1.7

Placing grounds

Parts AGND, EGND, GND_ANALOG, and GND_EARTH are all node 0 and functionally the same.

9. After additions or changes are made to a schematic, the chances are good that the circuit is out of position and incorrectly sized, and that portions of the circuit are fuzzy, splotchy, or missing. After reviewing *Schematics Note 1.3*, *refresh* or *refit* your present circuit, and whenever necessary in the future.

Schematics Note 1.3
How do I "refresh" or "refit" my circuit?

Zoom in Zoom out

Zoom all
or refit

- To clarify (refresh) your circuit at any time: **View, Redraw**.
- To cause the circuit to fill the screen (refit): **CLICKL** on the *Zooms to show all items on page* toolbar button, or **View, Fit**.
- To increase/decrease circuit size in stages: **CLICKL** on the *Zoom in/out about center of window* toolbar button, or **View, In/Out**, position cursor, **CLICKL**.

Note: When a circuit fills the screen (after refit), it will automatically move to allow placement of new components outside the border. When this happens, refit again.

10. The final step in our circuit construction is to complete the wiring. Referring to Figure 1.8(a), **CLICKL** on the *Draws a new wire* toolbar button (or **Draw, Wire**) to create the "pencil" cursor.

Draw Wire

Following the directions in the *status bar* at the bottom of the window, **DRAG** the pencil cursor to point 1 and **CLICKL** to anchor the wire to the top of V1, **DRAG** dotted wire straight up to point 2 and straight across to point 3, **CLICKL** to turn solid and anchor to left of R1. (Note that the pencil is still active.)

When done, the connection between V1 and R1 should be as shown in Figure 1.8(b). (If mistakes are made, delete appropriate items according to *Schematics Note 1.4* and redraw.)

11. Follow the sequence of step 10 to connect R1 with R2 and complete the circuit (as shown in Figure 1.9). When the wiring is complete, **CLICKR** to abort mode.

> Wires are normally drawn at 90° angles. To toggle between 90° drawing angles and any angle, and to review other schematic display options, see Appendix G.

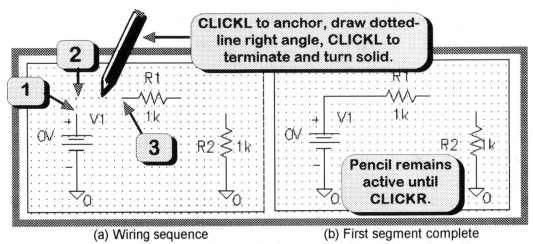

(a) Wiring sequence   (b) First segment complete

FIGURE 1.8

The *Wire* function
(a) Wiring sequence
(b) First segment complete

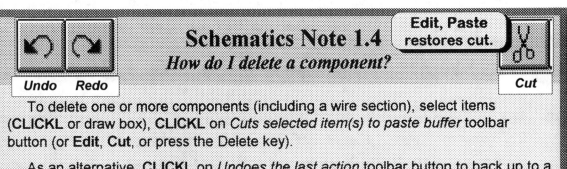

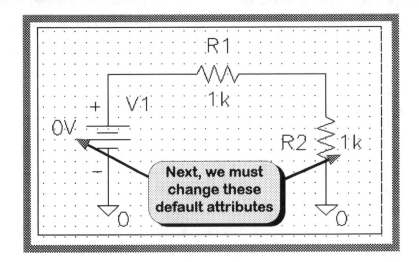

FIGURE 1.9

Circuit wiring
complete

12. The circuit wiring may be complete, but the attributes are not correct. For example, referring to Figure 1.1, R2's value should be 9k and V1's value should be +10V. Based on the process of *Schematics Note 1.5*, make the necessary changes.

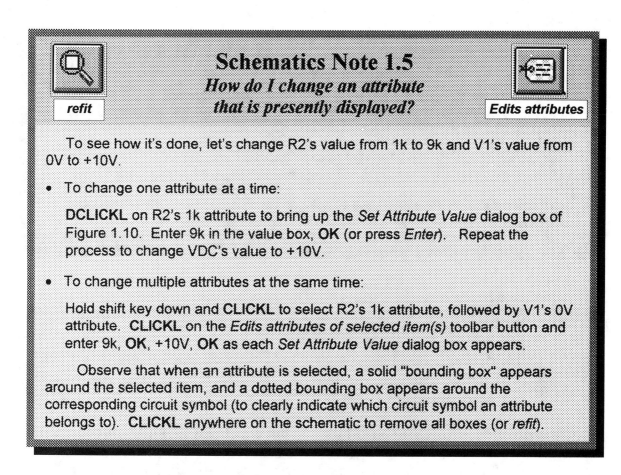

Schematics Note 1.5
How do I change an attribute that is presently displayed?

refit

Edits attributes

To see how it's done, let's change R2's value from 1k to 9k and V1's value from 0V to +10V.

• To change one attribute at a time:

DCLICKL on R2's 1k attribute to bring up the *Set Attribute Value* dialog box of Figure 1.10. Enter 9k in the value box, **OK** (or press *Enter*). Repeat the process to change VDC's value to +10V.

• To change multiple attributes at the same time:

Hold shift key down and **CLICKL** to select R2's 1k attribute, followed by V1's 0V attribute. **CLICKL** on the *Edits attributes of selected item(s)* toolbar button and enter 9k, **OK**, +10V, **OK** as each *Set Attribute Value* dialog box appears.

Observe that when an attribute is selected, a solid "bounding box" appears around the selected item, and a dotted bounding box appears around the corresponding circuit symbol (to clearly indicate which circuit symbol an attribute belongs to). **CLICKL** anywhere on the schematic to remove all boxes (or *refit*).

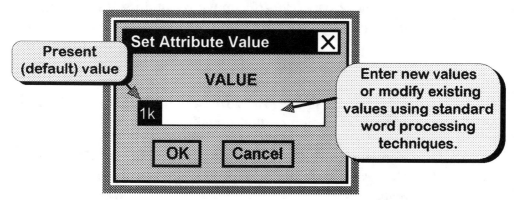

Present (default) value

Set Attribute Value

VALUE

1k

Enter new values or modify existing values using standard word processing techniques.

OK   **Cancel**

FIGURE 1.10

Set Attribute Value dialog box

13. The circuit is now complete, but the attributes may not be positioned as desired. To move any of the displayed attributes to a new location, follow the directions of *Schematics Note 1.6*. Your final circuit, ready for analysis, should closely resemble Figure 1.1.

Schematics Note 1.6
How do I relocate displayed attributes?

refit

To relocate an attribute to a new location: **CLICKL** on an <u>attribute</u> (not the symbol) to select (surround with solid boundary box), **CLICKLH** and move to new location, **CLICKL** anywhere on the schematic to remove all boundary boxes (or *refit*).

(Remember, when a <u>symbol</u> rather than an attribute is relocated, no boundary boxes are generated and all attributes simply "tag along.")

Step 2: Set the bias points

14. The circuit is now complete in all respects. But before we perform the calculations, we must tell the system which DC voltage and current solutions to display.

Select Part

To accomplish this, use the drawing techniques introduced in this chapter (**CLICKL** on *Selects a Part to Draw* toolbar button, etc.) to place parts *VIEWPOINT* and *IPROBE*— as shown Figure 1.11. (To place part *IPROBE*, move R2 and its associated ground back and forth.)

> Notes:
>
> Be aware that the *Part Browser Basic* dialog box can be moved to any location on the screen.
>
> If you wish, use **Place & Close** (instead of just **Place**) so the *Part Browser Basic* dialog box will not get in the way of the schematic.

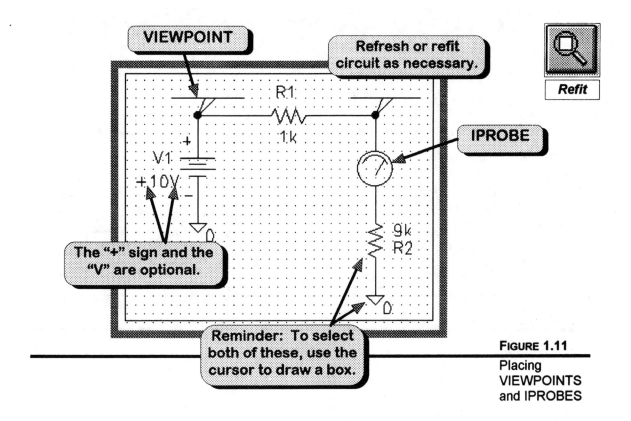

Refit

FIGURE 1.11

Placing
VIEWPOINTS
and IPROBES

15. The final step before analysis is to store the circuit file on disk. This requires us to select a disk/directory/file name. Based on file name *ohmslaw*, listed below are several possibilities.

- **C:\msimev71\ohmslaw.sch** to store in PSpice directory.

- **C:\mydir\ohmslaw.sch** to store in your own directory.

- **A:\ohmslaw.sch** to store on drive A.

To store your circuit file to one of the above locations (or other location of your choice): **CLICKL** on the *Saves the active schematic* toolbar button (or **File**, **Save as**) to bring up the *Save As* dialog box of Figure 1.12.

Save File

If necessary, **CLICKL** within the *Save in* and *Up one level* boxes to select the desired drive and directory pathway. Finally enter the desired file name (such as *ohmslaw.sch*) in the *File name* box, **Save**. (If you omit the ".sch" extension, the system will automatically add it.)

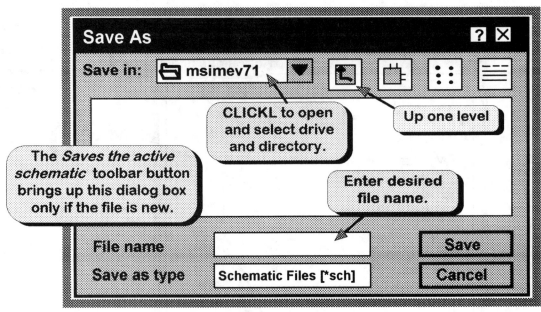

FIGURE 1.12
Save as dialog box

Step 3: Analyze the circuit

Simulate

16. We are finally ready to perform all calculations and display the results. To accomplish this: **CLICKL** on *Simulates the active schematic* toolbar button (or **Analysis**, **Simulate**, or press F11). The *PSpice* window opens during circuit calculations, and when finished, "bias point calculated" appears (and a beep may sound).

Step 4: Examine the results

17. Bring back the *schematics* window.

> To move from one window to another, **CLICKL** on any window portion or use *Alt/Tab* to scroll through the windows. Or, if using Windows 95, **CLICKL** on screen icons (usually found along the bottom of the screen).

Note the displayed voltage and current values. Are they correct?

Yes   **No**

18. As an alternative method of obtaining the bias point solution, we may examine the *output file*. To open the output file and analyze its contents, see *Schematics Note 1.7*. (If the output file does not open, see the *Special Note* at the back of the introduction.)

Schematics Note 1.7
What is contained in the output file?

The output file acts as an "audit trail" of the PSpice simulation and provides many services. For example, whenever an error occurs during simulation that does not involve the netlist or electrical rule check, it is explained within the output file.

The output file is organized sequentially into three major sections: *Schematics Netlist*, *Schematics Aliases*, and the *Small Signal Bias Solution*.

To examine the output file (after running PSpice): **Analysis**, **Examine Output** from Schematics Window (or **File**, **Examine Output** from PSpice Window). Based on the circuit of Figure 1.1, the following sections are generated:

Schematics Netlist

R_R1	$N_0002 $N_0001 1k
V_V1	$N_0002 0 10V
R_R2	0 $N_0003 9k
v_V2	$N_0001 $N_0003 0

Each line of the netlist represents a single component. For example, the second line uses *reference designator V_V1* to specify a voltage source between node 2 ($N_0002) and node 0 with a dc value of +10V. (v_V2 is the current probe.)

Schematics Aliases

R_R1	R1(1=$N_0002 2=$N_0001)
V_V1	V1(+=$N_0002–=0)
R_R2	R2(1=0 2=$N_0003)
v_V2	V2(+=$N_0001 –=$N_0003)

Aliases are useful as alternative methods of specifying nodes. Each component is assigned special (alias) designators that specify its two ends.   For example, the first line tells us that the left end of component R_R1 is at node $N_0002 and has alias R1:1, and the right end is at node $N_0001 and has alias R1:2. The second line tells us that the top end of V_V1 is at node $N_0002 and has the alias V1:+. The bottom end is at node 0 and has the alias V1:–.

Small Signal Bias Solution

NODE VOLTAGE		VOLTAGE SOURCE CURRENTS		TOTAL POWER DISSIPATION
($N_0001)	9.0000	NAME	CURRENT	1.00E-02 WATTS
($N_0002)	10.0000	V_V1	-1.000E-03	
($N_0003)	9.0000	v_V2	1.000E-03	

The small signal bias solution shows the DC voltages at all nodes, all DC circuit currents, and the total DC power dissipation.   To help determine the location of circuit nodes, we may refer to the section on aliases.   The values listed here should, of course, agree with those displayed with VIEWPOINTS and IPROBES. **File**, **Exit** (or, for Windows 95, **CLICKL** on "X") to exit the output file.

19.   Are the voltages and currents listed in the *small signal bias* section of the output file the same as those displayed on the schematic?

Yes   **No**

> Look at the output file currents. Why is the current positive for IPROBE (v_V2) and negative for VDC (V_V1)?
>
> For the answer, refer to *Schematics Note 1.8*.

Schematics Note 1.8
How do I determine the direction of conventional current?

First, locate side 1. Each two-terminal component that appears on the schematic has two sides: side 1 and side 2. For horizontal parts, side 1 is initially the left side; for vertical parts, side 1 is initially the top side. When a component is rotated, it moves counterclockwise.

Second, measure the current at side 1. If the current measured at side 1 is positive, conventional current is flowing through the device from side 1 to side 2; if negative, it is flowing through the device from side 2 to side 1. Whenever current is displayed by PSpice, its value is always with respect to component side 1.

   The current measured at the + terminal (side 1) of a voltage source is always negative. This is because conventional current flows through a voltage source from side 2 to side 1 (– to +).

Error correction

> PSpice recognizes two kinds of errors: Those involving *wiring* of the circuit, and those that occur during *analysis*. This chapter will cover only wiring errors—which are the most common.

Simulate

20.   To show how PSpice handles wiring errors, move the ground on V1 aside (so no contact is made with V1). Re-analyze the circuit, **OK** (on error box), and note the appearance of the *MicroSim Message Viewer* of Figure 1.13.

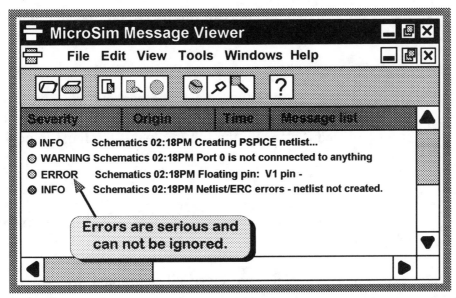

FIGURE 1.13

Message Viewer
dialog box

21. Looking at the Message Viewer:

(a) Did we receive both a WARNING and an ERROR?

   Yes   **No**

(b) Select (**CLICKL**) the WARNING and note the *message text*. Does it indicate that *Part 0 is not connected to anything*?

   Yes   **No**

(c) **CLICKL** on the *Find in Design* toolbar button (but do not move the mouse). Did the arrow cursor point to the error location?

   Yes   **No**

Find

(d) Bring back the *Message Viewer* window (e.g., *Alt/Tab*) and **CLICKL** on the *Help on* (?) toolbar button. Did the *MicroSim Schematic Error Messages* window come up, and did it indicate that the system "...encountered a port that was not connected to anything"?

   Yes   **No**

Help on

   When done, **File**, **Exit** to exit the *Error Messages* window (but not the *Message Viewer* window). (Windows 95 users can **CLICKL** on the "X" icon).

(e) Select the ERROR and note the *message text*. Does it indicate that V1 has a floating pin?

Yes   **No**

(f) **CLICKL** on the question mark toolbar button. Note the statement of the problem and the list of solutions. Is the first solution listed ("Connect the pin to a net") the most logical in our case?

Yes   **No**

Exit the *error messages* and *message viewer* dialog boxes when done.

22. The experiment complete, we close all additional windows. (If you wish to perform an *advanced activity* or *exercise,* skip this step until you are done.)

Advanced Activities

23. Calculate by hand the total power consumption of the circuit of Figure 1.1 and compare your result to the value given in the small signal bias solution of the output file. (For this and all future *advanced activities,* report all work and results on a separate paper.)

EXERCISE

• Referring to the combination circuit of Figure 1.14, use Kirchhoff's laws to calculate (by hand) the current through R2. Verify your prediction using an IPROBE under PSpice. (For this and all future *exercises,* report all work and results on separate paper.)

QUESTIONS AND PROBLEMS

1. Write "select item" or "perform action" after each of the following:

(a) **CLICKL** _____
(b) **DCLICKL** _____
(c) **CLICKR** _____

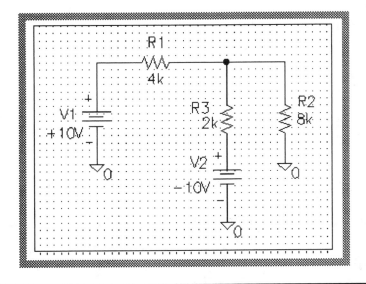

FIGURE 1.14

Applications
circuit

2. How do we know when a particular item on the *Schematics* window is selected?

3. Name two ways of determining a bias point voltage at a node.

4. Part V1 (VDC) is known as a *DC voltage source*. What does this mean? (Hint: What is the output impedance of a voltage source, and how does the voltage depend on the current?)

5. What are the two parts of every attribute.   Give several examples.

6. What are the three major sections of the *output file*?

7. What is a *bias point* solution?

8. Is it reasonable that MicroSim designed the IPROBE to be a "perfect" ammeter (one with no internal resistance)?

    Yes   **No**

9. For a resistor, what is the difference between the *part name* (R) and the *Package Reference Designator name* (such as R1)?   (<u>Hint</u>: Which one is general and which one is specific?)

10. What are the three parts of a file pathname?

11. Regarding Figure 1.11, the current through IPROBE is positive. After each of the following changes, would the current be positive or negative?

    (a) IPROBE alone were turned upside down.

    (b) V1 alone were turned upside down.

    (c) Both IPROBE and V1 were turned upside down.

12. When using DC sources, how is power determined in a resistor?   (Write the equation.)

CHAPTER 2

Introduction to Probe
The DC Sweep Mode

OBJECTIVES

- To prove that a resistor is a *linear* device.
- To determine maximum power transfer.
- To apply the *DC Sweep* mode of operation to DC circuits.
- To use *Probe* to display graphical information.

DISCUSSION

Are resistors *linear* devices? That is, is the relationship between voltage and current a straight line—as Ohm's law predicts?

To answer this question, we bring back the test circuit we used in Chapter 1 (reproduced in Figure 2.1). This time, however, we will vary (sweep) the voltage source (V1) across a *range* of values and use *Probe* to display the resulting current on a graph. If the current is a straight line, then resistors R1 and R2 are linear devices.

A second question we wish to investigate with this chapter involves *power*. Again referring to Figure 2.1, what value of R2 will result in maximum power transfer from V1 to R2? To find the answer, we will sweep R2 across a range of values, display R2's power on a graph, and look for the peak power point.

To sweep V1 and R2 over a range of values we adopt the *DC Sweep* mode under *Schematics*. We then use the facilities of *Probe* to graph the resulting current and power. (During a DC Sweep, if capacitors are present, they are opened; if inductors are present, they are shorted.)

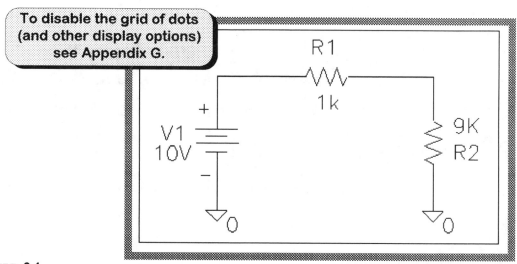

To disable the grid of dots
(and other display options)
see Appendix G.

FIGURE 2.1

Simple DC
test circuit

SIMULATION PRACTICE

Problem 1: Are resistors linear devices?

Step 1: Draw the circuit

Open File

Create File

Select Part

Draw Wire

1.   Draw or bring back the circuit of Figure 2.1, used in the previous experiment. (To bring it back, **CLICKL** on the *Opens an existing schematic* toolbar button, **CLICKL** on proper directory and file name, **OK.**   To create a new schematic, **CLICKL** on the *Creates a Schematic* toolbar button.)

> Note: If V1 is to be swept, the *10V* magnitude attribute is optional. If present (as shown in Figure 2.1), it writes an initial *bias point solution* to the output file.   It is ignored during the DC sweep process.

Step 2: Select the sweep mode

2.   To solve our linearity problem, we will perform a DC Sweep of voltage source V1 from 0 to 10 volts.

First, bring up the *Analysis Setup* menu of Figure 2.2 (**CLICKL** on *Sets up the simulation analysis for active* toolbar button, or **Analysis, Setup**), and enable the DC Sweep mode (**CLICKL** on *Enabled* box as shown).   (Do not perform *Close* yet.)

Analysis Setup

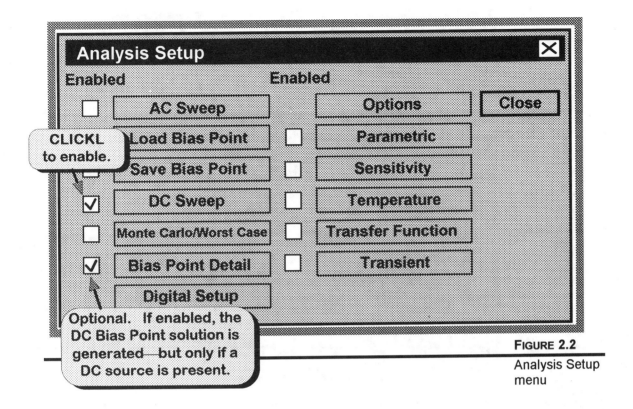

Analysis Setup

Enabled   Enabled

☐ AC Sweep   ☐ Options   Close

CLICKL to enable. Load Bias Point   ☐ Parametric

☐ Save Bias Point   ☐ Sensitivity

☑ DC Sweep   ☐ Temperature

☐ Monte Carlo/Worst Case   ☐ Transfer Function

☑ Bias Point Detail   ☐ Transient

☐ Digital Setup

Optional. If enabled, the DC Bias Point solution is generated—but only if a DC source is present.

FIGURE 2.2

Analysis Setup menu

3. Next, we **CLICKL** on the *DC Sweep* bar to bring up the *DC Sweep* dialog box of Figure 2.3 and fill in as shown:

- *Name:* V1 (The sweep variable.)

- *Swept Var. Type*: **Voltage Source**, because we are sweeping V1.

- *Sweep Type:* **Linear**, because we wish the voltage magnitude to increase in a linear manner.

- *Start Value, End Value, and Increment:* 0V, +10V, and .1V, meaning we wish to sweep V1 from 0V to +10V, in increments of .1V.

- *Model Type, Model Name, Param. Name,* and *Values:* not used by this application and are automatically disabled.

- *Nested Sweep:* not used by this chapter.

    OK (to exit the *DC Sweep* dialog box and save the parameters), **Close** (to exit the *Analysis Setup* menu with the DC Sweep mode enabled).

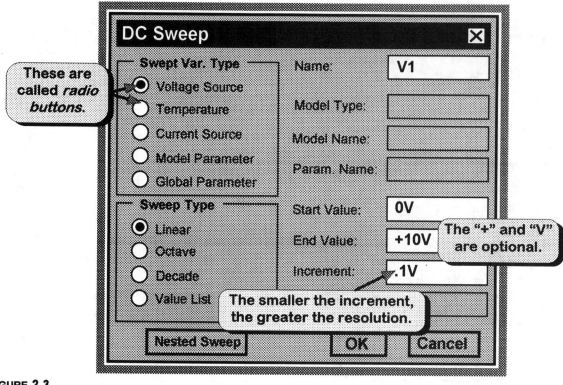

FIGURE 2.3

DC Sweep
dialog box

Save File

Simulate

Step 3: Analyze the circuit

4. Save the file to disk. (If necessary, see Chapter 1, step 15.)

5. We begin simulation (**CLICKL** on the *Simulates the active schematic* toolbar button, or **Analysis**, **Simulate**) and the PSpice window automatically appears (Figure 2.4). Note the calculation summary at the bottom, which gives the starting value, ending value, and a running account of the calculations.

> Reminder: If errors are found in circuit wiring, review the *Error correction* section of Chapter 1.

After completion of the calculations, and assuming no errors were found, the data base generated by PSpice (*ohmslaw.prb*) is sent to *Probe* and a window is opened (see Figure 2.5). The graph portion is the *initial* graph, in which the X-axis is automatically set by default to the DC sweep variable and range. As always, the Y-axis is initially blank.

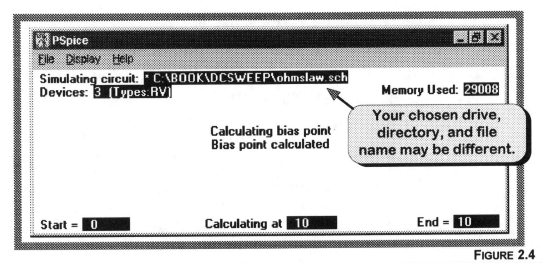

FIGURE 2.4

PSpice window

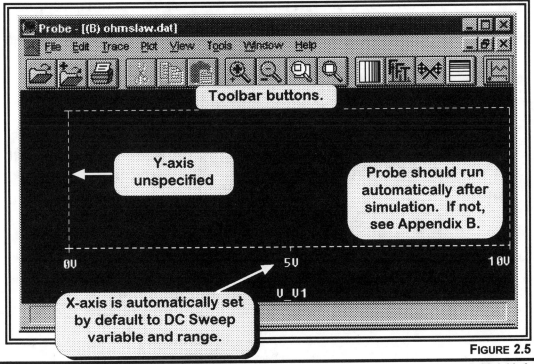

FIGURE 2.5

Initial (default) Probe
window showing DC
Sweep of V1

6. Before we plot our graph, take a couple of minutes and position the
    cursor over each of the toolbar buttons of the Probe window. Note
    that the description of each button appears at the bottom of the
    Probe window.

PSpice for Windows

Step 4: Select the X- and Y-axis variables

7. To determine the linearity of R1 and R2, convince yourself that the following X- and Y-axis assignments will do the job.

    *   The X-axis should be V1 (V_V1) from 0 to 10V.

    *   The Y-axis should be circuit current.

8. Looking at the *initial* graph of Figure 2.5, the default X-axis variable and range are proper and can remain as is.

9. To display the current waveform on the Y-axis, first bring back the *Schematics* window.

> Reminder: To move between windows, **CLICKL** on any window portion, or use *Alt/Tab* to scroll through the windows. Or, if using Windows 95, **CLICKL** on icons along the bottom of the screen.

Second, set a *marker* as follows: **Markers**, **Mark Current into Pin**, **DRAG** marker to the location shown in Figure 2.6, **CLICKL** (to set marker), and **CLICKR** to generate waveform and abort mode.

Bring the *Probe* graph to the forefront (Figure 2.7) and observe the waveform! (Note that the Y-axis *range* is automatically selected by Probe so the curve will fill the screen.)

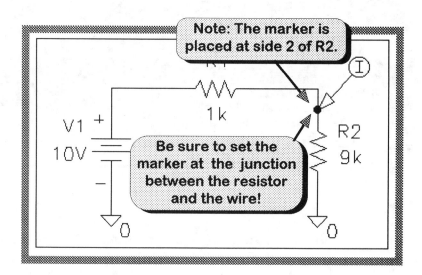

FIGURE 2.6

Setting a current marker

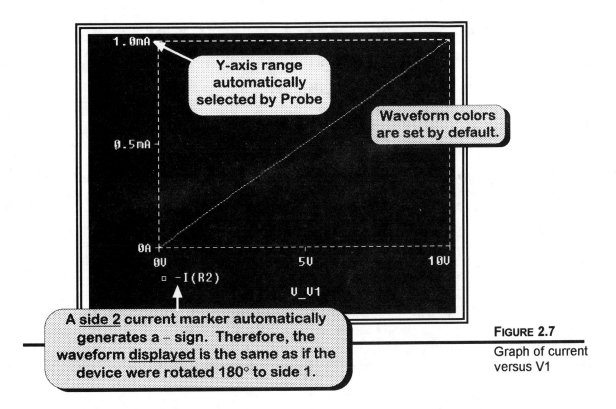

FIGURE 2.7

Graph of current
versus V1

10. Viewing the results (Figure 2.7), can we conclude that the two resistors collectively act as a 10kΩ linear resistive device that obeys Ohm's law?

               Yes   **No**

Problem 2: What value of R2 gives maximum power transfer?

Step 1: Draw the circuit

11. Return to the circuit of Figure 2.1. (We will not be sweeping V1's voltage, so the *10V* DC source voltage <u>is</u> necessary.) Be sure to erase the marker by **Markers**, **Clear All**. (If necessary, **View**, **Redraw** or refit.)

Refit

Step 2: Select the sweep mode

12. To generate a graph of power versus load resistance (R2), we must sweep resistor R2 through a range of values. To set up the system for such a *global parameter* sweep, follow the directions of *Schematics Note 2.1*.

PSpice for Windows

Schematics Note 2.1
How do I sweep a component value?

To sweep a component value (such as R2 of Figure 2.1), we follow a rather involved three-step process:

1. Substitute a variable for R2's constant value: **DCLICKL** on R2's magnitude value (presently 9k) to bring up the *Set Attribute Value* dialog box of Figure 2.8. Enter {RVAL}, **OK**.　(The "RVAL" value can be anything, but the curly braces are necessary.)

2. Define RVAL as a variable: **CLICKL** on the *Selects a part to draw* toolbar button, enter PARAM in *Part Name* box, **Place & Close**, **DRAG** "box" to any position, **CLICKL** to place, **CLICKR** to abort.　**DCLICKL** on "PARAMETERS" to bring up the *Part Name:PARAM* dialog box of Figure 2.9.　**CLICKL** on *NAME1=*, enter *RVAL* (no braces) in *Value* box, **Save Attr**.　**CLICKL** on *VALUE1=*, enter 9k in *Value* box, **Save Attr**, **OK**.

3. Enable a global sweep:　Bring up the DC Sweep dialog box (**CLICKL** on *Sets up the simulation analysis for active* toolbar button, or **Analysis**, **Setup**), DC **Sweep**, enter the items as shown in Figure 2.10 (to sweep global variable R2 from 10ohms to 10k ohms in units of 10), **OK** (be sure the *DC Sweep* box is enabled), **Close**.

After all three steps, the circuit schematic looks like Figure 2.11 and we are ready to proceed to the simulation step.

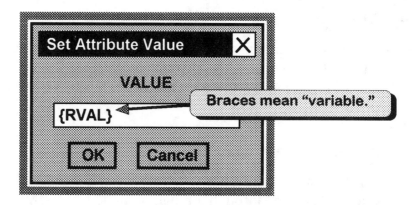

FIGURE 2.8

Set Attribute Value
dialog box

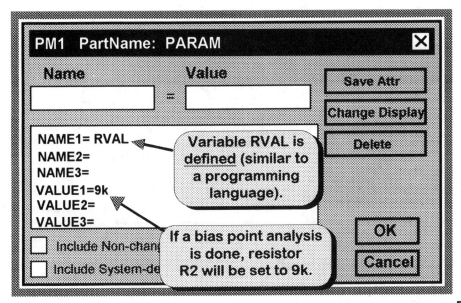

FIGURE 2.9

Part Name Param
dialog box

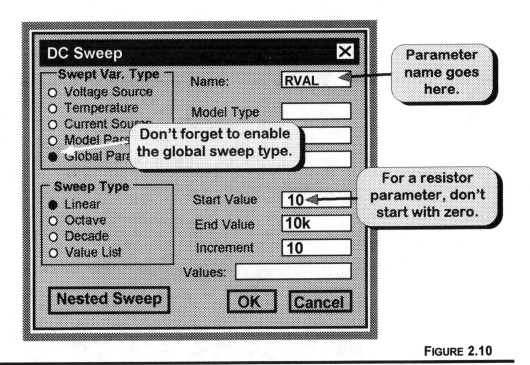

FIGURE 2.10

DC Sweep
dialog box

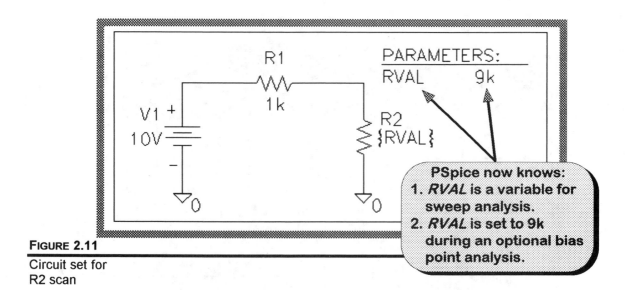

FIGURE 2.11

Circuit set for
R2 scan

Step 3: Analyze the circuit

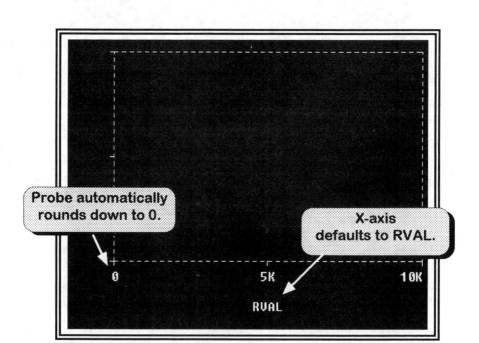

13. **CLICKL** on the *Simulates the active schematic* toolbar button (or **Analysis**, **simulate**) and generate the default Probe graph of Figure 2.12. Is the X-axis a linear sweep of R2 from 10 (0) to 10k?

        Yes   **No**

FIGURE 2.12

Default Probe
graph

Step 4: Select the X- and Y-axis variables

14. The default X-axis variable and range are proper. The Y-axis variable is power in R2, which cannot be selected with *markers* (which are limited to voltage and current). To see how power is graphed, follow the instructions of *Probe Note 2.1*.

Add Traces

Probe Note 2.1
How do I enter custom Y-axis variables?

1. From Probe, bring up the *Add Traces* dialog box of Figure 2.13 (**CLICKL** on the *Add trace(s) to the selected plot* toolbar button, or **Trace**, **Add**). Within the large left-hand box is a list of all available *trace variables*, and within the smaller right-hand box is a list of all available operators and functions.

    Let's study the format of the trace variables by looking at two examples:

    • V(R2:2) specifies the voltage at end "2" of resistor R2. (When a horizontal component is first placed, a "1" indicates "left-hand" and a "2" indicates "right-hand." After counterclockwise rotation, node "2" would be at the top.)

    • V(V1:+) clearly refers to the positive end of voltage source V1.

    CLICKL on *Alias Names* several times and note that some variables are toggled on and off. The additional trace variables are provided for convenience. For example, alias V(R1:1) refers to the same node as V(V1:+) and alias V2(R2) is equivalent to V(R2:2). Also note that we can **CLICKL** on *Voltages*, *Currents*, *Analog*, and *Digital* to isolate groups of variables.

2. To create a power variable, we combine the proper operators and functions with the proper trace variables to generate the desired power equation:

    Power developed in R2 = –V(R2:2)*I(R2)

3. To enter the power equation (as shown in Figure 2.13), simply go from left to right (starting with the minus sign) and **CLICKL** on each variable and operator in sequence, **OK**... and the power curve is drawn (Figure 2.14)!

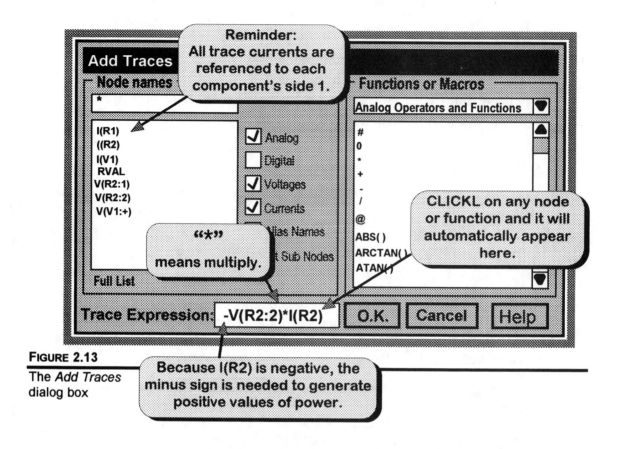

FIGURE 2.13

The *Add Traces*
dialog box

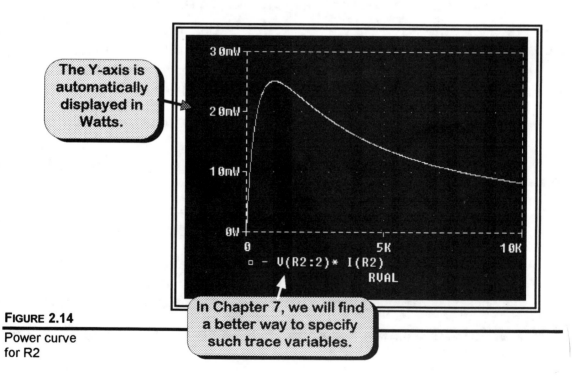

FIGURE 2.14

Power curve
for R2

15. Examine the graph of Figure 2.14. Approximately what value of R2 (*RVAL*) results in maximum power transfer?

    R2 (maximum power) = _____

16. Using the value of R2 determined in step 15, calculate the power developed in R2 by hand and compare to the graph. Are they approximately the same?

    Max power (hand calculation) = _____

    Max power (PSpice) = _____

17. If you wish, follow the directions of *Schematics/Probe Note 2.2* and print a copy of your circuit, graph, or output file.

Advanced Activities

18. If you enabled the *Bias Point Detail* in the *Analysis Setup* window, examine the SMALL SIGNAL BIAS SOLUTION of the output file (**Analysis, Examine Output** from Schematic). Are the DC voltage and current values correct?

    Yes   No

19. Add the power developed in V1 and R1 to the graph of Figure 2.14.   Does $P_{V1} = P_{R1} + P_{R2}$?

    > When using *Probe*, trace expression *V(R1:1)–V(R1:2)* is the same as *V(R1:1,R1:2)*.

EXERCISES

- Assuming that R2 (the load) can vary from 10 to 10kΩ, use PSpice to determine if R1 and R2 should be a 1/4W or 1/2W resistor. (Hint: What is the *worst case* power dissipated by R1 and R2?)

- A 5V power supply drives a 100Ω load. Design and test a PSpice circuit that will show how the output voltage changes for values of output impedance from 10Ω to 500Ω.   (Hint: A thevenized power supply consists of a perfect voltage source in series with a Z_{OUT} resistor.)

Refit

Schematics/Probe Note 2.2
How do I print my circuit, graph, or output file?

Print

In all cases, we assume that the computer system is properly matched to the printer. If not, **DCLICKL** on *My Computer* from the desktop (Windows 95), **DCLICKL** on *Printers*, **DCLICKL** on *Add Printer*, and follow the directions.

Schematics circuits

To print a full schematics page:

- Bring up the *Schematics* window.
- To view a schematics page and to see how it will look when printed: **View, Entire Page**. (Refit to return to the default view.)
- To print, **CLICKL** on *Prints the active schematic* toolbar button (or **File, Print**).

To print a selected portion of a schematics page:

- Bring up the schematics page.
- Draw a box around the entire circuit, or any portion of the circuit you wish to print (**CLICKLH** and drag).
- To print, **CLICKL** on *Prints the active schematic* toolbar button (or **File, Print**).

Probe graph

- Bring up the *Probe* window.
- To print the entire graph, **CLICKL** on the *Print plots* toolbar button (or **File, Print**).
- To print a selected portion of a graph, **CLICKL** on the *Zoom in on selected area of graph* toolbar button, draw a box around the desired portion (**CLICKLH** and drag), and **CLICKL** on the *Print plots* toolbar button (or **File, Print**). *Refit* to return to full plot.

Output file

- Bring up the *Schematics* window.
- Open the Output File (**Analysis, Examine Output**).
- To print, **CLICKL** on the *Prints the active document* toolbar button (or **File, Print**).

Zoom area

As an alternative to any of these, zoom (where applicable) to increase the desired size, copy to clipboard, paste to another document, and print as desired.

QUESTIONS AND PROBLEMS

1. What is the major function of each of the following software components?

    (a) Schematics

    (b) PSpice

    (c) Probe

2. Referring to the graph of Figure 2.7:

    (a) How was the X-axis specified?

    (b) How was the Y-axis specified?

3. Write *voltage marker* or *viewpoint* after each of the following:

    (a) Bias point (DC) voltages on schematic   _____

    (b) Changing (swept) voltages graphed under *Probe* _____

4. Based on the results of *Problem 2* in the text, is it true that maximum power is transferred when *impedances are matched*?

    Yes   **No**

5. *Using current and resistance*, give the custom Y-axis command that would print out the power across R1 of Figure 2.1.

    Power (R1) = _____

6.   Why is ohm's law (V = IR) a *linear* equation?

7.   A 9V flashlight gives off 2 watts of power.   What is the resistance of the lightbulb?

8.   Give two reasons for *defining* a parameter (such as *RVAL*).

9.   Regarding current values, are each of the following true or false?

   (a) Current markers must be placed at the junction of a component so the system will know if it's at side 1 or side 2.

   True   **False**

   (b) Regardless of where a current marker is placed (side 1 or side 2), the waveform <u>displayed</u> is always the same as if the marker were at a side 1 location.

   True   **False**

   (c) Current trace-variables always refer to side 1.

   True   **False**

CHAPTER 3

AC Circuits
The Transient Mode

OBJECTIVES

- To analyze steady-state sinusoidal AC circuits in the time domain.
- To generate Probe graphs in the transient mode.

DISCUSSION

In this chapter we move from DC to AC circuits. We switch from a constant to a sine wave voltage source, and we adopt the transient (time-domain) mode of display.

We begin with the simple RC circuit of Figure 3.1.

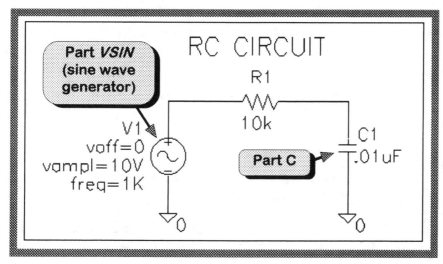

FIGURE 3.1

Simple RC circuit

THEORY

To predict the characteristics of the RC circuit of Figure 3.1, we have the choice of time-domain differential equations or frequency-domain algebraic equations. We choose the following frequency-domain solution because the mathematics is simplified.

Equation		Rectangular		Polar
V1	=	10V	=	10V $\angle 0°$
R1	=	10K	=	10K $\angle 0°$
$-jX_C$	=	$-j(1/(2\pi \times 1kHz \times .01\mu F)) = -j15.92k$	=	15.92K $\angle -90°$
$I = V1 / (R1 - jX_C)$	=	$10V / (10k - j15.92k)$	=	.532mA $\angle -58°$
$V_{out} = I \times -jX_C$	=	$(10V \times -j15.92k) / (10k - j15.92k)$	=	8.46V $\angle -32°$

INITIAL TRANSIENT SOLUTION

A transient analysis begins with an *Initial Transient Solution* at TIME = 0s. The values used in the calculation are the transient attribute values of the source (such as *VOFF = 0, VAMPL = 10V, and PHASE = 0*) at TIME = 0s. During initial transient calculations, all capacitors are opened and all inductors are shorted.

The initial transient solution—used as the starting point for a transient sweep—is displayed at the beginning of the Probe plot (at TIME = 0s) and is also written to the output file. (The *bias point* solution, which depends on *DC=* values, is in general not the same as the *initial transient* solution.)

Create File

Select Part

Draw Wire

SIMULATION PRACTICE

Step 1: Draw the circuit

1. Create a new schematics window, draw the initial circuit of Figure 3.1, and **DCLICKL** to set the resistor and capacitor attributes as shown. (The attributes of the voltage source will be set in step 2.)

2.   The next step is to assign amplitude, frequency, and offset attributes to V1 (as shown in Figure 3.1). *However, these attributes are not presently displayed.* To add these <u>new</u> attributes, follow the steps of *Schematics Note 3.1.*

Schematics Note 3.1
How do I set and change attributes that are <u>not</u> presently displayed?

Edit Attributes

As an example, let's assign to V1 the attributes of *VAMPL = 10V, VOFF = 0V,* and *VFREQ = 1k*:

- First, **DCLICKL** on V1's <u>symbol</u> to bring up the *Part Name* dialog box of Figure 3.2(a). (<u>Or</u> select V1's symbol, **CLICKL** on *Edits attributes of selected item(s)* toolbar button, <u>or</u> select, **Edit**, **Attributes**.)

- **CLICKL** on *VAMPL =* and fill in the *Value* box with 10V, **Save Attr.** (The "V" is optional.)

- We now have the <u>option</u> of displaying the name or value portion of the attribute—or both. **Change Display**, to bring up the *Change Attribute* dialog box of Figure 3.2(b), **CLICKL** on *Both name and value* (or another of your choice). (Experiment with the *Display Chracteristics* if you wish; they are generally left at their default states.)

      OK to return to *Part Name* dialog box.

- Repeat the previous two steps for *FREQ = 1k* and *VOFF = 0V*.   [*TD* (delay time), *DF* (damping factor), and *PHASE* will remain at their default values of zero, but can be assigned other values if desired. *DC =* (bias point) and *AC =* (frequency-domain) are not used for this purely transient analysis.]

- **OK** to return to schematic.   (Reposition attributes if necessary by select, **CLICKLH** and move.)

In summary: To modify an <u>existing</u> attribute, **DCLICKL** <u>on attribute</u> and change. To display and modify a <u>non-existing</u> attribute, **DCLICKL** <u>on symbol</u> and change. The display of attributes is optional.

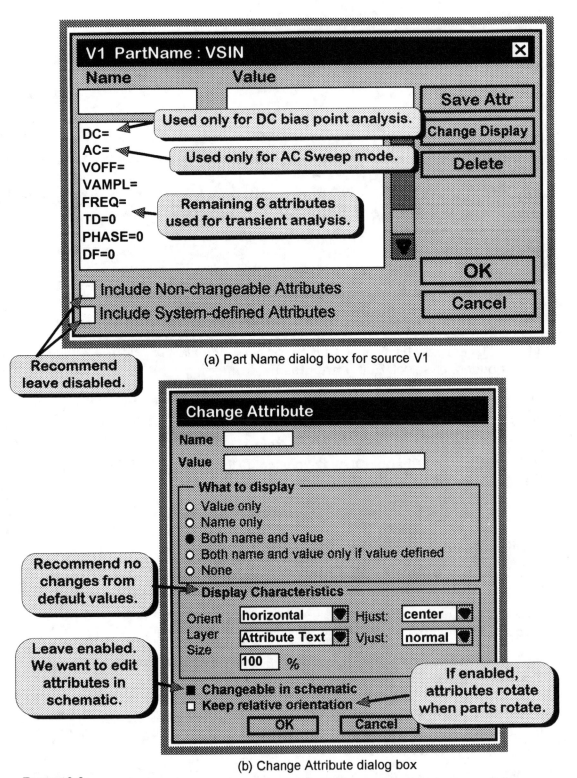

(a) Part Name dialog box for source V1

(b) Change Attribute dialog box

FIGURE 3.2

Attribute dialog boxes
(a) Part Name
(b) Change Attribute

PSpice for Windows

3. The circuit is now complete. However, to document the schematic, we wish to add the title "RC CIRCUIT" (shown in Figure 3.1). This is accomplished by: **CLICKL** on the *Draws text* toolbar button (or **Draw**, **Text**) to open up the *Place Text* window.   Enter text in the *Text* box, change size as desired, **OK**, **DRAG** text box to desired location, **CLICKL**, **CLICKR**. (*Select*, *cut* to remove text.)

Draw Text

Cut

Step 2: Select the sweep mode

4. We set the desired *transient* (time) mode as follows: **CLICKL** on the *Sets up the simulation analysis for active* toolbar button (or **Analysis**, **Setup**), **CLICKL** on the *enabled* box beside transient, **Transient** to open up the *Transient* dialog box and fill in as shown in Figure 3.3, **OK**, **Close**.

Analysis Setup

> Caution: <u>Do not set *Print Step* to zero</u>. (Print Step is not the start time; the start time is zero by default.) Refer to *PSpice Note 3.1* for a complete explanation of transient mode controls.)

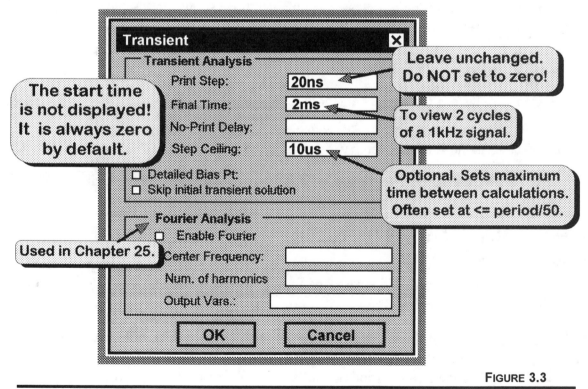

FIGURE 3.3

Transient mode dialog box

PSpice Note 3.1
What controls do I have over the transient analysis process?

Referring to the *Transient* dialog box of Figure 3.3, we have the following control over the calculation and display of data points:

- **Print Step** is used to determine the time step <u>only if there are no charge storage devices (such as capacitors) in the circuit</u>. Otherwise, *Print Step* refers to the print/plot of results to the <u>output file</u> (and not to Probe) when the special PRINT and PLOT *pseudocomponents* are placed on the schematic. When not required to set the time step, *Print Step* can be set to any value that is less than the *Final Time*. (The special pseudocomponents are explained in Chapter 5.)

- **No-Print Delay** is the amount of time (starting from 0) that is not graphed or printed.

- **Step Ceiling** is used to set the <u>maximum</u> *calculation* interval. All data points will be separated by no more than the value of step ceiling. (Step ceiling is useful for avoiding periods of low resolution.)   For repetitive waveforms, a good rule of thumb is: period/50 or less.

- **Detailed Bias Pt.** has no effect because the INITIAL TRANSIENT SOLUTION is always reported to the output file (unless *Skip initial transient solution* is enabled).

- **Skip initial transient** solution inhibits the reporting of the initial transient solution to the output file.

- **Fourier Analysis** is the subject of Chapter 25.

    Be aware that if a <u>DC</u> bias point solution is desired, enable the *Bias point detail* block in the *Analysis Setup* window.

Step 3: Analyze the circuit

Save File

Simulate

5.   The setup process is complete, so we save the file and begin PSpice simulation. (If errors are found, refer to the *Message Viewer* and *Output File*.)

When the PSpice window appears (Figure 3.4), note the summary at the bottom, which gives a running account of the *Time step* (time between calculations), the *Time* (present calculation time), and the *End* (finishing time). (To see how PSpice performs transient calculations, review *PSpice Note 3.2*.)

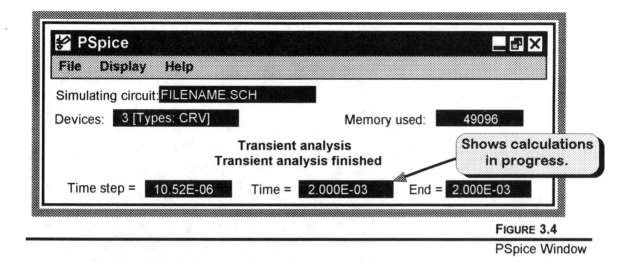

FIGURE 3.4
PSpice Window

PSpice Note 3.2
How does PSpice perform transient calculations?

Each transient calculation is called a *data point*. During transient analysis the time step between data points is automatically adjusted. When there is little activity, the time step is increased; during busy periods, the time step is reduced. Optional control *Step Ceiling* sets the maximum time between data points.

However, regardless of the circuit, at least 50 data points will be computed. All the data points calculated by *PSpice* are sent to *Probe* for display and printing.

6. After completion of the calculations, and assuming no errors were found, the initial *Probe* window is automatically opened (Figure 3.5). As expected, the X-axis defaults to the mode and value specified by Figure 3.3 (0 to 2ms), and the Y-axis is left blank.

Step 4: Select the X- and Y-axis variables

7. The default X-axis variable and range are proper.

To display the input and output voltages as Y-axis variables, we set two voltage "markers" as shown in Figure 3.6. (Bring up the *Schematics* window, **Markers**, **Mark Voltage/Level**, **DRAG** marker to first location, **CLICKL**, **DRAG** to second location, **CLICKL**, **CLICKR**, bring back the *Probe* window—and the waveforms of Figure 3.7 appear.)

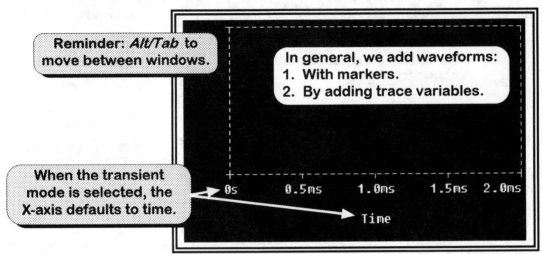

FIGURE 3.5

The initial
Probe window

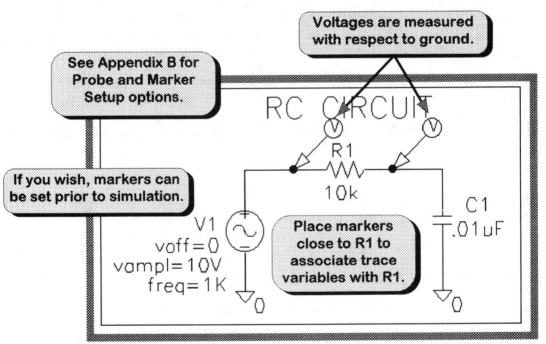

FIGURE 3.6

Setting voltage
markers

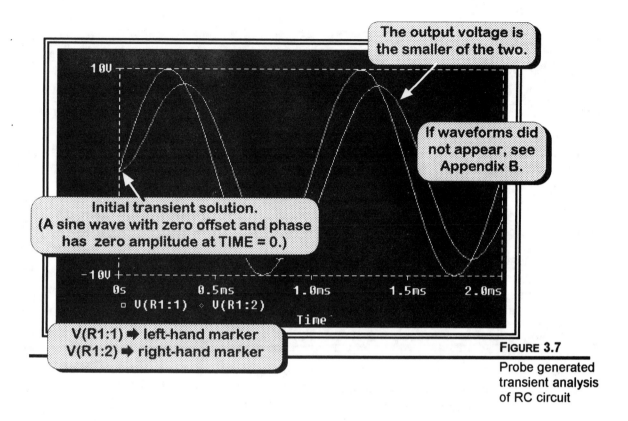

FIGURE 3.7

Probe generated transient analysis of RC circuit

8. After viewing the graph of Figure 3.7, *estimate* the following items. (<u>Hint</u>: For determining phase, 1ms = 360°.)

- V_{OUT} **(peak amplitude)** = _____

- **Phase difference between V_{IN} and V_{OUT} (degrees)** = _____

The cursor

9. In many cases, estimating values graphed under Probe is sufficient (as we did in step 8).   However, for those cases in which greater accuracy is required, we use the *cursor*.

Referring to *Probe Note 3.1* as necessary, use the cursors to again determine the following values as accurately as you can:

- V_{OUT} **(peak amplitude)** = _____

- **Phase difference between V_{IN} and V_{OUT} (degrees)** = _____

PSpice for Windows

Probe Note 3.1
How do I use the cursor?

Next peak

Cursor Display

To activate the *Probe* cursors: **CLICKL** on the *Toggle display of cursor* toolbar button, or **Tools**, **Cursor**, **Display**. Note the appearance of the cursors and the *Cursor* window (see Figure 3.8). If necessary, reposition the Cursor window (**CLICKLH** on the color bar and drag).

There are two cursors, A1 and A2. (If additional *Probe* windows are opened, both the windows and the cursors take on consecutive letters—A, B, C, ..., etc.)

- A1 is associated with closely spaced dotted lines and is controlled by the left-hand mouse button.
- A2 is associated with loosely spaced dotted lines and is controlled by the right-hand mouse button.

The first step is to associate a cursor with a waveform. This is done by a **CLICKL** (for cursor A1) or **CLICKR** (for cursor A2) on the appropriate color-coded legend symbols in front of the trace variables along the bottom of the graph. For example, on the graph of Figure 3.8, A1 has been associated with V(R1:1) and A2 has been associated with V(R1:2)—as shown in the blowup below.

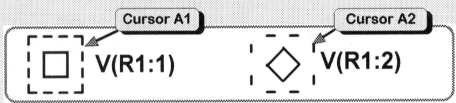

To position either cursor, **CLICKL** or **CLICKR** at any graph location and cursor A1 or A2 will move to that horizontal location along the corresponding waveform. If desired, **CLICKLH** (or **CLICKRH**) and drag either cursor. The X/Y coordinates of each cursor (as well as the difference) appear in the *Probe cursor* window. For example, referring to Figure 3.8, A1's cursor has an X coordinate of 101.010µs and a Y coordinate of 5.9003 volts.

To fine tune A1 (move A1's position in small steps), we use the arrow keys ($\rightarrow$ and $\leftarrow$). To fine tune A2, we hold down the Shift key and use the arrow keys.

To move either cursor to the nearest peak value, **CLICKL** (for A1) or **CLICKR** (for A2) to activate the desired cursor, followed by **CLICKL** on the *Position cursor at next peak value* toolbar button, or **Tools**, **Cursor**, **Peak**. Other cursor operations are available by **Tools**, **Cursor**, select option.

To deactivate the cursor, **CLICKL** on *Toggle display of cursor* toolbar button, or **Tools**, **Cursor**, **Display**.

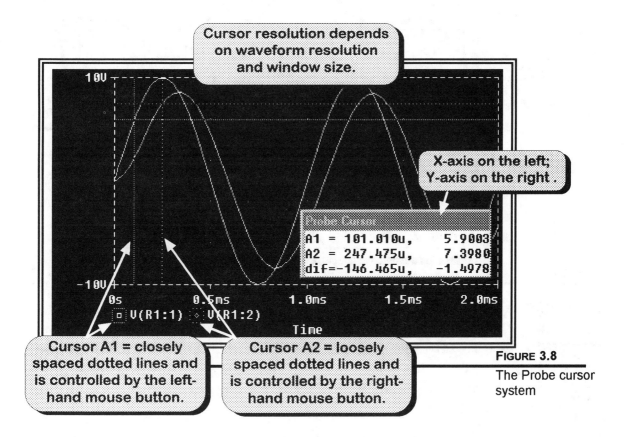

FIGURE 3.8

The Probe cursor system

10. What is the percent error between the cursor-obtained experimental values of step 9 and the theoretical values calculated in the discussion?

   • **V$_{OUT}$(ampl) % error =** _____

   • **Phase between V$_{IN}$ and V$_{OUT}$ (degrees) % error =** _____

Plotting current

11. By placing a current marker <u>at a component pin</u> as shown in Figure 3.9, add the circuit current to your graph (**Markers**, **Mark current into pin**, **DRAG** marker to pin, **CLICKL**, **CLICKR**).

   Oops! The resulting graph seems to show a constant current of nearly zero—and we know that is not correct! The problem is that the current *magnitude* is out of range—it's 1000 times less than the voltage magnitude, and PSpice always adjusts its curves according to the largest magnitude curve. (This happens quite often when mixing variables, such as voltages and currents.)

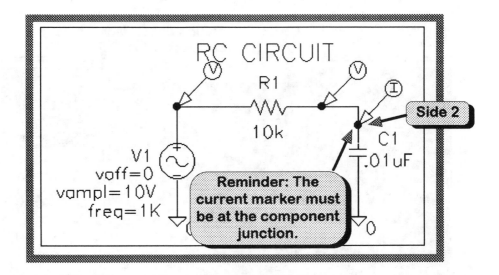

FIGURE 3.9

Placing a
current marker

Cut

12. To solve the problem, first delete the current waveform. (Select either the trace variable from *Probe* or the marker from *Schematics*, followed by **CLICKL** on *Cuts selected item(s)* toolbar button.)

13. To replace the current waveform correctly, review *Probe Note 3.2* and use a marker to redisplay the current <u>on a new Y-axis</u>. (The result is shown in Figure 3.10.)

Probe Note 3.2
How do I create multiple Y-axes?

To create a second (or third) Y-axis and associate a new waveform with this axis:

1. From Probe: **Plot, Add Y axis** to add new Y-axis to Probe graph.
2. Add desired curve (**DCLICKL** on existing marker, add new marker, or add trace variable).

Note the numerical code (1, 2, etc.) at the bottom of the *Probe* window that indicates which waveforms belong to which Y-axis. Also note the "axis marker" (>>), which indicates which Y-axis is active (which axis will receive the next action). To change the active Y-axis (and relocate the axis marker), **CLICKL** anywhere on the appropriate Y-axis scale.

To delete the selected Y-axis: **Plot, Delete Y Axis**.

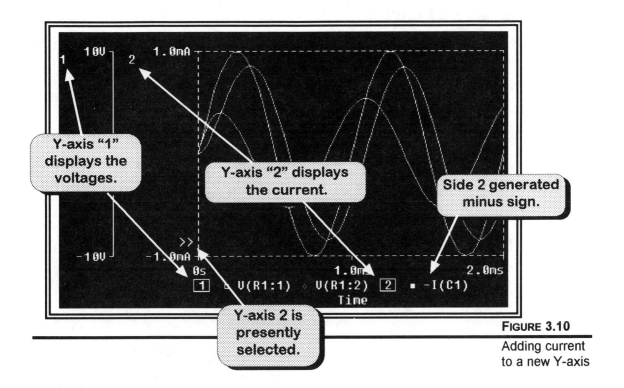

FIGURE 3.10

Adding current to a new Y-axis

14. Using the cursors, determine the following values as accurately as you can. (Use the second positive peak for all measurements, where the system has more closely approached a steady state.)

   • **I(peak) = _____**

   • **Phase between V_{IN} and I (degrees) = _____**

      Are these values approximately equal to those calculated in the discussion?

      Yes   No

Initial Transient Solution

15. Examine the output file (**Analysis, Examine Output** from Schematic) and locate the INITIAL TRANSIENT SOLUTION section. Do the initial values match those of Figure 3.10 (at 0s)?

      Yes   No

Advanced Activities

16. Perform a power analysis of the circuit of Figure 3.1 by generating the instantaneous waveforms of Figure 3.11.

- Is the resistor power "real" (always positive)?

   Yes   **No**

- Is the capacitor power "imaginary" (average of zero)?

   Yes   **No**

- Does the resistor power plus the capacitor power equal the source (apparent) power? (<u>Note</u>: V(R1:2) represents the same node as V(C1:2).)

   Yes   **No**

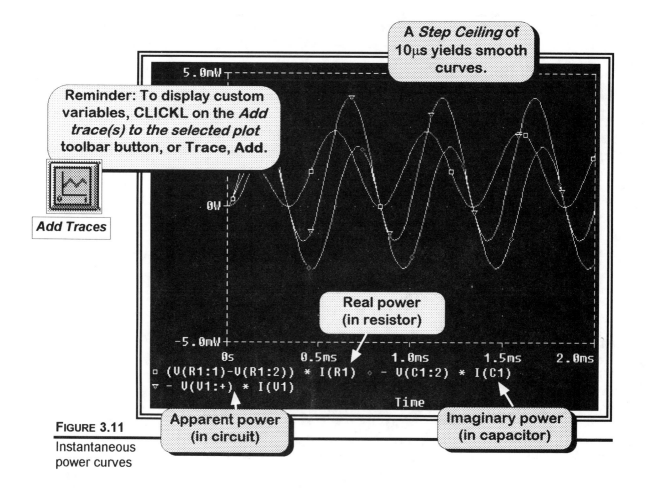

FIGURE 3.11
Instantaneous power curves

17. Use the AVG (running average) operator (Appendix B) to add plots of *average* power to Figure 3.11. (Pay special attention to the far right of the curves where the values are more closely approaching averages.)   Compare the instantaneous and average curves.

> To modify existing trace variables, **DCLICKL** on trace variable to bring up the *Modify Trace* dialog box, and modify the variable in the *Trace Expression* dialog box as desired.

18. Based on the circuit of Figure 3.12 (note the added TD, PHASE, and DC attributes), calculate by hand the INITIAL TRANSIENT and BIAS POINT values and record your predictions on a separate sheet of paper. Also, sketch the expected current and output voltage waveforms. Generate the same data and waveforms using PSpice and compare them with your predictions. (Be sure to enable the *Bias Point Detail* function, and to examine the output file for the INITIAL TRANSIENT and BIAS POINT solutions.)

19. Our task is completed for this chapter, so we exit all windows. (Reminder: Windows 95 users can **CLICKL** on "X" in the upper right of the window.)

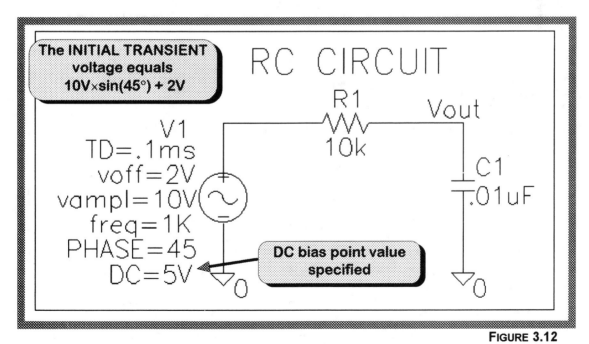

FIGURE 3.12

Attribute test circuit

EXERCISE

Referring to Figure 3.13, use complex numbers to calculate all necessary values required to sketch the following. Verify your results using PSpice.

(a) Draw the input and output voltage waveforms.

(b) Draw the *real* power output waveform (from R1).

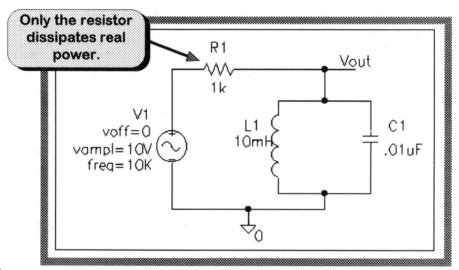

FIGURE 3.13

Applications circuit

QUESTIONS AND PROBLEMS

1.   When performing transient calculations, the starting time is always _____.

2.   In the complex term $-jX_c$, what does the $-j$ indicate about a capacitor?

3.   By drawing directly on Figure 3.1, show the location of the following *reference designators*: V(R1:1), V(R1:2), V(C1:1), and V(C1:2). (Which two are the same?)

4.   If voltage = 10 + j0 and current = 3 + j3, draw several cycles of the current and voltage waveforms on the following graph:

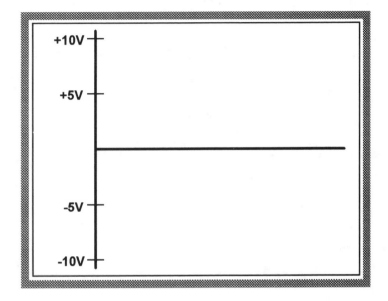

5.   What set of sine wave attributes (*Voff, Vampl,* and *Vfreq*) would generate the following input voltage (V1) curve?

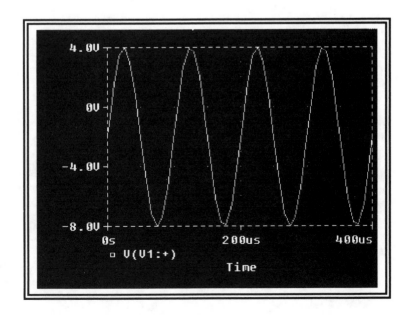

6. Referring to Figure 3.11, why is the resistor power always positive and the capacitor power always symmetric about zero? (<u>Hint</u>: What is the difference between *real* and *imaginary* power?)

CHAPTER 4

Complex Numbers
The AC Sweep Mode

OBJECTIVES

- To analyze a variety of RCL circuits using complex numbers.
- To generate and analyze Probe graphs in the frequency domain.
- To display complex values in both the polar and rectangular format.

DISCUSSION

When analyzing any circuit, such as the simple RC circuit of Figure 4.1, one of the most basic questions we can ask is this: Do we use the time-domain or the frequency-domain? The answer often depends on the application at hand.

If the RC circuit is found within a digital computer, it may be used as a 1's delay, and we would favor the time-domain analysis of the last chapter. If the same circuit is found within an analog system, such as a radio or TV set, it may be a simple low-pass filter and we would favor the frequency-domain analysis of this chapter.

Frequency-domain analysis means that the X-axis of our Probe display is frequency rather than time. To generate graphs in the frequency domain, we use the *AC Sweep* mode.

In the last chapter, we used complex numbers in a purely theoretical sense to perform hand calculations. In this chapter, we extend the use of complex numbers to PSpice.

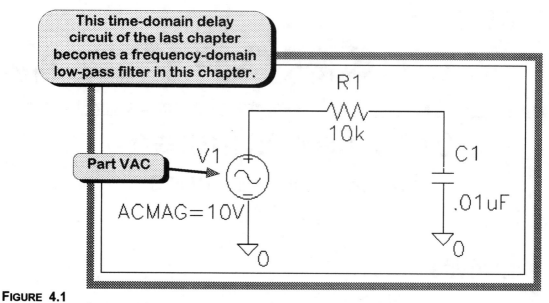

FIGURE 4.1

RC test circuit

Time domain versus frequency domain

In the time domain, the differential equations governing the operation of resistors, capacitors, and inductors are as follows—where all values of V and I are *instantaneous* values (lowercase):

THE TIME DOMAIN		
Resistor	Capacitor	Inductor
$v = i \times R$	$i = C dv/dt$	$v = L di/dt$

(Lowercase means instantaneous.)

However, if we substitute complex frequency ($e^{j2\pi ft}$) into these differential equations, a great simplification results: the more difficult differential equations of the time domain become the simpler algebraic equations of the frequency domain—where all values are complex, V and I are *peak* values (uppercase), and $X_C = 1/2\pi fC$ and $X_L = 2\pi fL$.

THE COMPLEX FREQUENCY DOMAIN		
Resistor	Capacitor	Inductor
$V = I \times R$	$V = -jX_C \times I$	$V = jX_L \times I$

(Uppercase means peak.)

Furthermore, the complex frequency-domain algebraic equations can often be further simplified by converting them from rectangular to polar format.

THEORY

In this chapter, we perform a frequency-domain analysis on the simple RC circuit used in the previous chapter (reproduced in Figure 4.1).

We will consider the circuit solved if we can plot current magnitude and phase versus frequency. Based on the three steps below, we start with Kirchhoff's voltage law in rectangular format, solve for complex current, and finally switch to polar format.

$$V = IR + -jIX_C$$

$$I = \frac{V}{(R - jX_C)} = \frac{V(R + jX_C)}{(R^2 + X_C^2)}$$

$$I = \frac{V}{\sqrt{R^2 + X_C^2}} \angle \left(0 - TAN^{-1}(\frac{-X_C}{R}) \right)$$

As a final step, we have the option of generating the current magnitude in decibels:

$$I(dB) = 20 \times LOG_{10}(I)$$

Using these equations, we can plot various graphs by hand for later comparison to PSpice-generated plots. However, since this can be quite time-consuming, let's just settle for the current and phase at a specific frequency—the *break* frequency.

The break frequency (f_B) is defined as the frequency in which the amplitude drops by 3dB, or the phase = 45°.

$$\frac{X_C}{R} = \frac{1}{(2\pi f_B CR)} = TAN(45°) = 1$$

$$f_B = 1592Hz$$

Therefore, at the break frequency of 1592Hz, we predict the following circuit values

Current	Value at f_B
I(magnitude)	$10V/(((10k)^2 + (10k)^2)^{1/2}) = 10V/14.1k = .707mA$
I(phase)	$45°$
I(imaginary)	$VR/(R^2 + X_c^2) = 10 \times 10k/(2 \times 10k^2) = .5mA$
I(real)	$VX_c/(R^2 + X_c^2) = 10 \times 10k/(2 \times 10k^2) = .5mA$

PSPICE COMPLEX ANALYSIS

All voltage and current variables processed by PSpice during an AC Sweep analysis are in complex form. By making use of the following *Probe* operators, we can display any circuit value in either polar or rectangular format.

Polar Operators	Description
M(x) or None	Magnitude of x
P(x)	Phase of x
Rectangular Operators	**Description**
R(x)	Real part of x
IMG(x)	Imaginary part of x

When using these complex operators, it is helpful to remember the following:

- When no operator is used, Probe displays the polar format magnitude (M) by default.

- Taking the phase (P) of the quotient of two trace variables returns the phase angle in degrees between them.

- When determining *real* power (peak), use the equation shown below, where the angle between voltage and current is in radians.

The "P" operator returns degrees, but the "cos" operator requires radians.

Real Power (peak) = V*I*cos(6.283/360*P(V/I))

Or simply determine the power in each resistive (real) component by $(I^2 \times R)/2$ and sum them together.

SIMULATION PRACTICE

Draw the circuit

Open File

1. Draw (or modify from the previous chapter) the simple RC circuit of Figure 4.1 and **DCLICKL** to set the attributes as shown.

> Note: Figure 4.1 uses part VAC for AC sweep analysis. Part *VSIN* can also be used for an AC sweep by specifying the *AC =* attribute; however, the transient attributes must also be set.

Create File

Select the sweep mode

Select Part

2. To analyze the RC circuit, we choose a logarithmic (decade) frequency sweep from 10Hz to 10kHz.

    We set up this AC Sweep mode as follows: **CLICKL** on the *Sets up the simulation analysis for active* toolbar button (or **Analysis**, **Setup**), **CLICKL** on *Enabled* box for AC Sweep, **AC Sweep** to bring up the *AC Sweep and Noise Analysis* dialog box of Figure 4.2, and enter data as shown.

Draw Wire

- *AC Sweep Type:* **CLICKL** on *Decade* (to make the X-axis plot logarithmic).

Analysis Setup

- *Sweep Parameters:*   Enter 200 in the *Pts/Decade* box (to command PSpice to calculate 200 points each decade).   Enter 10Hz in the *Start Freq:* box, and 10kHz in the *End Freq:* box, **OK**, **Close**.

Analyze the circuit

3. Simulate the circuit and note the calculation summary in the PSpice window.

    When the default Probe graph comes up, note the X-axis logarithmic range of frequency values. (Does it match your instructions?)

         Yes   **No**

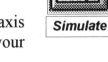
Simulate

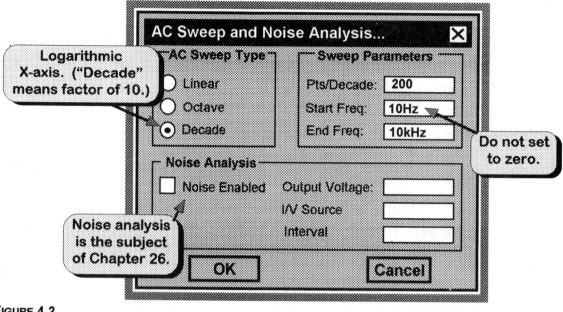

FIGURE 4.2

AC Sweep and
Noise Analysis
dialog box

Select the X- and Y-axes variables

4. The default X-axis variable and range are okay. For the Y-axis variable we choose circuit current. However, we are faced with several possibilities:

- We can choose either the polar or rectangular format for display.

- We can use either markers or trace variables to select items for display.

    For starters, set a current marker (Figure 4.3) for linear display of current magnitude in the polar format and generate the Probe graph of Figure 4.4 .

    Does the current magnitude (polar form) tend towards 1mA at high frequencies and 0mA at low frequencies—as expected?

    Yes   No

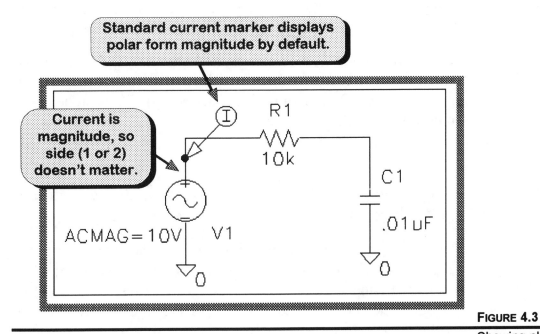

FIGURE 4.3

Showing placement of current marker

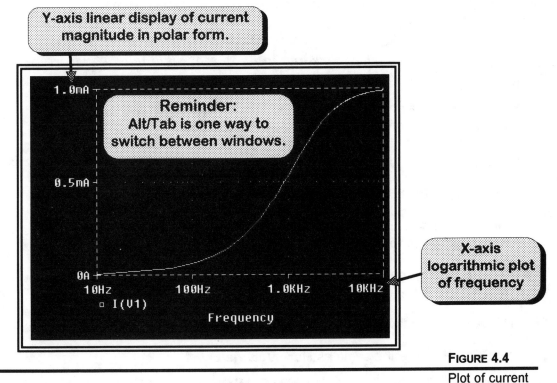

FIGURE 4.4

Plot of current magnitude in polar form

PSpice for Windows

5. To plot the phase between source voltage and current, we take advantage of the special *advanced markers* available under *Probe*.

Add a second Y-axis (**Plot**, **Add Y-axis**) and follow the guidelines of *Probe Note 4.1* to place the *iphase* marker as shown in Figure 4.5 (**Edit**, **Rotate**, or Ctrl/R if necessary). Your probe graph should resemble the plot of Figure 4.6.

NOTES

- The phase of any trace variable is always measured relative to the voltage source—which is always at zero phase.

- However, if the trace variable is current, all the polarity rules for current come into play. For example, current measured at the + terminal (side 1) of a voltage source is negative. Therefore, to display the correct phase of I(V1) (as shown in Figure 4.6), we add +180 to the trace variable.

Probe Note 4.1
What special markers are available to plot advanced waveforms?

To use the advanced markers, bring up the Schematics window, **Markers**, **Mark Advanced** to bring up the *Mark Advanced* dialog box, select the desired marker from the *Part* list (such as *iphase*), **OK**, place the marker at the desired location, **CLICKL**, **CLICKR**:

- The *db*, *phase*, *real*, and *imaginary* markers generate the indicated plots.

- IMARKER and VDIFFMARKER are the same as **Mark Current Into Pin** and **Mark Voltage Differential**.

- The groupdelay marker performs the negative derivative of the phase with respect to the frequency (–dPHASE/dFREQUENCY).

- POLARIS is used with *signal integrity analysis* (not covered in this text).

- NODEMARKER is the same as **Mark Voltage/Level**.

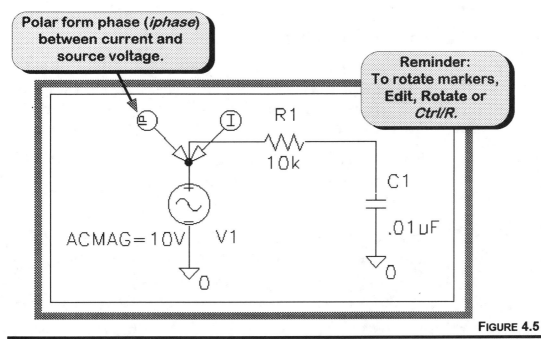

FIGURE 4.5

Phase marker added

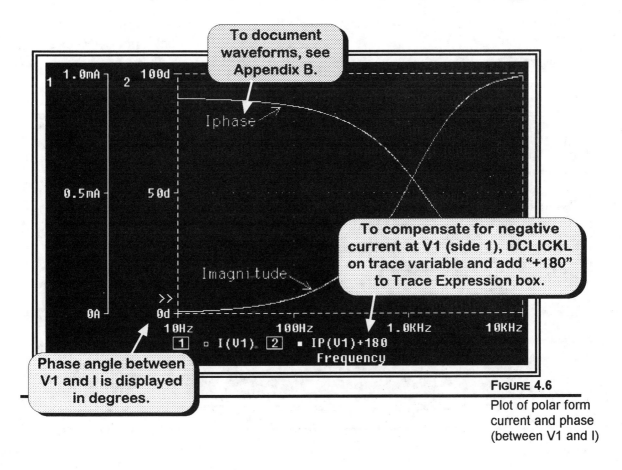

FIGURE 4.6

Plot of polar form current and phase (between V1 and I)

Adding rectangular format

6. The current magnitude and phase plots of Figure 4.6 are in polar format. To perform a complete complex analysis, we must also plot the current in rectangular format However, displaying both formats on a single graph would be confusing.

Based on *Probe Note 4.2*, open up a new window and arrange them in "tile" format—as shown by Figure 4.7.

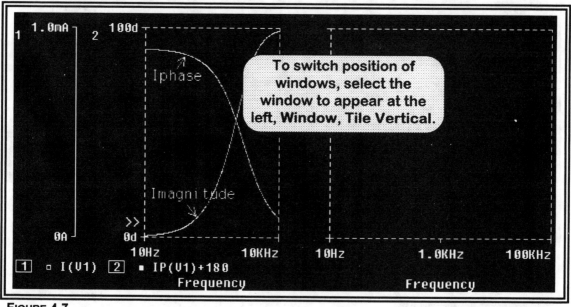

Probe Note 4.2
How do I open up multiple windows under Probe?

To open up a new window under Probe: **Window, New**. To arrange the windows in "tile" format (side by side): **Window, Tile Vertical**. (**Tile Horizontal** arranges the windows in horizontal layers, and **Cascade** arranges the windows like file folders.)

To select a given window for activity, **CLICKL** on that window (or **Window**, **CLICKL** on 1, 2, etc.). To remove any window: **CLICKL** to select, **Window, Close**.

FIGURE 4.7

Opening a second
window

7. To place the rectangular-format current components on the right-hand graph, select the right-hand graph (**CLICKL** on graph and note the border or title bar highlight), and return to the schematics window. Place advanced markers *ireal* and *imaginary*, as shown in Figure 4.8, and generate the plots of Figure 4.9. (Be sure to add minus signs to both trace variables.)

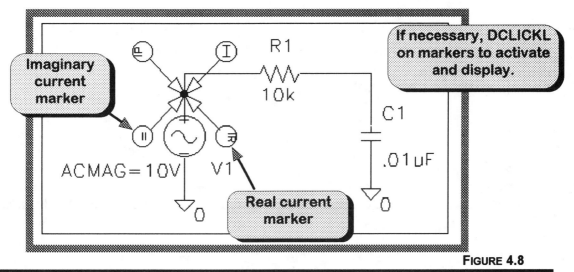

FIGURE 4.8

Placing rectangular-format current markers

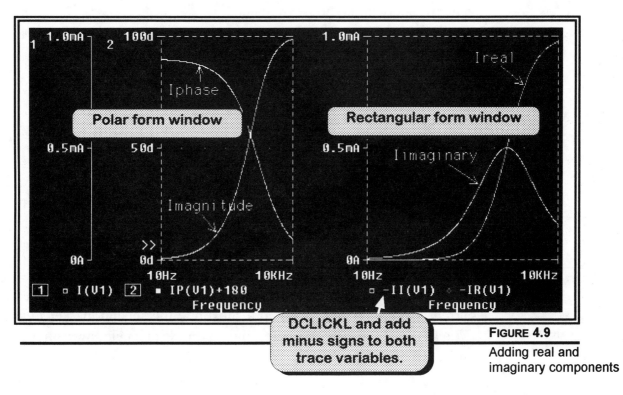

FIGURE 4.9

Adding real and imaginary components

8.   To document your waveforms as shown, see Appendix B.

Cursor Display

9.   Using the cursor, determine the following current values as close as possible to 1592Hz (the break frequency).

> Note: A separate set of cursors must be opened for each window. **CLICKL** on any window to select the corresponding cursor set.

Current	Value at f$_B$
I(magnitude)	
I(phase)	
I(imaginary)	
I(real)	

10.   Compare the values experimentally determined in step 9 with those calculated in the discussion.   Are they approximately the same?

Yes   **No**

11.   Using the data from step 9, do the following equations hold approximately at the break frequency?

$$I(magnitude) = \sqrt{I(real)^2 + I(img)^2}$$

$$I(phase) = \tan^{-1}(I(img)/I(real))$$

Yes   **No**

The Bode plot

12.   To generate a Bode plot, we must convert the Y-axis polar form magnitude plot from linear to logarithmic (decibels). (The other three plots will remain as is.)

Cut

To accomplish this, select the left-hand *Probe* window (and the correct Y-axis), switch to the *Schematics* window, delete the current magnitude marker (*I*), and substitute the special marker *idb* (**Markers**, **Mark advanced**, etc.).   Your Probe window should now resemble Figure 4.10.

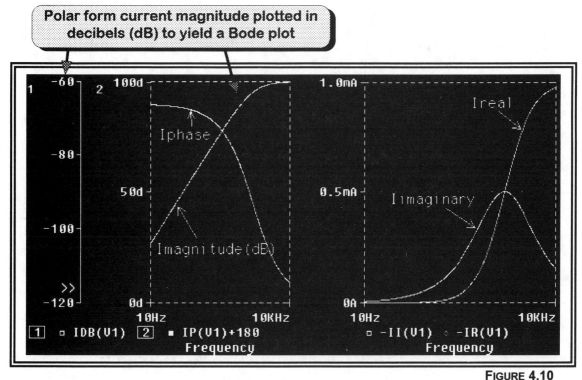

FIGURE 4.10

Default Bode plot

13. Examining the result:

(a) At high frequencies, does the current magnitude equal −60dB (1mA)? (Hint: Does $10^{-60dB/20dB} = 1mA$?)

  Yes   **No**

(b) Does the current "break" at −63dB?   (Remember: $f_{BREAK} = 1592Hz$.)

  Yes   **No**

(c) Well to the left of the breakpoint, does the current roll off at 20dB/decade? (1 decade = factor of 10.)

  Yes   **No**

Advanced Activities

14. To prove the equivalency of the polar and rectangular formats, we will generalize step 11 by generating complete polar waveforms from rectangular operators.

Add Traces

The following equations convert rectangular-form current into polar-form current. Enter the equations (separate Y-axes) into any clean AC sweep Probe graph and note the waveforms produced. Comparing the waveforms to Figure 4.6, what conclusions can you draw?

SQRT(PWR(R(I(V1)),2) + PWR(IMG(I(V1)),2))

ATAN(IMG(I(V1)) / R(I(V1)))*180/3.14

15. For the RC circuit of Figure 4.1, use the equations below to display the apparent, real, and imaginary power. Summarize your results. (When is real power the greatest? When does imaginary power peak? Is apparent power squared equal to real power squared plus imaginary power squared?)

Apparent power = V(V1:+)*I(V1)

Real power = (V(V1:+)–V(C1:2))*I(R1)

Imaginary power = V(C1:2)*I(C1)

EXERCISES

- The simple RC circuit of Figure 4.1 is also known as a *low-pass filter*. Using PSpice, generate a <u>gain</u> Bode plot (Vout/Vin with both axes logarithmic) and determine its *break frequency* (3dB down) and *rolloff* (slope of high-frequency portion in dB/dec).

- Design and test an RL low-pass filter with the same break frequency as the RC filter. (Hint: To determine the required value of L, remember that the break frequency occurs when X_L and R are equal, giving a phase shift of 45°.)

QUESTIONS AND PROBLEMS

1. What is the time-domain differential equation for the circuit of Figure 4.1?

2.   If I = 2 + j2, what do we know about the current magnitude and phase?

3.   Review Figure 4.6 and answer the following:

    (a) Why does the current tend toward 1mA at high frequencies?

    (b) Why does the current tend toward zero at low frequencies?

    (c) Why does the circuit phase tend towards 90° at low frequencies?

    (d) Why does the circuit phase tend toward 0° at high frequencies?

4.   For the RC circuit of Figure 4.1, determine the complex current (real and imaginary components) at 10Hz and 10kHz.   What do the results say about the characteristics of the circuit at these two frequencies?

5. When displaying *real* power (peak), why are the two equations below equivalent?

$$V(source:+)*I(source)*cos(6.28/360*P(V(source:+)/I(source)))$$

$$R*I(source)*I(source)/2$$

6. Referring to Figure 4.9, prove the equivalency of the polar and rectangular formats at 1kHz.

CHAPTER 5

The Tank Circuit
Resolution

OBJECTIVES

- To analyze a parallel RLC tank circuit.
- To use the print and plot *pseudocomponents*.
- To increase resolution by increasing the number of data points.

DISCUSSION

One of the most common and useful circuits in all of analog communications is the *tank* circuit of Figure 5.1. It is a natural bandpass *filter*, often used in high-frequency applications to single out a narrow band of frequencies or to establish a frequency of oscillation.

Because the tank circuit is most often found in analog communications systems, we will stay with the frequency-domain (*AC Sweep*) analysis of the last chapter.

THEORY

As in the last chapter, we analyze the tank circuit of Figure 5.1 in the frequency domain using Kirchhoff's laws and complex numbers:

$$I(\text{source}) \quad = \quad I(\text{C branch}) \quad + \quad I(\text{RL branch})$$

$$V(\text{source}) / Z \quad = \quad V(\text{source}) / -jX_C \quad + \quad V(\text{source}) / (R + jX_L)$$

The solution to this equation is quite involved. Fortunately, for small values of R, we can approximate its solution in terms of the tank's *resonant frequency* (f_r) and circuit Q (a measure of the circuit's selectivity).

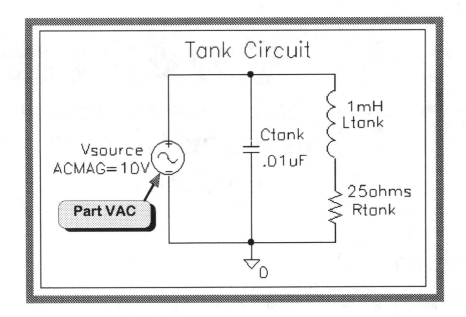

FIGURE 5.1

The tank circuit

For a high-Q circuit (above 10) the following solutions give satisfactory approximations:

f_r = 1/[2π(LC)$^{1/2}$] = 1 / [6.28 × (1mH × 0.01μF)$^{1/2}$] = <u>**50.33kHz**</u>

Q = X_L (at f_r) / r = (6.28 × 50.33kH × 1mH) /25Ω = <u>**12.65**</u>

BW (Bandwidth) = f_r /Q = 50.33kHz / 12.65 = <u>**4kHz**</u>

Z (at f_r) = Q × X_L = 12.65 x 316Ω = <u>**4kΩ**</u> = <u>**72dB**</u>

SIMULATION PRACTICE

Draw the circuit

Select Part

1.   Draw the circuit of Figure 5.1.

Draw Wire

To change *V1* to *Vsource*, *R1* to *Rtank*, etc., **DCLICKL** on each attribute to bring up the *Edit Reference Designator* dialog box of Figure 5.2. Enter the new attributes in the *Package Reference Designator* box, **OK**.   The *Gate* and *Package Type* boxes will not be used by this text.

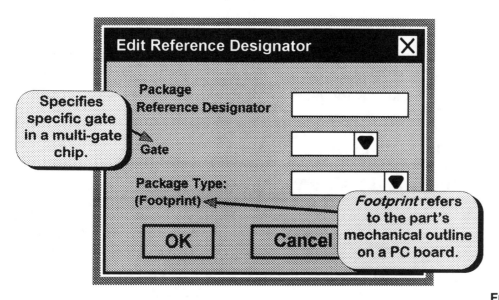

FIGURE 5.2

Edit Reference Designator dialog box

Select the sweep mode

2. Fill in the *AC Sweep and Noise Analysis* dialog box as shown in Figure 5.3. (The frequency range of 10kHz to 100kHz will contain the 50kHz predicted resonant frequency).

Analysis Setup

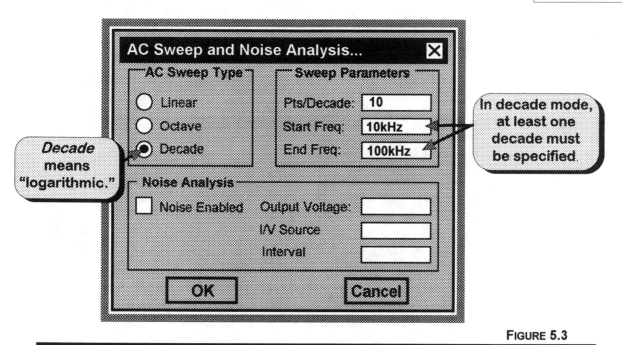

FIGURE 5.3

AC Sweep and Noise analysis dialog box

Save File

Simulate

Analyze the circuit

3. Save the file and simulate the circuit. Note the calculation summary in the PSpice window. When the default Probe graph comes up, note the X-axis logarithmic plot of frequency. Does it match your instructions?

Yes   **No**

Select the X- and Y-axes variables

Add Traces

4. The X-axis variable and range are proper and can remain as they are. To display circuit impedance on the Y-axis, **CLICKL** on the *Add traces to the selected plot* toolbar button (or **Trace**, **Add**) to bring up the *Add Traces* dialog box.

> Reminder: **CLICKL** on trace variables and operators when building equations in the trace box. Be especially careful when nested parentheses are used.

Enter the impedance equation shown below in the *trace* box—and the impedance waveform of Figure 5.4 appears!

$$DB(V(Vsource:+)/I(Vsource))$$

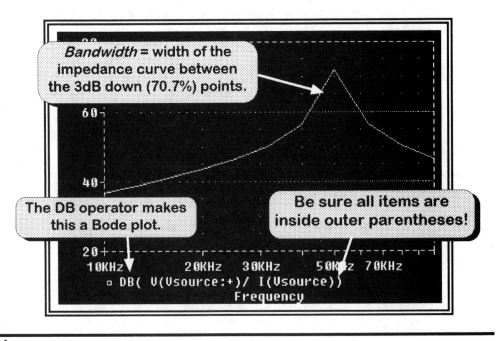

FIGURE 5.4

Bode plot of impedance

5. Based on the waveform of Figure 5.4, use the cursor to determine the following as accurately as you can:

$$f_r \quad\quad = \underline{\hspace{4cm}}$$

$$Z(dB \text{ at } f_r) \quad = \underline{\hspace{4cm}}$$

$$BW \quad\quad = \underline{\hspace{4cm}}$$

$$Q = f_r/BW \quad = \underline{\hspace{4cm}}$$

6. Do the PSpice values of step 5 approximately match the predicted values calculated in the discussion?

     Yes   **No**

Showing the data points

7. Reviewing Figure 5.4, we look at the very triangular shape of the impedance curve around resonance and we wonder if enough *data points* have been calculated to give good resolution.

     Fortunately, this dilemma is resolved easily. Just perform **Tools, Options, Mark Data Points, OK** from your Probe graph, and the data points appear (see Figure 5.5).

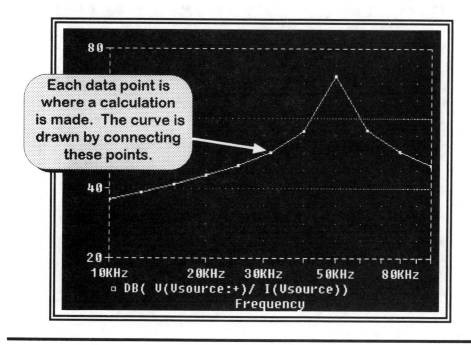

FIGURE 5.5

Graph showing
data points

8. The result (Figure 5.5) shows that our suspicions were correct! Only three data points define the important resonant portion of the graph.

Analysis Setup

To provide greater resolution (at the expense of more calculation time), return to *Schematics* and bring up the *AC Sweep and Noise Analysis* dialog box, increase the *Total Pts:* (per decade) from 10 to 100, re-simulate the circuit, and display the new dB curve (Figure 5.6).

(a) Approximately now many data points now mark the same resonant portion of the graph?

Data points near resonance = _____

(b) Go back and update the values of step 5. Are the new values closer to the theoretical predictions?

Yes   No

9. Our resolution study done, we remove the data points to make the waveforms easier to read (**Tools**, **Options**, **Mark Data Points** to disable, **OK**).

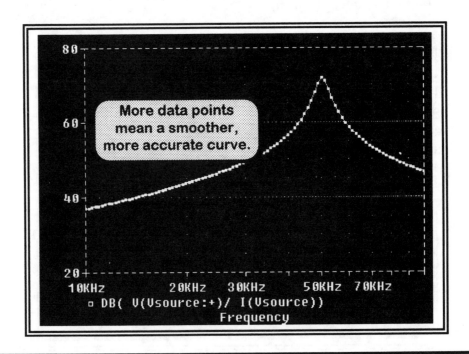

FIGURE 5.6

Increasing the number
of data points for
greater resolution

PSpice for Windows

Complex number analysis

10. Following the procedures of Chapter 4, perform a complex analysis of the tank circuit and create the graphs of Figure 5.7.

> The minus signs appearing with the *P*, *R*, and *IMG* operators are used to invert the current so the resulting plots will display correct values.

Add Traces

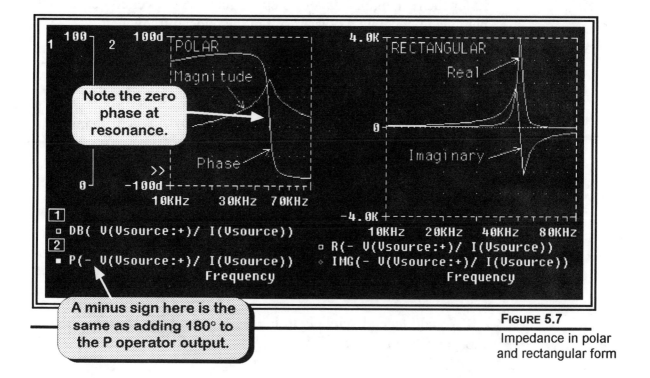

FIGURE 5.7

Impedance in polar and rectangular form

11. Based on the results of Figure 5.7, circle the two components listed below that are zero (or near zero) at the resonant frequency:

   Polar magnitude   **Rectangular real**

   Polar phase   **Rectangular imaginary**

   Is this as expected?

   Yes   **No**

12. Next, to prove the equivalence of the rectangular and polar formats, choose any convenient frequency (such as 45kHz), and use the cursors to fill in the following table.

Polar impedance	Rectangular impedance
Magnitude (dB) = _____	Real = _____
Phase = _____	Imaginary = _____

13. Enter the rectangular data of step 12 into the conversion equations below and generate a polar result at the chosen frequency.

   $$\text{Magnitude(dB)} = 20\log_{10}\{[Z(R)^2 + Z(IMG)^2]^{1/2}\} = \text{_____}$$

   $$\text{Phase}(°) = ATAN[Z(IMG)/Z(R)] = \text{_____}$$

   Do the calculated polar values *approximately* match the experimental polar values of step 12?

   Yes   **No**

Legend symbols

14. When a graph contains a large number of curves (as in Figure 5.7), it is convenient to place the legend symbols on the curves themselves. Adding descriptive text then becomes less important.

   To add legend symbols to Figure 5.7, read *Probe Note 5.1* and reproduce the graph of Figure 5.8.

Probe Note 5.1
How do I place legend symbols on the curves?

- To place legend symbols on the curves: **Tools**, **Options**, **Always** (under *Use Symbols* menu), **OK**.
- To remove the legend symbols: **Tools**, **Options**, **Auto** (or **Never**), **OK**.

When in the Auto mode, PSpice automatically places legend symbols when a given graph reaches a predetermined level of complexity.

To return to default options, **Tools**, **Options**, **Reset**, **OK**.

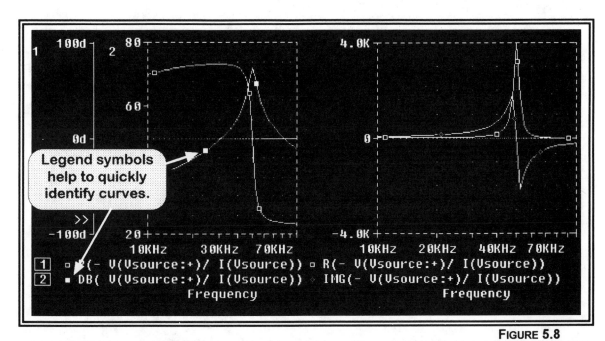

FIGURE 5.8

Adding legend
symbols

The Print and Plot pseudocomponents

Instead of using Probe, sometimes it is more convenient to send results
to the output file in the form of tables or plots.　For this purpose we can
select from the *pseudocomponents* of Table 5.1.

Symbol	Description
IPLOT	Plot showing current through a cut in the net (must be placed in series)
IPRINT	Table showing current through a cut in the net
PRINTDGTLCHG	Table showing digital changes during a transient analysis at the connect point
VPLOT1	Plot showing voltages at the connect point
VPLOT2	Plot showing voltage differentials between two connect points
VPRINT1	Table showing voltages at the connect point
VPRINT2	Table showing voltage differentials between two connect points

Table 5.1

Printpoint
pseudocomponents

15. As shown in Figure 5.9, add pseudocomponents *VPRINT1* and *VPLOT1* to your tank circuit and **DCLICKL** to set the attributes as shown. (VPRINT1 and VPLOT1 are from library *special.slb*.)

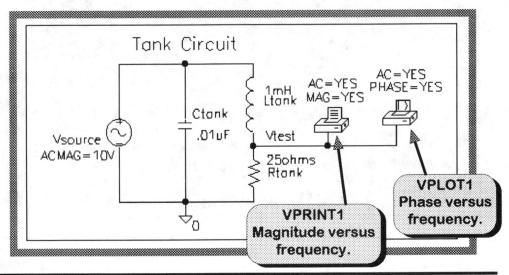

Figure 5.9

VPRINT1 and
VPLOT1 added

16. Run PSpice and note the results at the end of the output file. Did you observe a table of frequency versus voltage values and a plot of frequency versus phase values at the *Vtest* node? Did the number of entries equal the number of specified points (100)?

    Yes   **No**

Advanced Activities

17. Plot a graph of real, imaginary, and apparent power for the tank circuit of Figure 5.1. (Hint: Make use of the equations below.)

Apparent power (AP) =	Vsource*Isource
Real power (RP) =	Vsource*Isource*cos(6.28/360*P(Vsource/Isource)))
Imaginary power (IP) =	Vsource*Isource*sin(6.28/360*P(Vsource/Isource)))

Does $(AP)^2 = (RP)^2 + (IP)^2$?

    Yes   **No**

PSpice for Windows

EXERCISE

- Determine the impedance characteristics of the transformer coupled tank circuit of Figure 5.10.   How do the characteristics depend on the turns ratio and coupling coefficient?

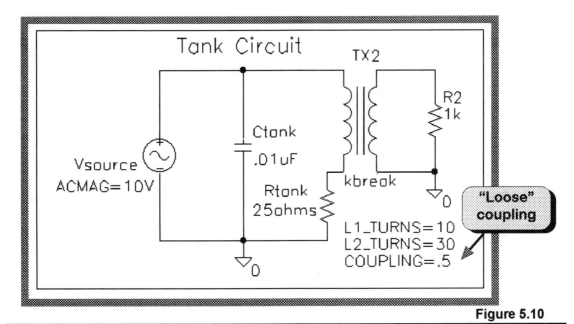

Figure 5.10

Tank circuit using transformer coupling to the load

QUESTIONS AND PROBLEMS

1. Why is the impedance of a tank circuit the greatest at the resonant frequency? (<u>Hint</u>: What happens to the current in the two branches near the resonant frequency?)

2.   An expression such as V(C1:2)*I(V1) produces what Y-axis unit of measurement?

3.   What voltage ratio is represented by +10dB?   −10dB?

4.   How does Figure 5.8 (rectangular format) prove that the tank circuit is:

     (a) resistive at the resonant frequency?

     (b) capacitive at frequencies above the resonant frequency, and inductive at frequencies below the resonant frequency?

5.   List two ways that circuit Q can be defined for a tank circuit.

6.   Why is real power generated in a tank circuit greatest at lower frequencies? (Hint: Which branch receives most of the current at low frequencies?)

7. Why are the two equations below equivalent?

$$DB(V(source:+)/I(source))$$
$$DB(M(V(source:+))/M(I(source)))$$

8. Would a circuit Q of 100 (compared to 12.65) produce a sharper impedance peak?

Yes **No**

CHAPTER 6

Families of Curves
The Parametric Mode

OBJECTIVES

- To use the *parametric* mode to plot a family of curves for the tank circuit of Chapter 5.
- To expand or compress waveforms for better viewing.

DISCUSSION

In Chapter 5 we analyzed the tank circuit of Figure 6.1 in the frequency domain, and we generated a Bode plot.

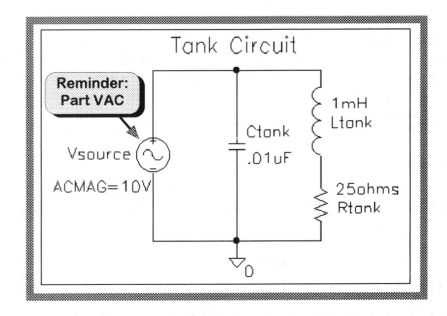

FIGURE 6.1

Tank circuit

However, for many applications, it becomes convenient and informative to show the properties of a tank circuit as a *family* of curves with various values of Q (X_L/Rtank). Such a plot is shown in Figure 6.2, and is the subject of this chapter.

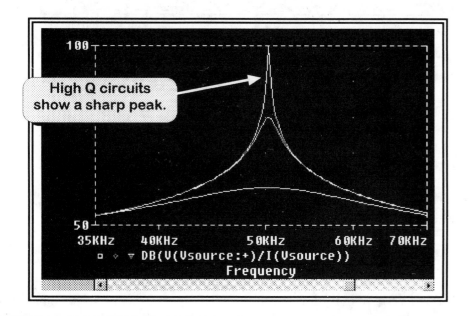

FIGURE 6.2

Family of curves of
various values of Q

NESTED CURVES

The plot of Figure 6.2 was created with a *nested* sweep (one sweep inside another). The first (outer) sweep is the *main* sweep, and the second (inner) sweep is the *nested* (parametric) sweep. The main sweep variable is usually related to the X-axis, and the nested sweep variable creates the family of curves. In Figure 6.2, the main sweep variable is frequency and the nested sweep variable is *Rtank*.

THEORY

In this experiment we will sweep *Rtank* through the values 1, 10, and 100Ω. For a resonant frequency of 50.33kHz, the following equations determine the circuit Qs.

Q(at 1Ω)   = X_L (at f_r) / Rtank = (6.28 x 50.33kH x 1mH) /1 = 316

Q(at 10Ω)   = X_L (at f_r) / Rtank = (6.28 x 50.33kH x 1mH) /10 = 31.6

Q(at 100Ω) = X_L (at f_r) / Rtank = (6.28 x 50.33kH x 1mH) /100 = 3.16

SIMULATION PRACTICE

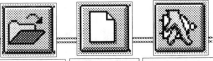

| Open File | Create File | Select Part | Draw Wire |

Draw the circuit

1. Draw or bring back the tank circuit of Figure 6.1 (from Chapter 5).

Select the sweep mode

Analysis Setup

2. Set up or modify the system for an AC sweep of *Vsource* from 10kHz to 100kHz at 500 points/decade.

3. To sweep a *global* variable (such as *Rtank*), we follow the three-step sequence used in Chapter 2 (*Schematics Note 2.2*). However, because *Rtank* is a *nested* sweep variable (and not an X-axis variable), we use the *Parametric* dialog box to set up the parameters in step 3.

   Step 1: Change *Rtank* from a constant (25ohms) to a variable ({RVAL}).

   Select Part

   Step 2: Define variable *RVAL*. (**CLICKL** on the *Selects a part to draw* toolbar button, **PARAM**, **Place & Close**, **DRAG** box to any location, **CLICKL**, **CLICKR**. **DCLICKL** on PARAMETERS, **Name1**, fill in RVAL in *Value* box, **Save Attr**, **Value1**, fill in 25 in *Value* box, **Save Attr**, **OK**).

   > Reminder: *Value1* = *25* sets the *Rtank* value to be used when the parametric analysis is disabled.

   Analysis Setup

   Step 3: Set up the parametric sweep: **CLICKL** on the *Sets up the simulation analysis for active* toolbar button (or **Analysis**, **Setup**), **CLICKL** on enabled box for Parametric mode, **Parametric** and enter parameters as shown in Figure 6.3, **OK**, **Close**.

   > Note: By enabling the *Value List*, we sweep Rtank through the numbers listed in the *Values* box.

   At the completion of all three steps, your schematic should resemble Figure 6.4.

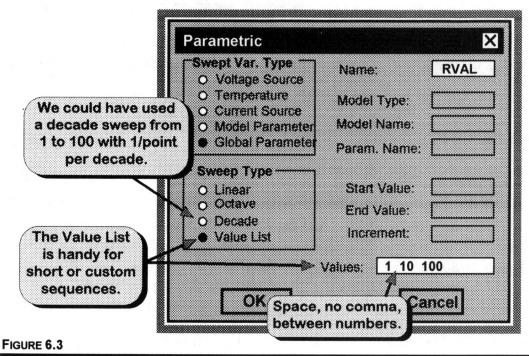

FIGURE 6.3

Parametric
dialog box

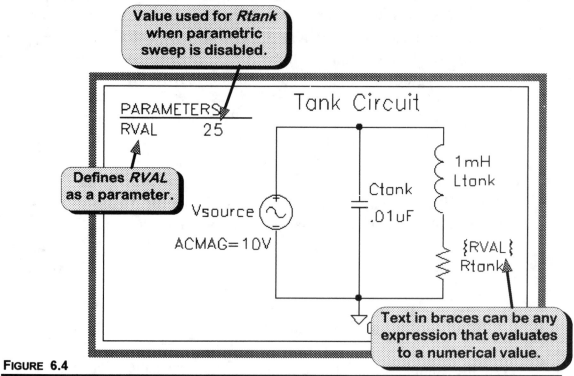

FIGURE 6.4

Tank circuit setup
for nested sweep

Analyze the circuit

4. Begin simulation and observe the PSpice window. Note how the frequency calculations repeat in a *nested* manner for *Rtank* values of 1, 10, and 100.

    After the calculations are done, the *Available Sections* dialog box appears (Figure 6.5), showing the range of parameter (RVAL) values and giving us an opportunity to select only those we wish to display. Since all are selected by default, **OK**.

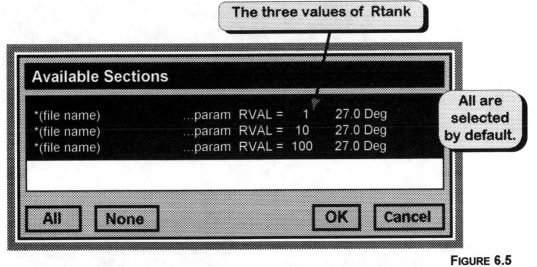

FIGURE 6.5

The Available Sections dialog box

5. The initial Probe graph appears (Figure 6.6) with the main sweep variable displayed by default.

Select the X- and Y-axes variables

Add Traces

6. The X-axis default variable and range are proper. To display a family of impedance curves on the Y-axis, as shown in Figure 6.7, enter trace variable *DB(V(Vsource:+)/I(Vsource))* into the *Trace Command* box, **OK**.

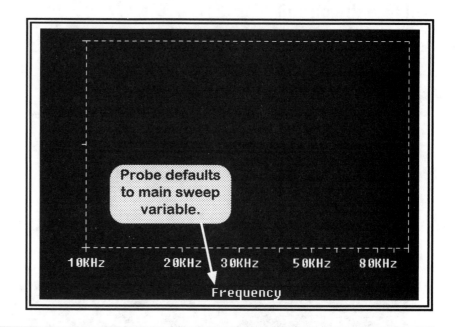

FIGURE 6.6

The initial
Probe graph

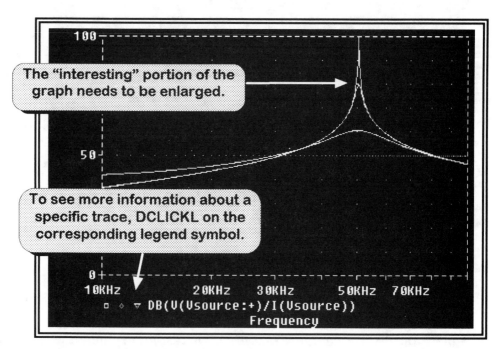

FIGURE 6.7

Family of curves
plot

7. From Figure 6.7, it is clear we have another resolution problem: Although smooth (due to an adequate number of data points), the "interesting" portion of the curve is too small for easy viewing. After reviewing *Probe Note 6.1,* use the "X-axis Settings" method to zoom in on the resonant portion of the curves so your graph resembles Figure 6.2.

Probe Note 6.1
How do I expand or compress waveforms?

Zoom Area   Refit   **Zoom In Zoom Out**

We have two techniques for accomplishing this: Change the X- and Y-axes ranges, or zoom in (or out) on portions of the waveform.

- To reset X- and Y-axes ranges: **Plot**, **X-axis Settings** or **Y-axis Settings**, **User Defined** (in *Data Range* section), enter the desired starting and ending ranges (such as 35k to 70k), **OK**.

- To zoom in (or out) on portions of a waveform: **CLICKL** on the *Zoom in on specified point (or Zoom out from specified point)* toolbar button, or **View**, **In** (or **Out**), **DRAG** crosshairs to desired point, **CLICKL**.

Another more versatile method of zooming in allows us to choose the exact area to expand. To accomplish this: **CLICKL** on *Zooms in on selected area of graph* toolbar button (or **View**, **Area)**, **DRAG** crosshairs to any *corner* of desired expansion area, **CLICKLH** and drag to create a box of the desired size, release button.

In all cases, refit by **CLICKL** on the *Zoom to show all traces and labels* toolbar button (or **View**, **Fit**) to bring back the original waveform, **View**, **Previous** to bring back previous waveforms, and **View**, **Pan - New Center** to set a new center-of-screen.

When either the X- or Y-axis is expanded, scroll bars automatically appear. The scroll bars enable us to scroll through the normal data range.

8. As suggested in *Probe Note 6.1*, use the X-axis scroll bar to scan the curves. Are all portions of the original curve available?

   Yes   No

9. To better document the graph, display legend symbols and label the curves as shown in Figure 6.8. (If necessary, review Appendix B and *Probe Note 5.1*.)

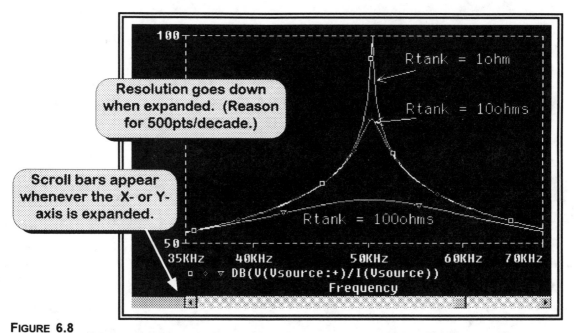

FIGURE 6.8

Final expanded and
documented graph

10. Based on your results (Figure 6.8), use cursors to fill in the resonant frequency and the Q of each plot below (Q = f_r/BW). Are the values close to those calculated in the discussion?

      Yes   **No**

      f_r =   _____

      Q(at 1Ω)   =   _____

      Q(at 10Ω) =   _____

      Q(at 100Ω) =   _____

Advanced Activities

11. In general, any attribute can be varied as a parameter. Draw the circuit of Figure 6.9 and write below the name of the attribute that is set up as a parameter.

      Parameter attribute = _____

12. Using primary turns ratios of 5, 10, and 20, generate the plots of Figure 6.10.

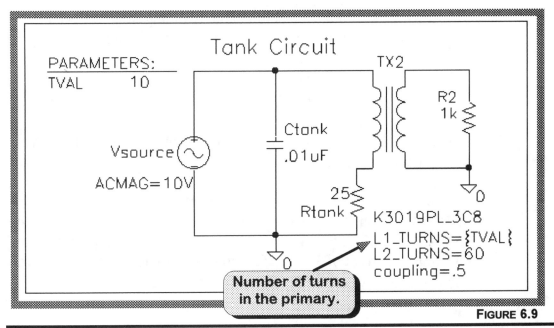

FIGURE 6.9

Attributes can
become parameters

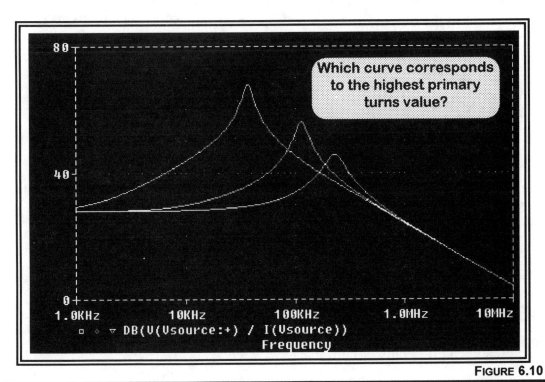

FIGURE 6.10

Impedance as a
function of primary
turns ratio

13. Reviewing the equation below and realizing that inductance is proportional to turns, properly label the three curves of Figure 6.10.

$$fr = \frac{1}{2\pi\sqrt{LC}}$$

14. Repeat using the coupling coefficient as a parameter. What conclusions can you draw?

15. To perform an optional bias point analysis, set *DC = 100V* (**DCLICKL** on *Vsource's* symbol) and run a simulation. Does the SMALL SIGNAL BIAS SOLUTION listed in the output file show a *Vsource* current of 100A, 10A, and 1A for each of the parametric values of *Rtank* (1Ω, 10Ω, and 100Ω)?

Yes   **No**

16. To perform an optional bias point analysis using *RVAL = 25*, disable all sweeps (AC and parametric), set *DC = 100V*, and run a simulation. Does the SMALL SIGNAL BIAS SOLUTION listed in the output file show a *Vsource* current of 4A (100V/25Ω)?

Yes   **No**

EXERCISES

● Treating the RC circuit of Chapter 4 as a *low-pass filter*, generate a Bode plot that gives a family of curves for various values of R1.

● With the help of the parametric mode, design a tank circuit suitable for an AM radio station. It must have a resonant frequency of 680kHz and a bandwidth of 6kHz.

QUESTIONS AND PROBLEMS

1. To create a high-Q tank circuit, use a

(a) low value of *Rtank*.
(b) high value of *Rtank*.

2. Can a resistor be a main sweep variable?

3. Which of the following analysis options is used to specify the variable that generates the family of curves?

    (a) Parametric
    (b) AC Sweep

4. What two general methods are available for expanding (zooming in on) a waveform?

5. At resonance, would you expect the real part of the impedance operator to be large or small when compared to the imaginary part?   Why?

CHAPTER 7

The RC Time Constant
Pulsed Waveforms

OBJECTIVES

- To determine the RC and L/R response to a square wave.
- To generate multiple plots within a single *Probe* window.

DISCUSSION

When a sine wave powers an AC circuit, it usually means an analog application in the frequency domain. When a *pulsed* waveform powers the same circuit, it usually means a digital application in the time domain.

In this chapter, we will determine the transient response of the simple RC circuit of Figure 7.1 to a pulsed voltage source.

LABELING NODES

Looking at Figure 7.1, we have often found it difficult to determine the reference designator of certain nodes. For example, is the output node V(R1:1) or V(R1:2) or V(C1:1) or V(C1:2)? Fortunately, there are two good solutions to this problem:

(1) Label appropriate wire segments.

(2) Assign and label a *bubble*.

Both solutions are demonstrated by *Vin* and *Vout* in Figure 7.1. In this and all future chapters, we will put these new labeling practices to good use.

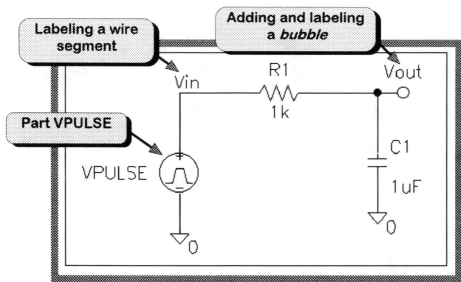

FIGURE 7.1

The pulsed RC circuit,
with input and output
labeling

THEORY

When working in the time domain, Kirchhoff's law generates the following time-domain differential equation for the circuit of Figure 7.1:

$$V_{IN} = V_{PULSE} = R\frac{dQ}{dt} + \frac{Q}{C}$$

For a pulsed input, we obtain the following solutions for the rise and fall times.   (The term "RC" is known as a *time constant* and in our case has the value 1ms.)

$$VOUT(rise) = V_C = V_{PEAK}(1 - e^{-t/RC})$$

$$VOUT(fall) = V_C = V_{PEAK}e^{-t/RC}$$

Create File

Select Part

Draw Wire

SIMULATION PRACTICE

Draw the circuit

1.   Draw the RC test circuit of Figure 7.1 and set the attributes as shown. (Be sure to label the input and output nodes using the techniques of *Schematics Note 7.1*.)

Schematics Note 7.1
How do I label wire segments and bubbles?

Select Part

- To label any wire segment: **DCLICKL** on a wire segment to bring up the *Set Attribute Value* dialog box, enter any desired label (such as Vin), **OK**.

- To assign and label a bubble, select part BUBBLE and place at desired location (if necessary, Ctrl/R to rotate).   **DCLICKL** on part BUBBLE to bring up *Set Attribute Value* dialog box, enter *Vout* (or label of your choice), **OK**.

  These wire and bubble attributes turn into trace variables [such as V(Vin) and V(Vout)] and can be used by *Probe* to generate waveforms.

2.   To generate the desired input waveform, program VPULSE as follows: **DCLICKL** on the VPULSE symbol to open up its *Part Name* dialog box, and enter the seven values specified by Figure 7.2. (<u>Display</u> any or all of these attributes if you wish.)

3.   The pulse width is equal to how many RC time constants?

   PW (pulse width) = _____ time constants

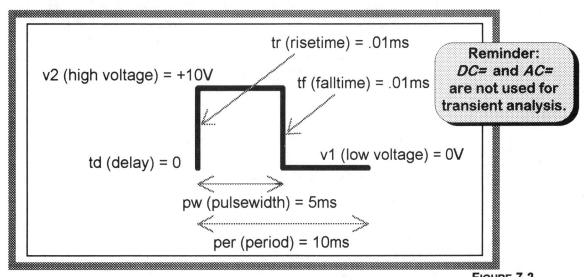

FIGURE 7.2

VPULSE attribute specifications

PSpice for Windows

Select the sweep mode

Analysis Setup

4. Bring up the transient dialog box, and set up the sweep variable as time from 0 to 10ms. (Remember: Do not place zero into *Print Step*—the initial time is zero by default.)

Analyze the circuit and set the X- and Y-axes variables

Simulate

5. Run PSpice and generate the default *Probe* graph. This time, instead of markers, use the new wire segment and bubble trace variables (*V(Vin) and V(Vout)*) to display the curves of Figure 7.3.

Add Traces

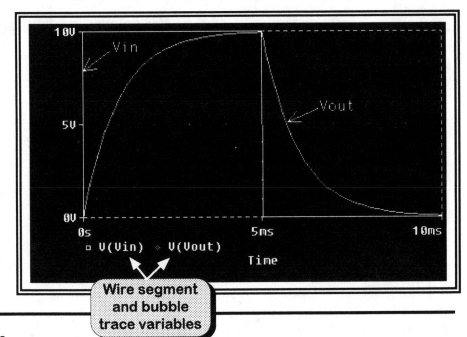

FIGURE 7.3

RC response for
five time constants

Cursor Display

6. Using the cursors, carefully measure the rise and fall voltage levels for each of the time constants listed next: (Hint: Refer to *Probe Note 7.1* to generate the *marked points* of Figure 7.4.)

1 time constant (1ms) = _____

4 time constants (4ms) = _____

6 time constants (6ms) = _____

9 time constants (9ms) = _____

Probe Note 7.1
How do I mark coordinate values on my graphs?

Cut

Cursor Display

To mark the coordinate values of any point on a graph:

1. Activate the cursor.

2. Assign each cursor to the desired reference designator, place the cursor at the desired location, and **Tools, Label, Mark**.

   To reposition a marked point: freeze the cursor (**Tools, Cursor, Freeze**), select the marked point, **CLICKLH** and drag to the new location.   To remove a marked point, select and cut.   Unfreeze the cursor as required.

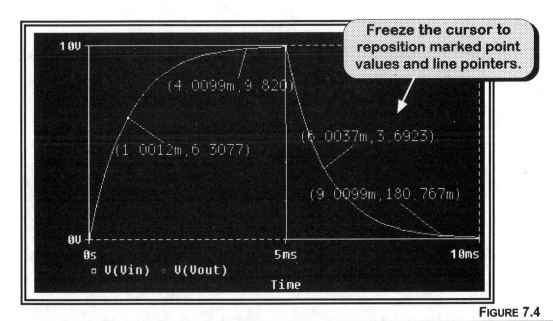

FIGURE 7.4

Marked points

7. Repeat step 6 using a calculator on the theoretical equations developed in the discussion. (Do they match Figure 7.4?)

    At 1 time constant   (1ms), Vout = _____

    At 4 time constants (4ms), Vout = _____

    At 6 time constants (6ms), Vout = _____

    At 9 time constants (9ms), Vout = _____

8. Using the *Mark Voltage Differential* marker as shown in Figure 7.5 [or enter V(Vin,Vout) in the *Add Traces* dialog box], generate a plot of the voltage *across* R1 (Figure 7.6).

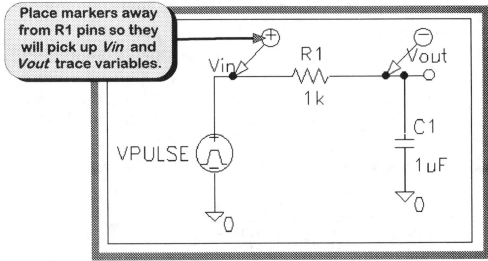

FIGURE 7.5

Marking a
differential voltage

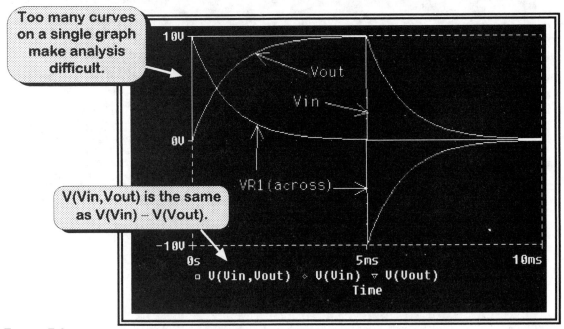

FIGURE 7.6

Vr and Vc waveforms

PSpice for Windows

9. A possible problem with Figure 7.6 is that there are too many curves on a single graph. To solve the problem, first clear the *Probe* window (cut all items or rerun PSpice). Based on *Probe Note 7.2*, generate the multiple-plot graph of Figure 7.7.

Cut

Probe Note 7.2
*How do I generate multiple plots
within a single Probe window?*

Add Traces

To add up to three additional plots to your Probe window (for a total of four): **Plot**, **Add Plot**, etc. (up to three times).

To select a plot, **CLICKL** anywhere within the desired plot. Note that "SEL>>" moves to the selected plot.

To add curves to the selected plot, follow the usual sequence (Markers, or *Add traces*).

To delete plots: select plot, **Plot**, **Delete Plot**.

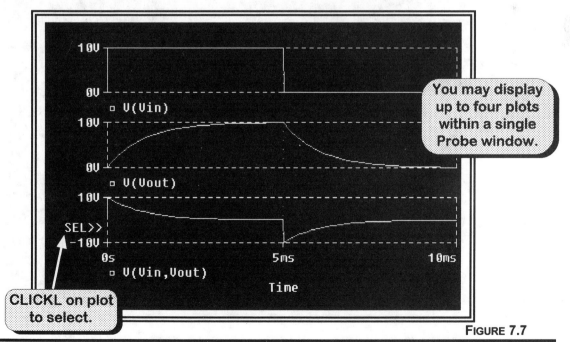

FIGURE 7.7

Display of voltages using multiple plots

10. Using the techniques of *Probe Note 7.3*, label the Y-axis of each of the graphs of Figure 7.7. (A possible result is shown in Figure 7.8.)

Probe Note 7.3
How do I label the Y-axis?

To label any Y-axis, select the desired plot (**CLICKL** within plot), **Plot, Y-Axis Settings** to bring up the "Y-axis Settings" dialog box, enter desired label into "Axis Title" block, **OK**.   If a given plot contains more than one Y-axis, enter the appropriate number into the *Y-axis Number* box.

Any label can be changed by repeating the process.

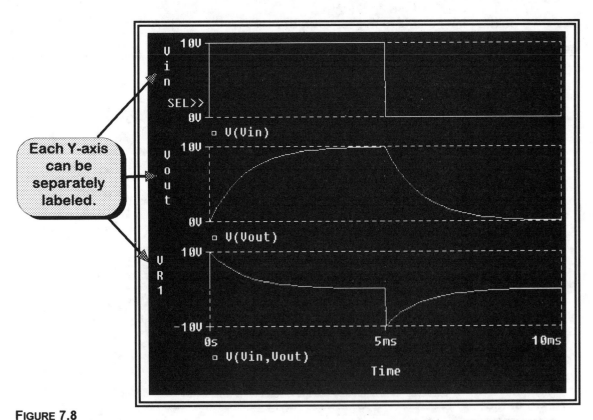

FIGURE 7.8

Adding labels
to graphs

Long and short RC time constants

11. The curves of Figure 7.8 were generated by choosing the RC time constant value to equal one-fifth the pulse width (PW). This is a *medium* RC time constant value.

    If C1 remains constant, use ratios to complete the following table and determine the values of R1 that will produce the *short* and *long* RC conditions indicated:

	Definition	Formula	R1
Medium	RC = PW / 5	(R1 × 1µF) = 5ms / 5	1kΩ
Short	RC = PW / 25	(R1 × 1µF) = 5ms / 25	
Long	RC = PW / 1	(R1 × 1µF) = 5ms / 1	

Solve for R1.

12. To show these three cases, sweep R1 as a *nested* (parametric) variable with the values determined in step 11 and generate the graph of Figure 7.9. If necessary, refer to the three-step process outlined below, or review Chapters 2 and 5.

    1) Set R1's <u>value</u> (presently 1k) to *{RVAL}*.

    2) Define the parameter. (Place part **PARAM** and enter *NAME1 = RVAL*, and *VALUE1 = 1k*, etc.)

    3) Set up the parametric sweep mode. (Bring up and enable the *Parametric* dialog box, enter the values developed in step 11, etc.)

Advanced Activities

13. Using the "s" (integrate) and "d" (differentiate) operators, differentiate and integrate VPULSE to generate the curves of Figure 7.10. (Remember, the independent variable is always the X-axis unit—time, in this case.)

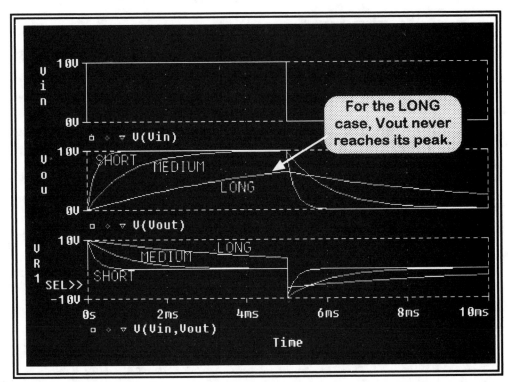

FIGURE 7.9

Short, medium, and
long time constants

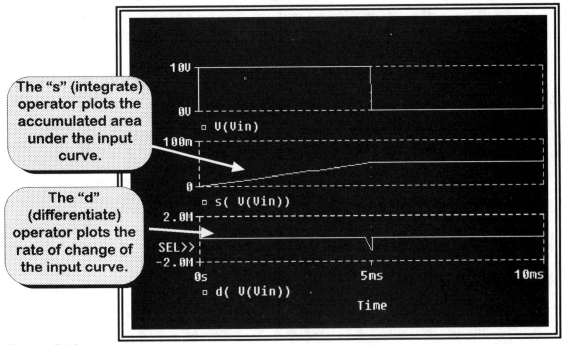

FIGURE 7.10

Using the "s" (integrate)
and "d" (differentiate)
math operators

PSpice for Windows

14. Comparing Figures 7.9 and 7.10, which of the choices below best demonstrates each of the following? (Circle the correct answer.)

   • A *differentiator* in which the output voltage waveform is a measure of the *rate of change* of the input waveform.

   V(C1)$_{LONG}$ V(C1)$_{SHORT}$ V(R1)$_{LONG}$ V(R1)$_{SHORT}$

   • An *integrator* in which the output voltage waveform is a measure of how the input voltage *accumulates over time.*

   V(C1)$_{LONG}$ V(C1)$_{SHORT}$ V(R1)$_{LONG}$ V(R1)$_{SHORT}$

15. By repeating the steps used for the RC circuit, generate a graph for the L/R circuit of Figure 7.11 that is similar to Figure 7.9. (Under what conditions does the L/R circuit approximate differentiator or integrator action?)

16. By entering the following equations (based on those developed in the discussion) in the trace expressions dialog box, generate RC rise and fall curves and compare to those of Figure 7.3. (Note: 2.7 is the natural logarithm base.)

$$\text{VOUT(rise)} = V_C = 10 * (1 - \text{PWR}(2.7, -\text{Time}/.001))$$

$$\text{VOUT(fall)} = V_C = 10 * \text{PWR}(2.7, -\text{Time}/.001)$$

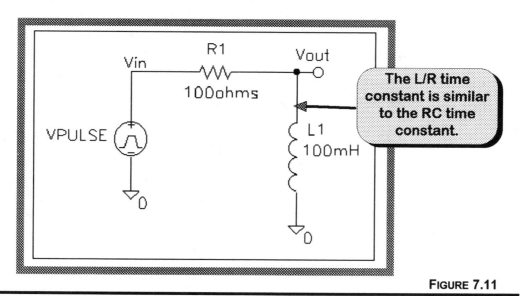

FIGURE 7.11

The L/R circuit

EXERCISE

- Using an RC combination, design a "ones-delay" circuit that delays the logic one 5V pulse to a TTL gate by 5μs. (<u>Note</u>: The logic 1 threshold is 2.73V.)

QUESTIONS AND PROBLEMS

1. When the input to an RC circuit suddenly changes, across what component does most of the change *initially* occur?

    (a) the resistor
    (b) the capacitor

2. In order for the output from the RC circuit of Figure 7.1 to resemble the input, which of the following would you choose?

    (a) a very long RC time constant
    (b) a very short RC time constant

3. Based on the results of Figure 7.10, what is the difference between *integration* and *differentiation*?

4. In one RC time constant, the voltage rises to _____% of the way from the initial to the final steady-state voltage.

5. Referring to the simple RC circuit of Figure 7.1, the break frequency equals $1/(2\pi RC)$ and the rise time (from 10% to 90%) equals 2.2RC. Derive an equation that relates the break frequency (f_B) to the rise time (T_R).

6.   Referring to Figure 7.6, does Vin = VR + VC?

7.   The Vin waveform of Figure 7.12 drives the RC circuit of Figure 7.1. Sketch directly on the graph the *approximate* Vr and Vc curves (assuming a medium RC time constant).

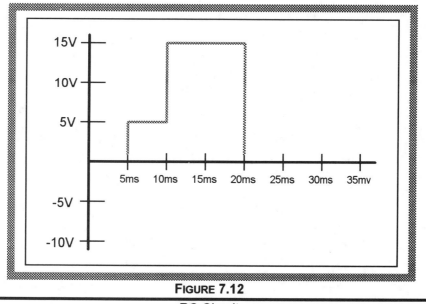

FIGURE 7.12

RC Circuit
waveforms

8.   Repeat step 7 by plotting on the graph of Figure 7.12 the (mathematically perfect) *integrated* and *differentiated* waveforms.

CHAPTER 8

Device Models
Temperature Coefficient

OBJECTIVES

- To change and display the temperature model coefficients of R devices.
- To change and display the temperature and voltage coefficients of C and L devices.

DISCUSSION

All the devices used by PSpice rely on mathematical models and model parameters to determine their characteristics. Initially, these model parameters are set to default values, but they can be changed as desired.

In this chapter, we set and modify model parameters for the passive devices: resistors, capacitors, and inductors. The models for the passive devices are relatively simple, and the number of parameters are few in number.

In future chapters, we will examine the more complex models of such active devices as diodes and transistors. We will see that their mathematical models are quite complex and involve a large number of model parameters.

The resistor model

In the case of the resistor, the mathematical model is based on Ohm's law, and the only parameters that can be varied are three *temperature coefficients* (TC1, TC2, and TCE).

If TCE (the exponential coefficient) is *not* specified, then the resistance is given as follows, where TC1 is the linear temperature coefficient and TC2 is the quadratic temperature coefficient.

$$R = R(nom) \ (1 + \textbf{\textit{TC1}} \times \Delta T + \textbf{\textit{TC2}} \times \Delta T^2)$$

If TCE is specified, then the resistance is given as follows, where TCE is the exponential temperature coefficient.

$$R = R(nom) \times 1.01^{TCE \times \Delta T}$$

In all cases R(nom) is the resistance value at nominal temperature (usually 27°C), and ΔT is the change in temperature from the nominal value. When TC1, TC2, and TCE assume their default values, R = R(nom).

Resistor examples

Our first example assumes that TC1 = .001, and both TC2 and TCE are zero (by default). If the temperature of a 1kΩ resistor changes by 10°C (from 27° to 37°C), then the resistance calculation is as follows:

$$R = 1k\Omega \ (1 + .001 \times (37° - 27°) + 0 \times (37° - 27°)^2) = 1.01k\Omega$$

Our second example assumes that TC2 = .001, and both TC1 and TCE are zero. Given the same parameters as the first example (1kΩ and 10°), the resistance calculation is as follows:

$$R = 1k\Omega \ (1 + 0 \times (37° - 27°) + .001 \times (37° - 27°)^2) = 1.10k\Omega$$

Our third and last example assumes that TCE = 4, and both TC1 and TC2 are zero. Under the same conditions as before, we obtain:

$$R = 1k\Omega \times 1.01^{4 \times 10} = 1.49k\Omega$$

Capacitor and inductor model parameters

In addition to temperature coefficients TC1 and TC2, both the capacitor and inductor have voltage and current model parameters (*VC1*, *VC2*, *IL1*, *IL2*) that are defined as shown below.

$$C = C(nom)(1 + \textbf{\textit{VC1}} \times V + \textbf{\textit{VC2}} \times V^2)(1 + \textbf{\textit{TC1}} \times \Delta T + \textbf{\textit{TC2}} \times \Delta T^2)$$

$$L = L(nom)(1 + \textbf{\textit{IL1}} \times I + \textbf{\textit{IL2}} \times I^2)(1 + \textbf{\textit{TC1}} \times \Delta T + \textbf{\textit{TC2}} \times \Delta T^2)$$

Based on these equations, the value of a capacitor depends on the voltage across it, and the value of an inductor depends on the current through it—in addition to the usual temperature dependency.

Parameters VC1 and VC2 are the linear and quadratic voltage coefficients for a capacitor, and IL1 and IL2 are the linear and quadratic current coefficients for an inductor. As with the temperature coefficients, their default values are zero.

For example, suppose we are designing a circuit with a capacitor of nominal value $1\mu F$ (at V = 0 and T = 27°). Furthermore, we assume that coefficients TC1 and VC1 are both .001. If we then apply a voltage of 5V and a temperature of 37°C, the value of C becomes:

$$C = 1\mu F(1 + .001 \times 5 + 0 \times 10^2)(1 + .001 \times 10 + 0 \times 10^2) = 1.015\mu F$$

Global versus local models

In order to set and change model parameters (*TC1*, *VC1*, *IL1*, etc.), the corresponding parts must have a model. Conventional parts R, C, and L do not have accessible models, and the only parameters that can be changed are their attributes (*value* and *tolerance*).

Special "breakout" parts *Rbreak, Cbreak,* and *Lbreak,* however, do have accessible models that allow us to set and change model parameters. They are found in model library *breakout.lib*. All parts that offer models have a model name (in addition to their part names). In most cases, the part name and model name are the same (such as *Rbreak*).

When a part's model is first accessed, it comes from a *global* library of models, such as *msimev71/lib/breakout.lib*. (A global model is accessible to all schematics.) However, to protect this original model for future use, it automatically becomes a *local base* model of the same name (valid only within the present schematic).

Under various conditions, an "X" may be automatically appended to a local model name. Since this can lead to some confusion, we recommend that a unique model name be assigned to each part. When a change is made to a model definition, all parts with the same model name are also changed.

SIMULATION PRACTICE

Resistor models

Select Part

Draw Wire

1. Draw the simple test circuit of Figure 8.1, and **DCLICKL** to set the attributes as shown. (Reminder: Use part *Rbreak* for the resistor.)

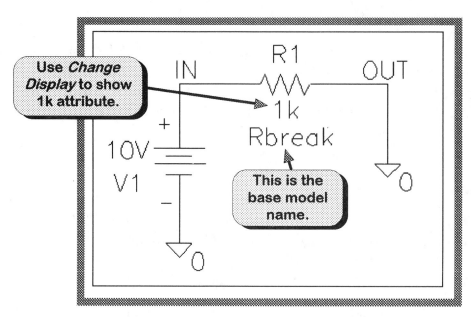

FIGURE 8.1

Resistor
test circuit

Linear temperature coefficient

2. For linear analysis, we will set temperature coefficient TC1 to .001°C^{-1}. (TC2 and TCE will remain at their default values of 0.)

    To set the temperature coefficient (and change the local model name), select part *Rbreak*, **Edit, Model** to bring up the *Edit Model* dialog box, **Edit Instance Model [text]** to bring up the *Model Editor* dialog box.   As shown below, change the model name from *Rbreak* to *myR* (or another name of your choice), and add TC1 = .001. (Do not activate OK yet.)

    .model myR RES
    R=1 ◄━━━━ **Weighting factor**
    TC1 = .001
    *\$

3.   By examining the *Model Editor* window:

(a)   Was the model copied <u>from</u> a *global* library file, and was it assigned the model name *Rbreak*?

   Yes   **No**

(b)   Was the model copied <u>to</u> a local library file with the same name as your schematic file?

   Yes   **No**

4.   CLICKL on **OK** to exit the window.   When done, the circuit will resemble Figure 8.2.

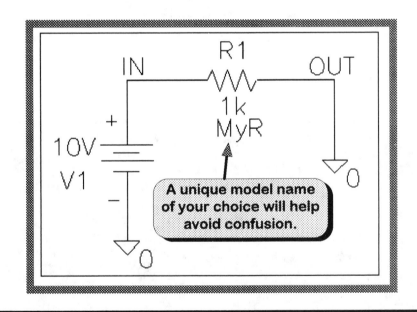

FIGURE 8.2

Test circuit showing local model name

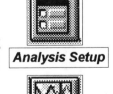

Analysis Setup

5.   Following the guidelines of Figure 8.3, set up the DC Sweep dialog box for a temperature sweep from 0°C to +50°C in units of .1°C (which corresponds to 32°F to 122°F in units of 1.8°F).

Simulate

6.   Simulate the circuit and generate the graph of Figure 8.4. (Resistance is obtained by plotting voltage/current.)

PSpice for Windows

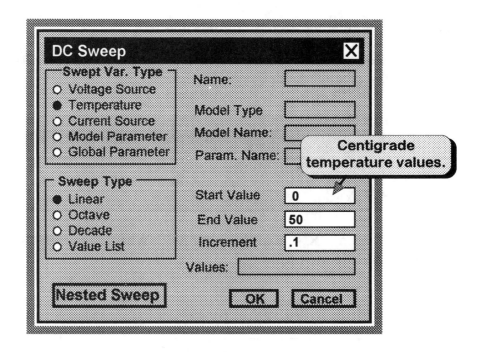

FIGURE 8.3

DC Sweep dialog box
for temperature sweep

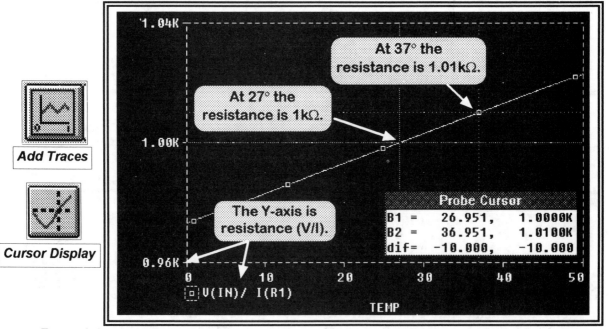

FIGURE 8.4

Results of linear
temperature
coefficient test

7. Looking at the graph, answer the following:

    a) Does the resistance increase linearly as temperature rises?

        Yes   **No**

    b) Is the circuit resistance at the nominal temperature of 27°C approximately equal to 1kΩ? (Note the cursor.)

        Yes   **No**

    c) Does the resistance at 37°C approximately equal the value calculated in the discussion (1.01kΩ)?

        Yes   **No**

Quadratic temperature coefficient

8. As shown below, replace TC1 with TC2 in the resistor model. (If necessary, see step 2.)

    ```
    .model myR RES
    R=1
    TC2 = .001
    *$
    ```

9. Simulate the circuit and generate the graph of Figure 8.5.

10. Looking at the graph (and the cursor values), answer the following:

    a) Does the resistance seem to vary in a quadratic (parabolic) relationship with temperature?

        Yes   **No**

    b) Does the circuit resistance at the nominal temperature of 27°C appear to be approximately 1kΩ?

        Yes   **No**

    c) Does the resistance at 37°C approximately equal the value calculated in the discussion (1.10kΩ)?

        Yes   **No**

Exponential temperature coefficient

11. Finally, replace TC2 = .001 with TCE = 4 and generate the graph of Figure 8.6.

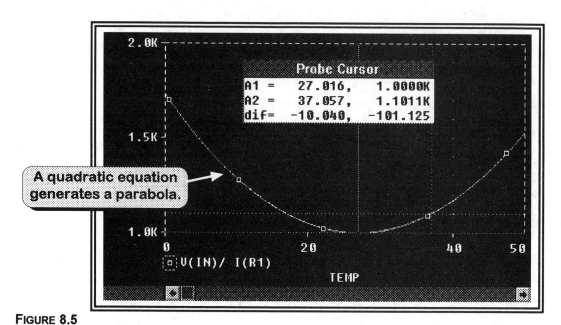

FIGURE 8.5

Quadratic temperature
coefficient test

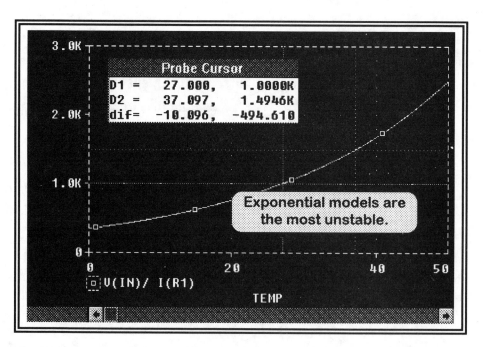

FIGURE 8.6

Exponential temperature
coefficient test

12. Looking at the graph and the cursor values in Figure 8.6, answer the following:

    a) Does the resistance seem to rise in an exponential relationship with temperature?

        Yes   **No**

    b) Does the measured resistance at the nominal temperature of 27°C appear to be approximately 1kΩ?

        Yes   **No**

    c) Does the measured resistance at 37°C approximately equal that calculated in the discussion (1.49kΩ)?

        Yes   **No**

Advanced Activities

Capacitor models

To graph C versus temperature and voltage, we can choose from among the three possible equations listed below:

$$Q = CV \qquad I = C \times dV/dt \qquad V_{PEAK} = I_{PEAK}/2\pi fC$$

Because Q cannot be directly measured, and VPEAK and IPEAK cannot be varied, we must choose the middle relationship, where voltage will be set to a linear ramp function to give a constant dV/dt:

$$I = C \times dV/dt$$

We perform a transient analysis, with temperature as a parametric variable. We finally plot C = I/(dV/dt) and generate a family of curves of capacitance versus time at various selected temperatures.

A careful analysis of the resulting graph will show how capacitance varies with both voltage and temperature.

13. Draw the circuit of Figure 8.7 and set the attributes as shown. (V1 is part *VPWL*, and is programmed to generate a ramp function from 0 to 10V when going from 0 to 1μs.)

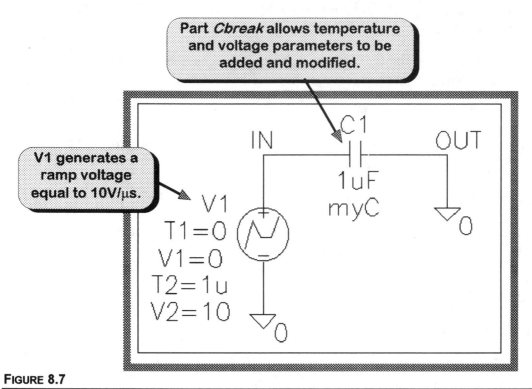

FIGURE 8.7

Capacitor test
circuit

14. As shown below, set both the linear temperature and voltage coefficients of C1 to .001, and change the local model name to *myC*. (VC2 and TC2 will remain at their default values of zero.)

> **.model myC CAP**
> **TC1 = .001**
> **VC1 = .001**
> ***$**

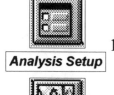

Analysis Setup

15. Perform a transient analysis from 0 to 1μs, and a parametric analysis using the temperature sequence 17, 27, 37, and 47. (See Figure 8.8.)

Simulate

16. Plot capacitance (I/(dV)) and generate the family of capacitance curves of Figure 8.9. (Be sure to expand the Y-axis and display the legend symbols, as shown.)

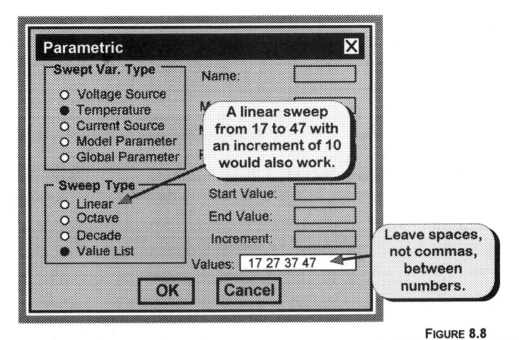

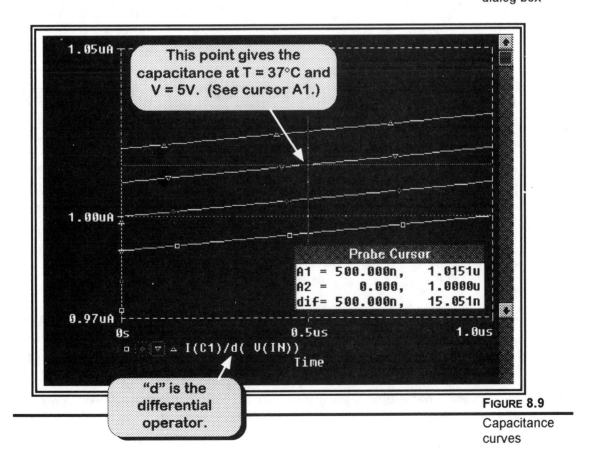

17. Because Vin was programmed to be a linear ramp function, it follows that Vin goes from 0 to 10V as time goes from 0 to 1μs. Therefore, using a pen or pencil, label the X-axis from 0 to 10V— as well as the default 0 to 1μs.

18. Looking at the graph of Figure 8.9, answer the following (remember that the Y-axis represents capacitance values):

    a) Does the capacitance increase in a linear fashion as *temperature* rises? (Hint: Are the curves approximately evenly spaced with 17°C at the bottom?)

    Yes   **No**

    b) Does the capacitance increase in a linear fashion as *voltage* (and time) increase? (Hint: Are the curves straight lines?)

    Yes   **No**

    c) Does the circuit capacitance at the nominal temperature of 27°C and 0V appear to be approximately 1μF? (Note cursor A2.)

    Yes   **No**

    d) Does the resistance at 37°C and 5V (.5μs) equal the value calculated in the discussion (1.015μF)? (Note cursor A1.)

    Yes   **No**

19. Generate a family of curves similar to Figure 8.9 for an inductor.

> To determine inductance, we use the following time-domain differential equation:
> $$V = L \times dI / dt$$

20. To view all the library files that are available to any given schematic (such as Figure 8.7): **Analysis, Library and Include Files**, and bring up the *Library and Include Files* dialog box. The local libraries created by this experiment should be listed, along with the global library *nom.lib*. (Note the asterisk after *nom.lib*, indicating that it indeed is a global library.)

21. Examine the contents of any of the library files that contain the models (extension *.lib*). (Hint: Use the *File Manager* or *Windows Explorer* and **DCLICKL** on the library file name.)

EXERCISES

- Using the techniques of your choice, and setting the temperature and voltage/current model coefficients of your choice, plot a graph of tank circuit resonant frequency versus temperature from 0°C to 50°C.

- Using any methods available (heat from soldering iron or hair dryer; cold from refrigerator or air conditioner), plot the resistance versus temperature characteristics of a real 1k resistor. Using the data, determine the coefficient mix (TC1/ TC2 or TCE) that most closely matches your results. Using these coefficients, plot R versus T using PSpice and compare to the experimental results.

QUESTIONS AND PROBLEMS

1. If TC1 = .001^{-1}°C for a 10k resistor, at what temperature will the resistance double? (Is this temperature realistic?)

2. Repeat question 1 for TC2 = .001^{-1}°C.

3. When the applied voltage to a capacitor increases in a linear fashion, why is the current constant?

4.   (a) A local model is accessible to all schematics.

   True   **False**

   (b) A global model is accessible to all schematics.

   True   **False**

5.   In general terms, why should capacitance depend on applied voltage?

CHAPTER 9

An Analog Computer
Series Resonance

OBJECTIVES

- To analyze and design an automotive suspension system using an LCR resonant circuit as an analog computer.

- To review and apply the *Schematic*, *PSpice*, and *Probe* techniques of Chapters 1 through 8.

DISCUSSION

This is the last chapter involving only DC/AC circuits. New material is included, but our primary purpose is to review past chapters and to test your readiness to start Part II of this book. Therefore, expect to carry out many of the PSpice activities yourself, without the detailed directions of the earlier chapters. (Refer to earlier material as necessary.)

THE AUTOMOTIVE SUSPENSION / LCR CIRCUIT ANALOGY

Our task is to construct an analog computer, one that uses an LCR series circuit to simulate the mass/spring/shock-absorber combination of an automotive suspension system. Such a system exhibits a *damped resonant* response when "hit" with a force. When hit with a <u>repetitive</u> force field, energy buildup becomes a significant factor.

When designing our suspension system, the major problem will be to choose the correct level of damping. *Underdamping* will cause unwanted oscillations; *overdamping* will make the response too stiff. When damping is just right, the system will absorb the shock, but with minimal bouncing.

Looking at Figure 9.1, we choose a series resonant circuit because all three components of a real suspension system (mass, spring, and shock) are connected at the same point (wheel hub) and therefore have the same velocity. Since velocity is analogous to current, a series circuit is required. Table 9.1 compares a real mechanical system and its electronic equivalent.

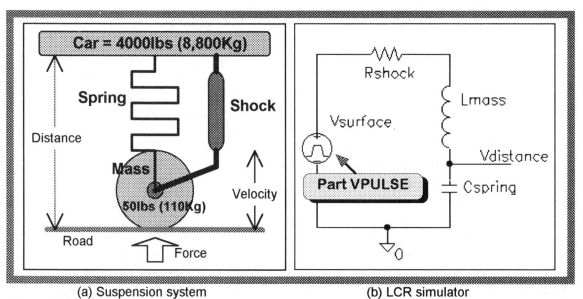

(a) Suspension system   (b) LCR simulator

FIGURE 9.1

Mechanical/simulation comparison
(a) Suspension system
(b) LCR simulator

Mechanical	Electronic
D (Distance)	Q (Charge)
V (Velocity)	I (Current)
F (Force)	V (Voltage)
M (Mass)	L (Inductance)
K_S (Spring constant)	1/C (Inverse capacitance)
K_F (Coefficient of friction)	R (Resistance)
F (Force on spring) = $K_S D$	V = 1/C x Q
F (Force of friction) = $K_F V$	V = IR (Ohm's law)
F = Mdv/dt (Newton's second law)	V = LdI/dt (Inductor voltage)
$1/2MV^2$ (Kinetic energy)	$1/2LI^2$ (Magnetic energy)
$1/2K_S D^2$ (Potential energy)	$1/2CV^2$ (Capacitive energy)

TABLE 9.1

The mechanical/electronic
equivalency

THEORY

To analyze the system theoretically, we see from Figure 9.1(b) that L represents the tire mass, 1/C represents the spring constant, and R represents the shock coefficient of friction. Because Q (charge) is analogous to distance and proportional to voltage (Q = CV), graphing the capacitor voltage gives a profile of the wheel motion. As designers, our task is to choose appropriate values for R, L, and C.

The calculations are as follows:

- When a 4000lb car (1000lbs/tire) is placed on its springs, the springs compress approximately 0.5 feet. Therefore K_S = 1000lbs/0.5ft = 2000lbs/ft. Since M (the mass of a tire) is approximately 2 slugs (64lbs/32ft/sec^2), the ratio of K_S/M is 2000/2 = 1000. It follows that the ratio of 1/C to L (or 1/LC) is also approximately 1000. We choose C = 100μF and L = 10H.

- Because R is our design variable, we choose a low value to begin with—one that represents a very worn set of shocks (such as 10Ω).

- Based on the calculated values for L and C, the resonant frequency of the system is:

$$f_R = \frac{1}{2\pi\sqrt{LC}} = \frac{1}{2\pi\sqrt{10H \times 100\mu F}} \cong 5Hz$$

SIMULATION PRACTICE

The railroad tie hazard

The first test of our shock absorber system will be a worst case test. We will drive over railroad ties at a speed that is harmonically related to the system's resonant frequency. Therefore, we should see evidence of energy buildup.

1. Draw the circuit of Figure 9.1(b), and set the R, L, and C components to the values calculated in the discussion (R = 10Ω, C = 100μF, L = 10H). Be sure to label the output wire segment *Vdistance*, and to change VPULSE's *Package Reference Designator* from the generic *Vsurface* to the specific *Vrailroad*.

2. Program *Vrailroad* as specified by Figure 9.2.

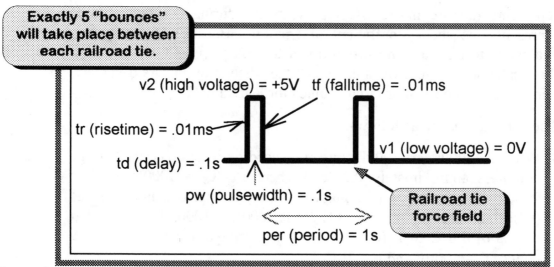

Exactly 5 "bounces" will take place between each railroad tie.

v2 (high voltage) = +5V   tf (falltime) = .01ms

tr (risetime) = .01ms

td (delay) = .1s

v1 (low voltage) = 0V

pw (pulsewidth) = .1s

Railroad tie force field

per (period) = 1s

FIGURE 9.2

VPULSE programmed
for a railroad tie
force field.

3. Set up the system for a transient mode sweep from 0 to 3 seconds (to display approximately three VPULSE cycles).   (Suggestion: To smooth out the waveforms, set *Step Ceiling* to on or about .001s.)

4. Run PSpice and create the motion graph of Figure 9.3.

5. As we expected, the waveforms make it clear that the wheel oscillates way too strongly. Circle the correct response below:

   • **The system is *underdamped*.**   • **The system is *overdamped*.**

6. Does the system show energy buildup, consistent with a resonant system in which the input frequency is harmonically related to the natural resonant frequency?

   Yes   **No**

7. Step 5 tells us that the value of *Rshock* is too small. Change *Rshock* to 1k, and generate the new waveforms of Figure 9.4.

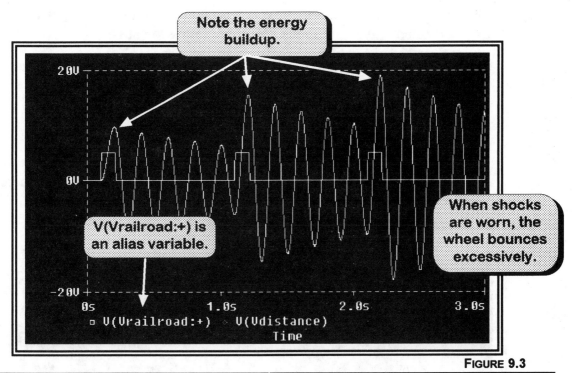

FIGURE **9.3**

Response for
Rshock = 10Ω

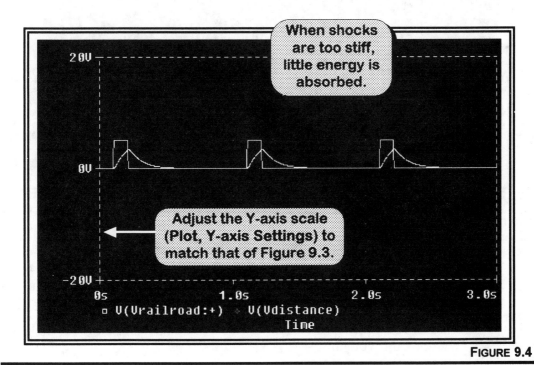

FIGURE **9.4**

Response for
Rshock = 1k

8. After viewing the new waveforms, it is clear that we went too far the other way. The shock absorber is now too stiff.

    • **The system is *underdamped*.**   • **The system is *overdamped.***

Adding a nested sweep variable

9. Clearly, there is an intermediate value between 10Ω and 1kΩ that is just right. To help find the right value, make *Rshock* a parametric (nested) variable and sweep its value over the following range: *Rshock* = 50, 100, 300, 500, and 800. The resulting waveform set is shown in Figure 9.5.

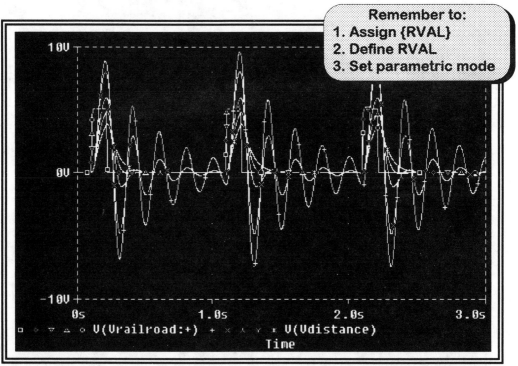

FIGURE 9.5

Waveform set
for various values
of Rshock

10. From the waveform set of Figure 9.5, select the one curve that you believe to be the best. (The best system absorbs the greatest amount of shock, but without *excessive* oscillation.) What value of *Rshock* did you choose?

      ***Rshock* (best curve) = _____**

11. We wish to display this one chosen curve, but we do not wish to repeat the analysis process. Delete the present curves, and review *Probe Note 9.1* to display the single best curve (such as the curve shown in Figure 9.6 for *Rshock* = 300Ω).

Probe Note 9.1
How do I single out individual curves from a family of curves?

To single out individual curves, we use the "at" symbol (@). For example, the graph of Figure 9.5 contains five curves in each group, numbered from 1 to 5.   Curve 1 corresponds to R1 = 50Ω and curve 5 corresponds to Rshock = 800Ω.   For our "best" curve, we choose curve 3 (*Rshock* = 300Ω).

- To draw curve 3 of Vsurface: **CLICKL** on the *Add traces to the selected plot* icon, enter V(Vdistance)@3, **OK**.

- Repeat the process for V(Vrailroad:+).

    The result of these two operations is shown in Figure 9.6.

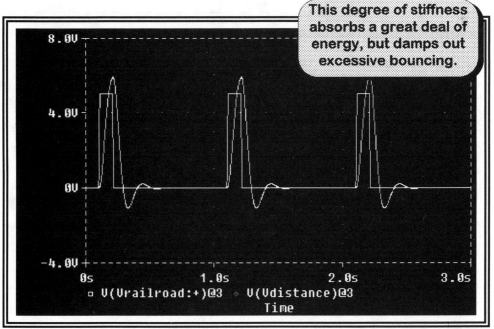

This degree of stiffness absorbs a great deal of energy, but damps out excessive bouncing.

FIGURE 9.6

Displaying individual curves

Testing to another road hazard

Having successfully designed our suspension system for a series of railroad ties, we now wish to test our design on another hazard—the single pothole surface hazard of Figure 9.7. Because the waveform is one-time-only (nonrepetitive), we will choose the PWL (piecewise linear) voltage source.

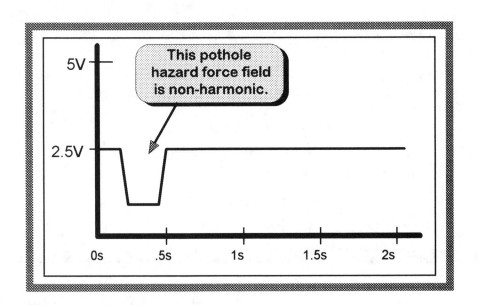

FIGURE 9.7

Pothole road
surface hazard

12. Return to the Schematics window, and change *Rshock* from {RVAL} to the best value (300Ω?). Replace source VPULSE with VPWL, and disable the parametric analysis.

13. Program VPWL (Vpothole) to match the pothole hazard of Figure 9.7. Your circuit should resemble Figure 9.8.

14. Run PSpice and generate the curves of Figure 9.9. (If you wish, switch to parametric analysis and add curves for the *worn* and *too-stiff* cases.)

15. After viewing the results, does the suspension system appear to handle the pothole as well as it did the railroad ties?

        Yes   **No**

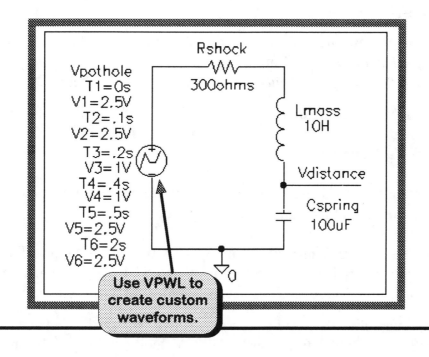

FIGURE 9.8

VPWL
programmed
for a pothole
force field

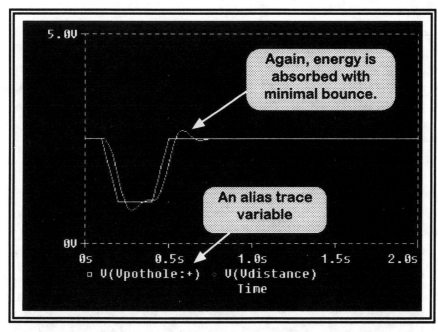

FIGURE 9.9

Pothole test
results

Advanced Activities

16. Do an energy study of the suspension system. (Add the waveforms of the *kinetic energy* of the wheel ($1/2\ LI^2$), *potential energy* of the spring ($1/2CV^2$), and *heat energy* of the shock absorber ($1/2\ I^2R$).

    Does it appear that properly functioning shock absorbers must dissipate a great deal of energy? Do the spring and wheel energies trade back and forth?

17. Change the speed (width and period) of the car as it negotiates the railroad and pothole hazards and report on the results.

18. To the best response curve of Figure 9.6, add a graph of best wheel velocity (*Lmass* current) to generate a plot like that of Figure 9.10. (Note: The X-axis has been expanded for easier viewing.)

    Examining the results, do you see any relationship between the distance and velocity curves? (Hint: Velocity = slope of distance.) If you wish, use the horizontal scroll bar to scan through the waveform.

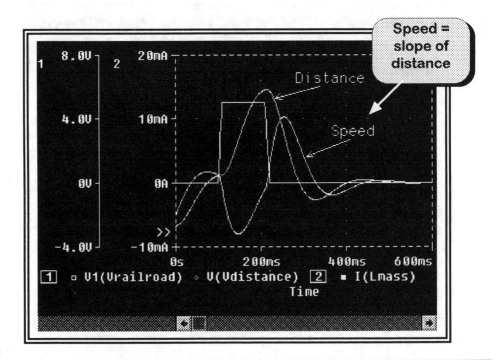

FIGURE 9.10

Adding a plot of "velocity" (current)

19. Using the "d" (differentiate) operator, generate the velocity (speed) curve by differentiating the distance curve. Is the resulting curve equal to the velocity curve generated in step 18?

EXERCISES

- Test your suspension design on a new or modified road surface of your choosing. Report the road hazard and the resulting motion.

- Do a frequency analysis of the suspension system computer of this chapter and generate a family of Bode plots (of distance, velocity, or variables of your choice). Do the curves show strong resonance properties? How does the magnitude, Q, and bandwidth of your best system compare to the underdamped and overdamped cases?

QUESTIONS AND PROBLEMS

1. What is the difference between an *analog* computer and a *digital* computer?

2. Based on the analogy of this experiment, how does an inductor simulate Newton's first law (an object in motion tends to stay in motion, and an object at rest tends to remain at rest—unless acted on by an external force)?

3. When shocks are worn, the system is

   (a) underdamped
   (b) overdamped

4. Why does a *series* LRC circuit (rather than a *parallel* tank circuit) simulate the suspension system? (Hint: Do all components of the suspension system have the same instantaneous velocity?)

5. Reviewing Figure 9.3, why is the second bounce of the wheel greater than the first?

6. Why is driving over railroad ties at a harmonic speed a worst case condition?

7. Why could the activities of this chapter be called a *double simulation*?

8. If the railroad ties of Figure 9.2 are 10 feet apart, how fast is the car traveling?

PART II

Diode Circuits

In Part II, we move from the simple passive **DC** and **AC** components to the active devices of solid-state electronics.

Because we assume that the major **PS**pice techniques of Part I are second nature, we condense the more detailed four-step sequence into a two-step "process summary":

1. What sweep mode will I use?
2. What variables will I assign to the X- and Y-axes?

CHAPTER 10

The Diode
Switching Speed

OBJECTIVES

- To plot diode curves.
- To design a zener diode voltage regulator.
- To determine diode temperature effects.
- To examine and modify a diode's model.
- To determine a diode's switching speed.

DISCUSSION

As shown in Figure 10.1, a diode is an active device with a single PN junction.

Using the waterfall analogy, electrons in the high-energy conduction band can fall easily to the holes in the low-energy valence band when passing from the N to the P region (forward bias voltage). However, electrons cannot easily flow uphill from the P to the N region (reverse bias voltage). Therefore, the PN junction offers a low resistance in the forward direction and a high resistance in the reverse direction.

Note that the *schematic symbol* arrow points in the forward bias direction for *conventional* current flow (Figure 10.1).

If enough voltage is applied in the reverse direction, a conventional diode will break down, and chain-reaction ionization (avalanching) will destroy the diode. A *zener diode*, on the other hand, avoids avalanche and is designed to work in the reverse breakdown region as a *voltage source* (or *voltage regulator*).

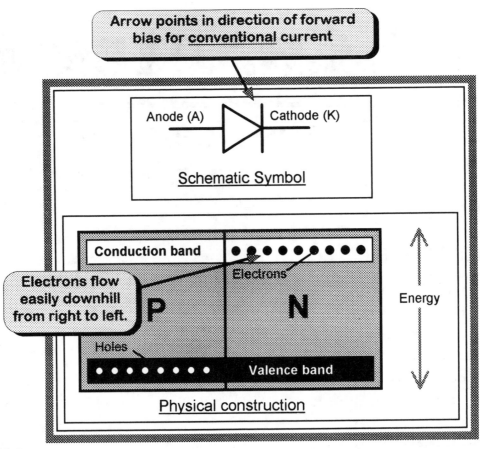

FIGURE 10.1

The PN junction

The best way to display the characteristics of a diode is through the *diode curve*, in which diode voltage and current are plotted on the X- and Y-axes. In this chapter, we draw diode curves for both the small signal diode and the zener diode.

DEVICE MODELS

As we learned in Chapter 8, all PSpice devices use mathematical *models* and model *parameters* to determine their characteristics. In the case of the simpler devices used so far (parts R, C, and L), the model parameters are simple and few in number.

In contrast, parts such as diodes have more complex models and many accessible parameters, and they give us the ability to modify parameters as needed.

PSpice for Windows

In the case of the 1N4148 and 1N750 diodes, the model parameters are contained in *global* file *eval.lib* in directory *msimev71\lib* (or later version). (A global file is accessible to all schematics.)

The local library

Recall from Chapter 8 that when a model library is accessed for the first time (**Edit, Model, Edit Instance Model**), it is assumed that changes will be made. Therefore, to protect the original *global* model, a copy is automatically written to a *local* model library. (A *local* library is accessible only to the corresponding schematic.)

The new local library is automatically given the same file name as the schematic (with extension *.lib*) and is placed in the same directory. When the same part model is accessed again, the local library model appears automatically in the dialog box. As before, we strongly suggest that the user change the local model name during the edit process.

Although we will never take this step, the user may also change the underlying *global* representation of a model by way of the *symbol editor*. (Generally speaking, we wish to protect—not modify—the original global model.)

MODEL PARAMETERS

For the 1N4148 diode of Figure 10.1, the model parameters are listed next:

Parameter	Description	Value
Is	Saturation current	0.1pA
Rs	Parasitic resistance	16Ω
CJO	PN capacitance	2pF
Tt	Transit time	12ns
Bv	Breakdown voltage	100V
ibv	Reverse knee current	0.1A

In this chapter, we will access these model parameters and modify the value of the reverse breakdown voltage (Bv).

SIMULATION PRACTICE

The small signal diode

1. Draw the test circuit of Figure 10.2, and set the attributes as shown.

   - D1N4148 is the part name of the small signal diode (found in library **eval.slb**).

     > The model name is also D1N4148, but it does not appear on the schematic.   Symbol D1 is the attribute.

   - Because V1 will be swept, and we don't require a bias point solution, its *DC=* voltage value need not be specified.

   - As shown, be sure to label the appropriate wire segment *Vanode*.

   - If you wish, title your schematic as shown.

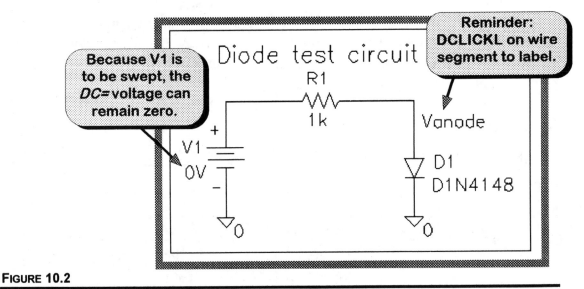

FIGURE 10.2

Diode test circuit

The diode curve

2. To draw a diode curve, select V1 as the <u>main</u> sweep variable and set up a linear DC Sweep from −110V to +10V in increments of .01V. (Do not program the nested sweep.)

3. Run PSpice, and generate the initial Probe graph of Figure 10.3.

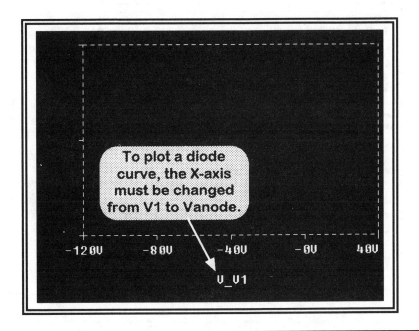

FIGURE 10.3

Initial Probe graph

4. This time, looking at Figure 10.3, the default X-axis variable (V_V1) is not what we need—instead, the X-axis must be the diode's anode-to-cathode voltage [V(Vanode)]. Review *Probe Note 10.1* and make the change.

Probe Note 10.1
How do I change the X-axis variable?

To change the X-axis to any available variable: **Plot, X Axis Settings, Axis Variable**, CLICKL on the desired trace variable [such as V(Vanode)], **OK, OK.** (Be aware that, if appropriate, the X-axis *range* will automatically be adjusted to match the data base.)

5. Plot diode current [I(D1)] on your graph and generate the curve of Figure 10.4. (Use a marker, toolbar button, or menu.)

PSpice for Windows

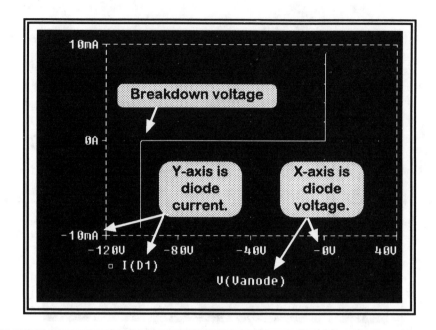

FIGURE 10.4

The diode curve

6. Based on the results of Figure 10.4, use the cursor to determine the following:

    (a) *Breakdown voltage* (V_{RSM})

    > V_{RSM} is also known as the *non-repetitive peak reverse voltage*. We will measure V_{RSM} at a typical test current of approximately $-75\mu A \pm 50\mu A$.

    V_{RSM} (at $\approx -75\mu A \pm 50\mu A$) = _____

    (b) *Maximum reverse current* (I_R)   (We will measure I_R at a typical test voltage of $-90V$):

    I_R (at $\approx -90V$) = _____

7. When the diode curve is viewed from a distance (as in Figure 10.4), it appears to exhibit *ideal* characteristics; that is, a short in the forward direction, and (before breakdown) an open in the reverse direction.

    To bring out the details in the critical forward direction, zoom in on the curve by adjusting the X-axis range as shown in Figure 10.5. (Reminder: Select the **Plot** menu.)

PSpice for Windows

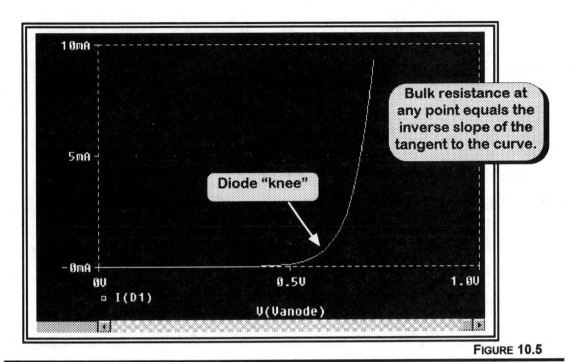

FIGURE **10.5**

Forward bias details

8. From your graph, determine *approximate* values for the following (Hint: Use the cursors):

    (a) The knee voltage (at 1mA): _____

    (b) The forward (bulk) resistance of the diode at 1mA: _____

    > Hint: Place cursor A1 just below 1mA and A2 just above 1mA, and determine 1/slope as $\Delta V/\Delta I$, **or** use the "d" (differentiate) operator to plot 1/d(I(D1)) on a second Y-axis from .6V to 1V.

    (c) The forward resistance of the diode at 5mA: _____

    (d) Does the forward resistance go down as the current goes up?

    >   **Yes**   **No**

Temperature effects

9. All active devices (such as diodes) are sensitive to temperature. To see how temperature can be changed, review *Schematics Note 10.1* and change the temperature of the diode test circuit from the default 27°C (80.6°F) to 60°C (140°F).

Schematics Note 10.1
How do I change the circuit's temperature parameter?

To change the temperature of your circuit: From the *Schematics* window bring up the *Analysis Setup* dialog box (*sets up the simulation analysis for active* toolbar button), **CLICKL** on "Enabled" beside the temperature box, **Temperature** to open up the *Temperature Analysis* dialog box, enter the new temperature, **OK**, **Close**.

10.   Generate a new diode curve for 60°C, compare to steps 6 and 8, and fill in the blanks below.

V_{KNEE} (at $\approx$ 1mA, 60°C)   = _____   % change (from 27°C)   = _____

$I_{REVERSE}$ (at $\approx$ −90V, 60°C)   = _____   % change (from 27°C)   = _____

DC Sweep nesting

11.   A better method of evaluating temperature effects is to generate a family of curves. Follow *Schematics Note 10.2* and set up the diode temperature as a nested variable.

Schematics Note 10.2
How do I set up the DC Sweep nested mode?

When adding a nested sweep to the DC Sweep mode, we use the DC sweep *nested* mode (instead of the *parametric* mode that is used with the *AC Sweep* and *Transient* modes).

   As an example of the nested mode, we set up the nested diode curves of step 11 as follows: *Sets up the simulation analysis for active* toolbar button, **DC Sweep** to bring up the (Main) DC Sweep dialog box and fill in as shown in Figure 10.6(a); **Nested Sweep** to bring up the *DC Nested Sweep* dialog box and fill in as shown in Figure 10.6(b). **Enable Nested Sweep, OK, Close**.

   (CLICKL on the *Nested Sweep* or *Main Sweep* buttons to toggle between boxes.)

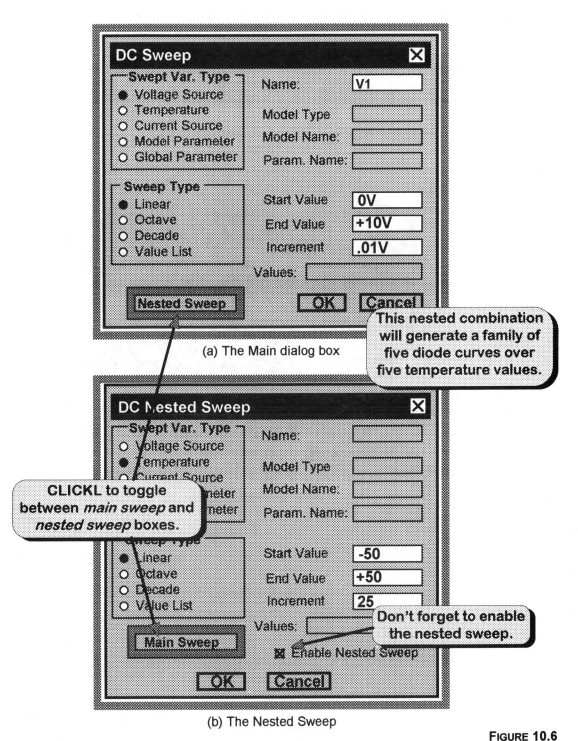

(a) The Main dialog box

(b) The Nested Sweep

FIGURE 10.6

DC Sweep dialog boxes
(a) The Main dialog box
(b) The Nested Sweep

PSpice for Windows

12. Check to make sure the standard temperature analysis of step 9 is disabled because it interferes with a temperature sweep.

> When the standard temperature is disabled, and no temperature sweep is set, the system reverts to a default temperature of 27°C.

13. Run PSpice and create the curves of Figure 10.7.

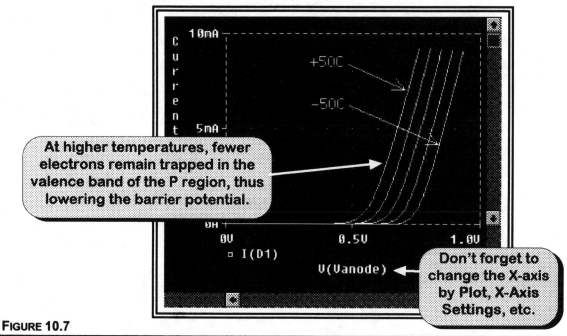

FIGURE 10.7

Family of diode curves

14. Based on the results:

(a) By what *approximate* percentage does the knee voltage (at 1mA) change for each degree C?

% change in knee voltage/°C = _____

(b) Based on simple inspection of the curves, do the impedance characteristics (1/slope) depend on temperature?

          Yes   **No**

Model parameters

15. Referring to *Schematics Note 10.3*, view the model parameters of the 1N4148 and change the reverse breakdown voltage (Bv) from 100 to 150.   (Change the local model name if you wish.)

Schematics Note 10.3
How do I examine and change model parameters?

To change a model parameter: Select the component (**CLICKL** to turn red), **Edit, Model, Edit Instance Model[text]** to bring up the *Model Editor* dialog box of Figure 10.8.   Change the parameter values as desired (i.e., Bv from 100 to 150), **OK**.

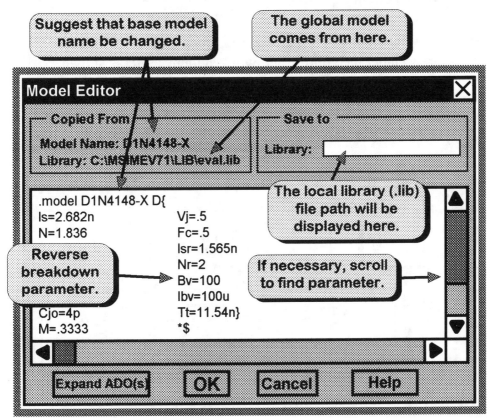

FIGURE 10.8

Diode model parameters

16. Generate a graph similar to that of Figure 10.4.

> Be sure to sweep from −160V to +10V, and to disable the DC nested sweep.

Does the breakdown now occur at −150V?

Yes   **No**

17. Return parameter *Bv* to its original default value of 100V. (Select diode, **Edit**, **Model**, **Edit Instance Model [text]**, etc.)

The zener diode

> The only zener available in the evaluation version is the 1N750. This popular zener breaks down at 4.7V and is therefore widely used in +5V digital circuits.

18. Draw the voltage-regulator zener diode circuit of Figure 10.9. Be sure to label the appropriate wire segment *Vout*, as shown.

Is the diode reverse biased?

Yes   **No**

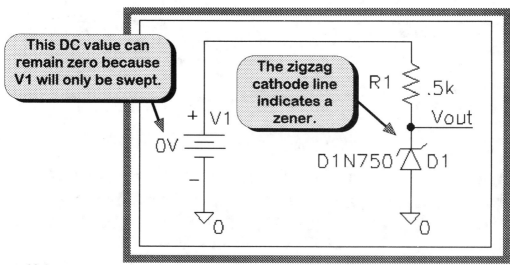

FIGURE 10.9

Zener diode
voltage regulator

19. Generate the zener graph of Figure 10.10. (If necessary, refer to the *process summary* that follows.)

> Listed here is our first *Process Summary*, which condenses the creation of the zener graph of Figure 10.10 into the following two essential steps: (1) Specify the sweep mode and (2) select the X- and Y-axes variables.
>
> *Here and in the future, you should try to generate all curves on your own, referring to these process summaries only as necessary.*
>
> ### Process Summary for Zener Curve
>
> • The <u>main sweep</u> variable is V1, generated by a DC Main Sweep from 0V to +20V in steps of .01V. (The nested sweep is disabled.)
>
> • The X-axis variable is the negative zener voltage [−V(Vout)], and the Y-axis variable is the zener current [I(D1)].

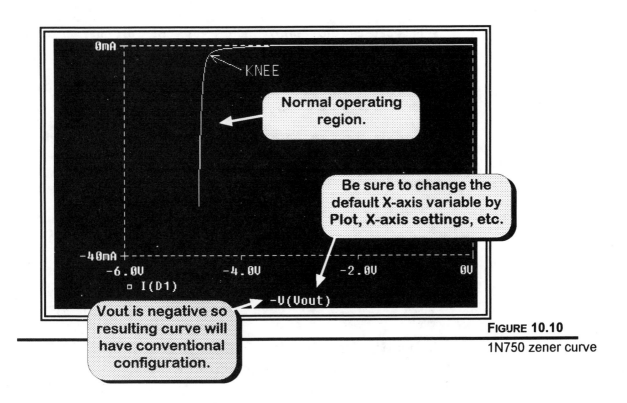

FIGURE 10.10

1N750 zener curve

20. Use the cursor to determine accurately the zener current at a zener voltage of as close as possible to 4.7V.   Compare your answer with the 1N750 spec sheet in Appendix D.

    I$_Z$ (at 4.7V) = _____　　　I$_Z$ (spec sheet) = _____

21. By using the cursor method (see step 8b), determine the zener impedance at the 4.7V test condition and compare to the spec sheet. (Suggestion: Choose test points ≈ 1mA apart.)

    Z (at 4.7V) = _____　　　Z (spec sheet) = _____

22. In the operating region, is the zener a *voltage source*? (Is the voltage approximately independent of the current?)

    Yes　　　　　　　　**No**

Advanced Activities

23. In digital circuits, diode switching speed is important. Draw the pulsed circuit of Figure 10.11, and generate the curves of Figure 10.12.

    (a) What causes the approximately 8ns of *reverse delay* in *Vanode* when V1 switches from forward to reverse bias?

    (b) What causes the slight delay (≈3nS) when V1 switches from reverse to forward bias?

    (c) Based on the waveform results, what is the approximate typical (average) value of the diode's reverse-biased capacitance? (Hint: $I = C \, dV/dt$.)

24. To show how complicated component modeling can be, below is the equation for just the forward current for our "simple" 1N4148 small signal diode. (Note that many of the parameters are listed in Figure 10.8.)

$$Ifwd = IS(e^{Vd/NVt} - 1) + ISR(e^{Vd/NRVt} - 1)((1 - Vd/VJ))^2 + 0.005)^{M/2}$$

    Change **IS** (the saturation current) from 2.682n to 10n and summarize below the changes in the forward diode curve. (If desired, change other parameters and note the changes.)

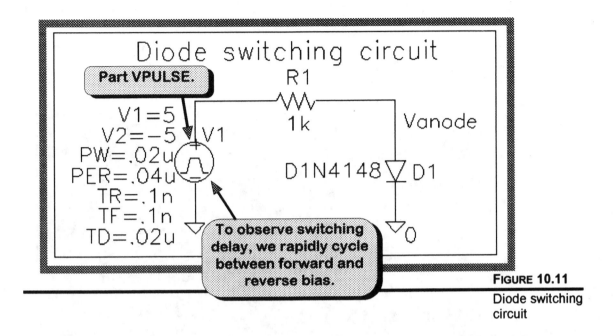

FIGURE 10.11

Diode switching
circuit

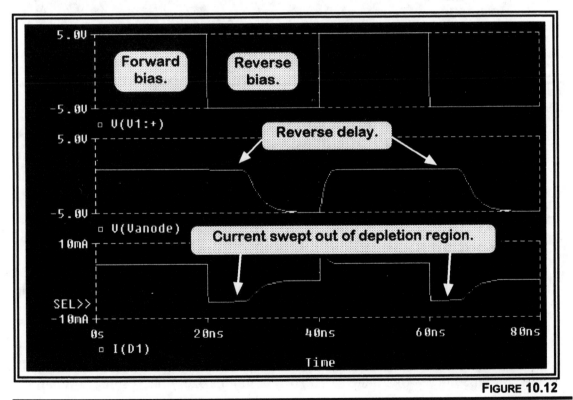

FIGURE 10.12

Switching waveforms

PSpice for Windows

25.   Using the "/" (divide) and "d" (differentiation) operators, add a plot of zener impedance to the zener curve of Figure 10.10 and generate the expanded plot of Figure 10.13. Do the results agree with step 21?

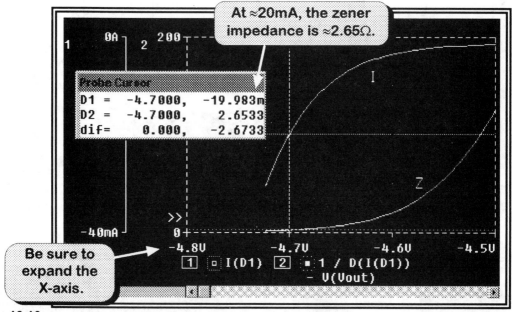

FIGURE 10.13

Adding zener
impedance

26.   By way of its model parameters, change the reverse breakdown voltage of the 1N750 zener diode from 4.7V to 10V and test the results.   At what reverse current is the zener voltage 10V?

EXERCISES

• Test the switching characteristics of the D1N914 small signal diode and compare it to the D1N4148 of Figure 10.12.

• Test the voltage regulation characteristics of a zener diode under a varying load. (Hint: Draw the circuit of Figure 10.14(a) and generate the curves of Figure 10.14(b).)   Summarize your results. (What are the values of RL, I_{ZENER}, and I_{RL} when the zener comes out of regulation?)

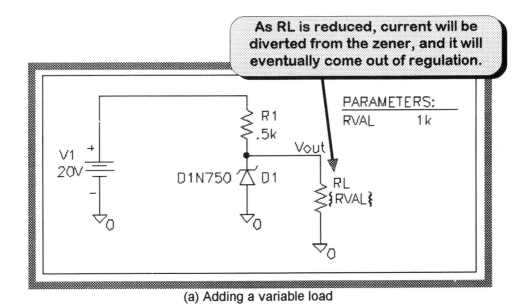

(a) Adding a variable load

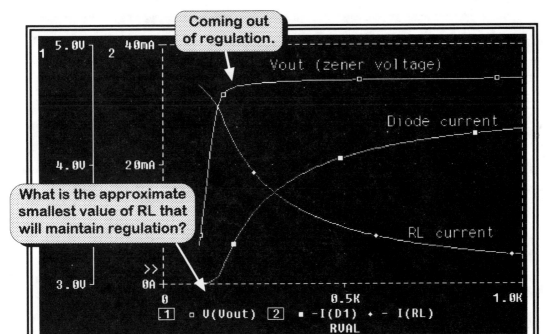

(b) How regulation is affected by load

FIGURE 10.14

Zener regulation
test circuit
(a) Adding a
    variable load
(b) How regulation
    is affected by load

PSpice for Windows

QUESTIONS AND PROBLEMS

1. The forward-biased AC resistance of a diode is lowest at

    (a) low currents
    (b) high currents

2. As the temperature goes up, the barrier potential goes

    (a) up
    (b) down

3. Using an ohmmeter, give a quick and simple method for checking a diode.

4. What is the difference between a small-signal diode and an *LED*?

5. Based on the results of step 6b, how long would it take 1 coulomb of charge to pass through a reverse-biased diode?

6. A zener diode normally operates

    (a) in forward bias
    (b) in reverse bias

7. Referring to Figure 10.14(b), approximately what is the smallest load value that will maintain zener regulation?

8. Referring to Figure 10.15, why is the diode circuit on the left called an OR gate and the circuit on the right an AND gate?

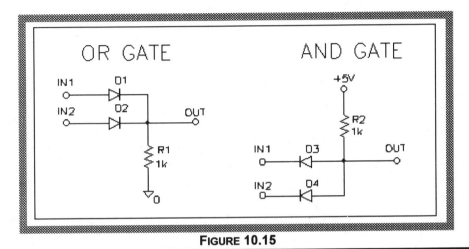

FIGURE 10.15

Diode OR and
AND gates

CHAPTER 11

The Power Supply
Voltage Regulation

OBJECTIVES

- To design a power supply, complete with filter and regulator.
- To measure output ripple and regulation efficiency.

DISCUSSION

A "perfect" power supply provides a constant desired voltage, regardless of the value of the load. A "real" power supply, on the other hand, has a ripple and generates an output voltage that varies with the load.

Our goal in this chapter is to design a power supply that approaches "perfection," but without exceeding reasonable size, cost, and complexity limits. Our design philosophy will be to start simple, and to add components and circuits gradually until we achieve our goal.

A REAL VOLTAGE SOURCE

For safety reasons, it is common practice in the laboratory to use a signal generator to simulate the output from a wall socket and step-down transformer. The problem is that such laboratory voltage sources usually have a significant output impedance value. However, the voltage sources used by PSpice are "perfect" and have zero output impedance.

To simulate a laboratory voltage source using PSpice, we have the option of adding a resistor in series with the voltage source, as shown in Figure 11.1. Commonly found values of Zout are 50Ω and 600Ω.

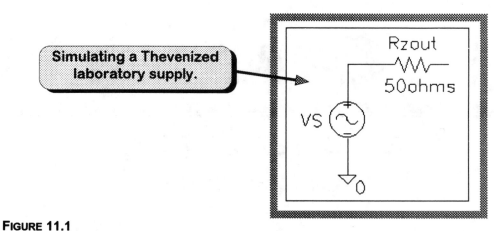

FIGURE 11.1

Simulating Zout of
a power source

Therefore, in this chapter the AC voltage source includes a 50Ω Zout resistor. In future chapters this resistor is optional, but should be added whenever a PSpice simulation is to be directly compared with the same circuit built and tested in the laboratory.

SIMULATION PRACTICE

1. Draw the initial design of Figure 11.2, which is known as a *half-wave rectifier*. (Suggestion: Since we will consistently be displaying *Vout*, set a permanent voltage marker, as shown.)

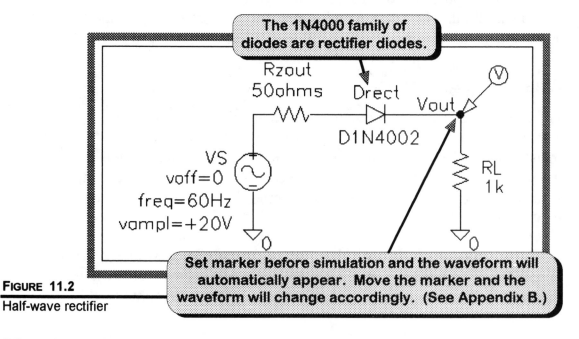

FIGURE 11.2

Half-wave rectifier

PSpice for Windows

2.   Using PSpice, generate the output waveform of Figure 11.3.   (If necessary, refer to the *Process Summary* below.)

> ### Process Summary for Half-Wave Rectifier
>
> - The main sweep variable is time, generated by a transient sweep from 0 to 83ms ($5 \times 1/60 = 83$ms).
>
> - The X-axis is time (by main sweep default), and the Y-axis is Vout [V(Vout)].

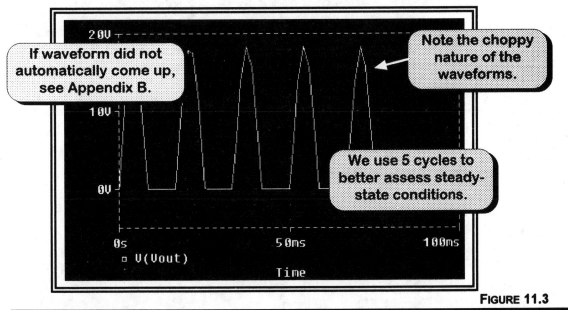

FIGURE 11.3

Half-wave rectifier waveforms

3.   The waveforms are almost as expected—except they are not smooth, especially near the peaks.   Suspecting the problem may related to the calculation points, we display the same graph with data points shown.   (**Tools, Options, Mark data points, OK.**)

4.   Figure 11.4 shows that our suspicions were correct.   To generate more data points we must set a *step ceiling*.   A reasonable value is 1% of the waveform period ($1\% \times 1/60$s $\cong 150\mu$s).   (**CLICKL** on the *Sets up the simulation analysis for active* toolbar button, **Transient**, enter 150μs in the *Step Ceiling* box, **OK**, **Close**.)

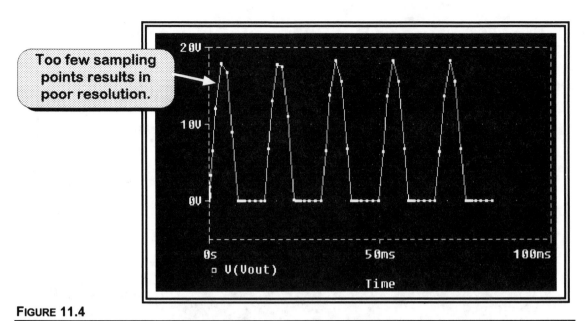

FIGURE 11.4

Showing data points

5. Re-analyze the circuit. The result (Figure 11.5) shows a smooth waveform of high resolution. (To remove the marked data points, **Tools**, **Options**, **Mark data points**, **OK**.)

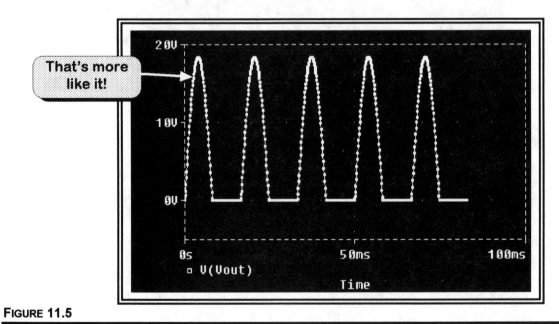

FIGURE 11.5

High resolution
waveform

PSpice for Windows

6. <u>Sketch</u> the half-wave rectifier waveform of Figure 11.5 on the graph of Figure 11.6 and label it as "*Half-wave rectifier.*"

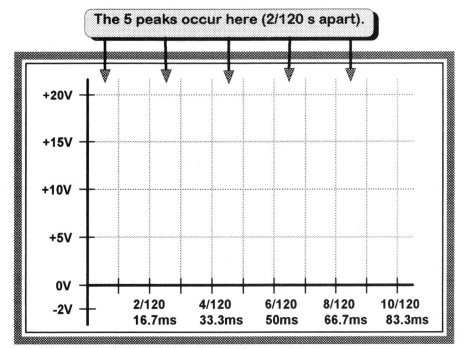

FIGURE 11.6

Power supply
output waveforms

Peak rectifier

7. Figure 11.6 clearly tells us that we are a long way from our goal. Let's improve the circuit in two ways:

    • Use a *full-wave rectifier* so both the positive and negative input cycles will power the output.

    • Add a *filter capacitor* to smooth out the waveform.

    Make these changes and create the circuit of Figure 11.7, which is known as a *full-wave peak rectifier.*

    The circuit acts like a leaky bucket: Each wave of voltage fills up the capacitor bucket with charge—which then leaks out through RL. Due to the blocking diodes, the charge cannot return to the source. The rising and falling portion of the output signal is known as the *ripple* voltage.

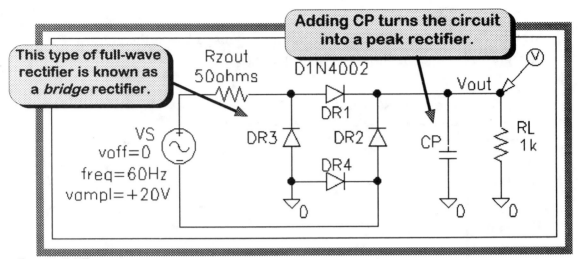

FIGURE 11.7

Full-wave peak
rectifier

8. To complete the design, what value will we choose for CP? A highly accurate answer would require some advanced mathematics. Fortunately, we are only after a ballpark estimate and can make some assumptions:

    - We assume that a 1V output ripple is acceptable.
    - We assume that Vout (average) $\cong$ 16V (after R_{ZOUT} and two diode drops).
    - We assume that each capacitive discharge lasts for a worst case maximum time of 1/120 sec.

    Using these assumptions on the differential form of $Q = CV$ ($I = C\Delta V/\Delta t$), solve the equation below and determine the approximate value of C:

    I (discharge current) = CΔV / Δt = V$_{OUT}$ / RL, where

ΔV	=	ripple voltage	=	1V
Δt	=	maximum discharge time	=	1/120 sec
RL	=	load	=	1kΩ
Vout	=	output voltage	=	+16V

    Solving for C yields approximately _____

9. Round off the value of C determined in step 8 and assign it to CP. Generate the output waveform of Figure 11.8, and add your new output voltage curve to Figure 11.6. Be sure to label the curve "*Peak rectifier.*" (Hint: CP $\approx$ 133μF.)

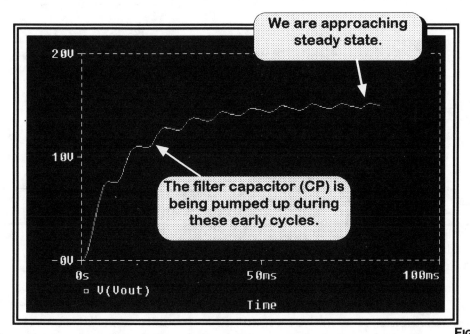

FIGURE 11.8

Peak rectifier
waveform

10. Determine the ripple voltage at the far right of the curve as it approaches steady-state conditions. (Suggestion: Position cursors at a peak and trough and report the difference.)

$$V_{RIPPLE} = \underline{\hspace{2cm}}$$

Is the ripple less than 1V, as predicted by our previous calculations?

    Yes   **No**

Low-pass filter

11. Still we are not satisfied with the output. The ripple voltage is too large—yet we don't wish to increase the size of the expensive and bulky *filter capacitor* (CP)..

    The solution is to add a *low-pass filter*, which passes the DC voltage and shorts the AC ripple to ground. Make the necessary changes and create the circuit of Figure 11.9.

PSpice for Windows

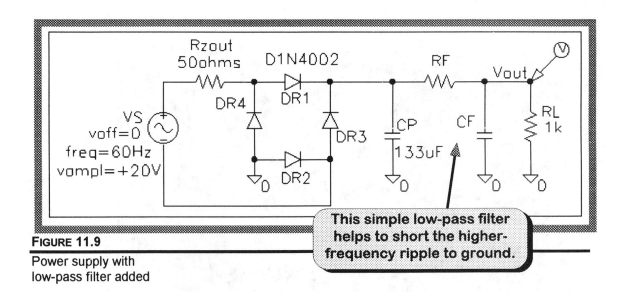

FIGURE 11.9

Power supply with
low-pass filter added

This simple low-pass filter
helps to short the higher-
frequency ripple to ground.

12. Our next task is to choose values for RF and CF. Again, advanced mathematics would be required for a highly accurate answer. As before, estimated values will give satisfactory results. Using the following design guidelines, determine the required value of C:

   - RF cannot be too large compared to the load (RL) because it would drop too much voltage. We arbitrarily choose 200Ω.

   - CF must have a reactance (X_C) at the ripple frequency of 120Hz that is small when compared to RF. We arbitrarily choose a 10-to-1 ratio, giving X_C = 20Ω. Therefore:

   1 / 2πfC = 20Ω, where π = 3.14 and f (ripple frequency) = 120Hz

   C = approximately _____

13. Assign to RF and CF the values determined in step 12. Generate the new (filtered) V_{OUT} of Figure 11.10, add your curve to Figure 11.6, and tag it "*Filter added*." (<u>Hint</u>: CF ≈ 66μF.)

14. Determine the <u>approximate</u> ripple voltage at the far right of the curve as it approaches steady-state conditions. (Be sure to factor out as best you can the background slope of the curve.)

   V_{RIPPLE} ≅ _____

   Has the ripple been reduced by about 90%?

         Yes   **No**

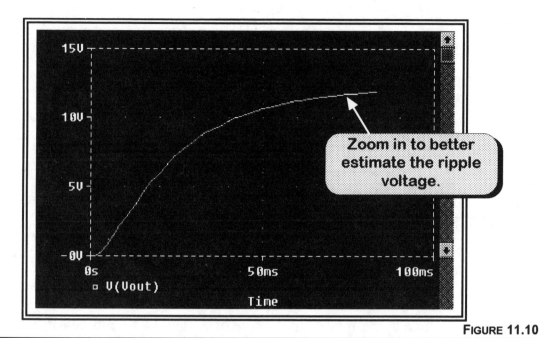

FIGURE 11.10

Filtered output
waveform

Voltage regulator

15. The ripple is now quite low, but the output voltage is nowhere near
    our 4.7V design goal. Furthermore, the output is not regulated
    because Vout varies considerably as the load (RL) changes.

    To solve both problems, add the zener regulator circuit
    developed in Chapter 10. As an added bonus, we will find that the
    ripple voltage is further reduced. Our final design is given in
    Figure 11.11.

16. To determine RZ, we use Ohm's law to design the circuit for the
    ideal zener current of 20mA:

    - *The current through RZ:* From Chapter 8, the approximate value
      of current that gives a zener voltage of 4.7V is 20mA. The 1kΩ
      load adds about 5mA, for a total of 25mA through RZ.

    - *The voltage across RZ:* From the original 20V, we subtract 5V
      for the R_{ZOUT}/diode drop, 5V for the 25mA flowing through the
      200Ω filter resistor, and 4.7V across the zener diode. This leaves
      approximately 5V across RZ.   Therefore:

        RZ $\cong$ **5V/25mA** $\cong$ _____

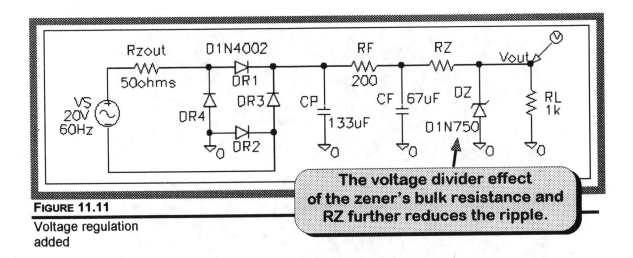

FIGURE 11.11

Voltage regulation
added

17. Set the value of RZ according to step 16. (Hint: RZ ≈ 200Ω.)

18. Generate the final output curve of Figure 11.12 and add to Figure
     11.6. Label this last curve "Regulator added." Also, determine the
     following by using steady-state values to the far right of the curve:

     Vout = _____   **Vripple = _____**

     Is the output voltage near 4.7 and is the ripple very small?

          Yes   **No**

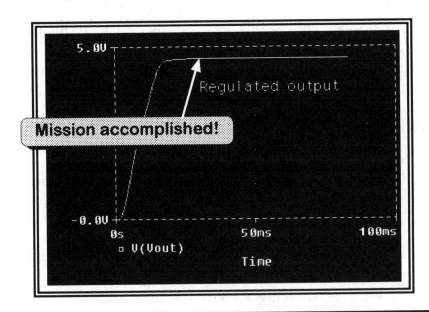

FIGURE 11.12

Regulated
output

Surge current

19. Open a second Y-axis on the graph of Figure 11.12 and add a graph of current through rectifier diodes DR1 or DR2. You will find that the highest current occurs during the initial (surge) cycle.

Record this *maximum surge current* (ISurge) below and compare with the spec sheet value (*nonrepetitive peak surge current*).

I_{SURGE} = _____ I_{SURGE} (SPEC) = __**50mA**__

Is the surge current above the maximum allowed value of 50mA (especially the first cycle)?

Yes   No

20. To lower the surge current, add a small *surge resistor* (RS) to your circuit (between the output of the bridge rectifier and CP). Determine its value by using the worst case equation below:

VS (peak) / I (nonrepetitive peak) = 20V / 50mA = _____

Measure the maximum surge current again. Is it now below the spec sheet value? (Note: It now takes about 150ms to reach steady state output.)

Yes   No

Regulation test

21. To test the voltage regulation characteristics of our final design, generate the family of curves of Figure 11.13 by adding a nested sweep of the load value (RL). (If necessary, review the *Process Summary* below.)

> **Process Summary for Regulation Test**
>
> • The main sweep variable is time, generated by a transient sweep from 0 to 83ms (≈400ms if a surge resistor is present). The nested sweep variable is RL, generated by a parametric sweep from 200Ω to 1kΩ in increments of 200Ω.
>
> • The X-axis is time (primary sweep default), and the Y-axis is Vout [V(Vout)].

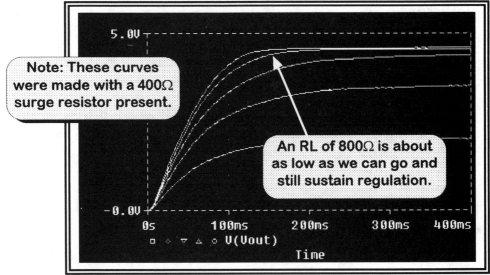

FIGURE 11.13

Regulated output
as a function of RL

22. Based on your results:

- At what approximate value of RL does the system appear to come out of regulation?

    Minimum RL for regulation = _____

- How good is the regulation when RL is near 1kΩ? (<u>Suggestion</u>: Zoom in on the regulated output and determine ΔVout when RL goes from 800Ω to 1kΩ.)

    $\Delta V_{OUT} / \Delta RL$ = _____

Advanced Activities

23. Add a front-end transformer (from library *analog.slb*) to your power supply, as shown in Figure 11.14. In addition to its output voltage, measure the primary and secondary voltages [vp and v(vs1,vs2)] and verify the turns ratio.

> <u>Note</u>: Should you encounter a convergence problem during calculation (time step goes below the minimum allowed value of 200×E-15), force the system to take larger minimum steps by setting the *Step Ceiling* in the transient analysis to an appropriate value (say, 5µs).

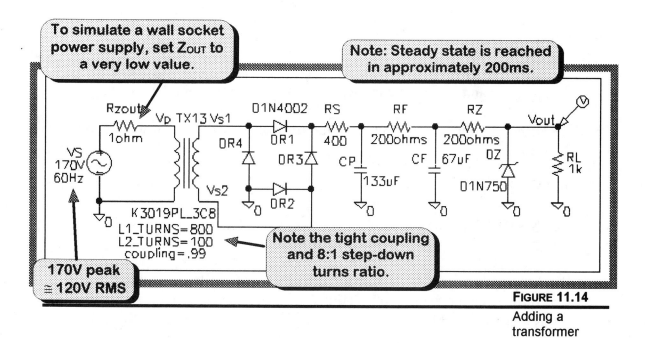

FIGURE 11.14

Adding a transformer

24. For each of the following malfunctions to the circuit of Figure 11.14, predict the approximate output voltage waveform. Make the change to the circuit and compare to the PSpice-generated result.

    (a) Diode DR1 opens

    (b) CP opens

    (c) RZ shorts

EXERCISE

• Perform a heat analysis on various components (Rs and diodes) in the circuit. Compare to spec sheet and rated values. (Hint: Graph V*I or I^2R.)

QUESTIONS AND PROBLEMS

1. Besides the power supply and load, what two components are required for a peak rectifier?

2. Fill in the blanks below with *resistor* or *capacitor*.

    With an RC low-pass filter, the DC component appears across the
    _____ and the AC component (ripple) appears across the _____ .

3. Referring to Figure 11.9, circle all the following processes that will decrease the ripple:

    (a) increase CP
    (b) decrease CP
    (c) increase CF
    (d) decrease CF

4. Besides regulating the voltage, why does the zener voltage regulator circuit also further reduce the ripple?   (Hint: How does the zener RZ combination act as a voltage divider?)

5. Why is an LC filter more efficient than an RC filter?

6. Why is the surge current greatest during the first cycle?

CHAPTER 12

Clippers, Clampers, and Multipliers
Component Initialization

OBJECTIVES

- To design and analyze a variety of clippers, clampers, and multipliers.
- To initialize components and more quickly reach steady state.
- To generate *marching* waveforms.

DISCUSSION

Three of the most common applications of the diode are *clippers*, *clampers*, and *multipliers*. They are defined as follows:

- A *clipper* is a combination of diodes and resistors that limits the magnitude of a time-domain waveform.

- A *clamper* is a series combination of a diode and capacitor that adds a DC component to a time-domain waveform.

- A *multiplier* is a combination of diodes and capacitors yielding a DC voltage that is a multiple of the peak input voltage.

COMPONENT INITIALIZATION

Quite often we are interested in a circuit's steady-state response. However, based on the results of the power supply of Chapter 11, a great deal of computing time is often needed just to reach steady state. A case in point will be the multiplier circuit of this chapter. One solution is to *initialize* the capacitors to near full charge before computation begins.

MARCHING WAVEFORMS

So far, all Probe-generated waveforms have been drawn at one time after all calculations were complete. In some cases, it makes sense to generate *marching waveforms*, which plot consecutive segments of the waveform while the calculations are under way. During time-consuming calculations, this gives us an opportunity to view results as they are available and to terminate simulation early. Since our calculations are short, we will use the marching waveform feature to give a degree of "animation" to our waveforms.

SIMULATION PRACTICE

Clippers

1. Figure 12.1 shows a simple clipper and a *biased* clipper. In each case, predict the output time-domain waveforms for a +5V sine wave input. Sketch your predictions on the graphs of Figure 12.2.

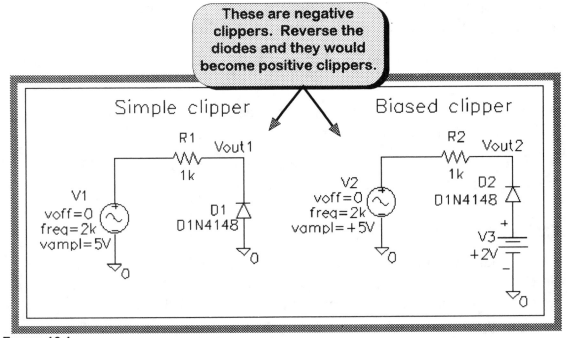

FIGURE 12.1

Clipper circuits

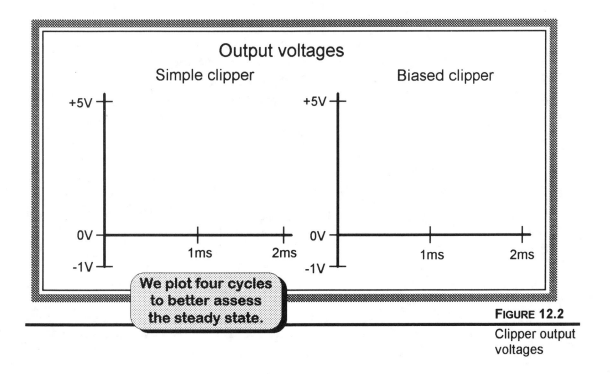

FIGURE 12.2

Clipper output voltages

2. Using PSpice, draw the circuits (both on the same schematic) and generate transient output waveforms. (Suggestion: To smooth out the waveforms, set the *Step Ceiling* to approximately 10μs.)

3. Add the PSpice-generated waveforms to the graphs of Figure 12.2. Clearly label all curves. Did your predicted curves match the experimental (PSpice) curves?

     Yes   **No**

Clampers

4. Figure 12.3 shows a simple clamper and a biased clamper. In each case, predict the output waveforms and sketch your predictions on the graphs of Figure 12.4.

5. Using PSpice, generate output waveforms and add them to the graphs of Figure 12.4. Did your predictions match the experimental curves (except for the first cycle)?

     Yes   **No**

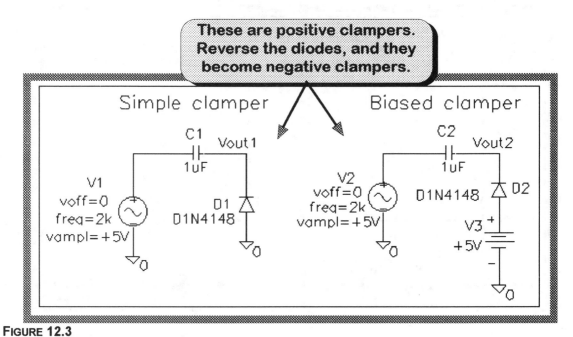

FIGURE 12.3

Clamper circuits

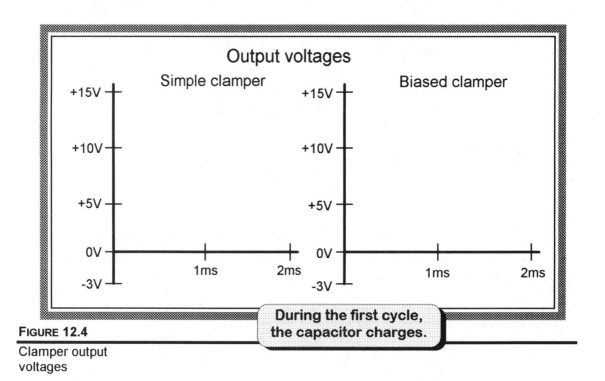

FIGURE 12.4

Clamper output
voltages

Multipliers

6.   Figure 12.5 shows a common form of multiplier. In essence, it is a positive clamper followed by a peak rectifier. Predict the output voltage waveform and sketch on the graph of Figure 12.6.

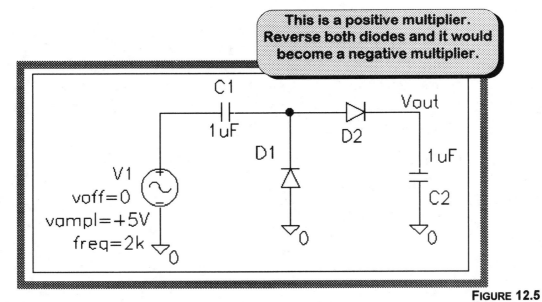

FIGURE 12.5

Multiplier circuit

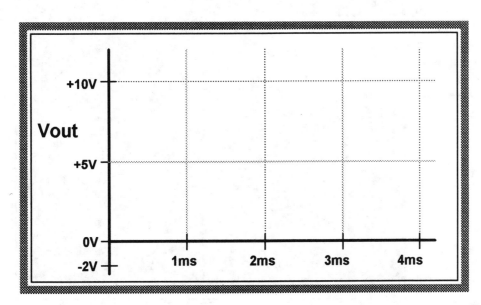

FIGURE 12.6

Multiplier waveform

PSpice for Windows

7. Using PSpice, generate the output waveform (from 0 to 4ms) and add to the graph of Figure 12.6.

8. Chances are that step 7 revealed large differences between the predicted and actual (PSpice) waveforms because the capacitors must be pumped up during the earlier cycles to approach their steady-state values.

    Using the *No-Print Delay* option, generate the waveform of Figure 12.7, which shows the output from approximately 50 to 55 cycles (25ms to 27.5ms) as it approaches steady state. (Hint: Within the transient dialog box, set *Final Time* to 27.5ms and *No-Print Delay* to 25ms.)

    - **What is the average value of Vout between 25ms and 27.5ms?** _____

    - **Is Vout still increasing?**

        Yes   **No**

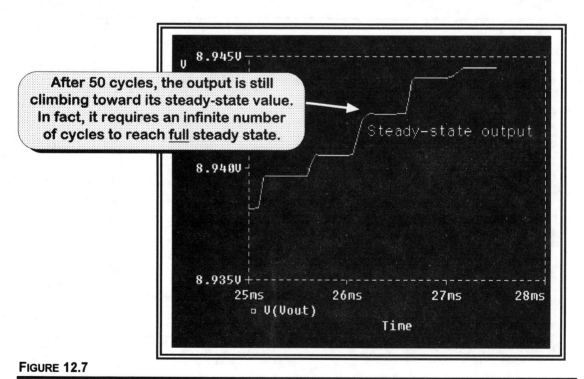

FIGURE 12.7

Steady-state output

Component initialization

9. To approach steady-state conditions more quickly in the multiplier circuit of Figure 12.5, we can initialize C1 and C2.

    Following *Schematics Note 12.1*, pre-charge capacitor C1 to 4.4V and C2 to 8.7V, as shown by Figure 12.8. (We use 4.4V and 8.7V because of the barrier potentials of D1 and D2.)

Schematics Note 12.1
How do I initialize a component value?

PSpice offers two methods for initializing components. Method one is the preferred technique.

*   Method One: *Place initial condition setpoints (IC1 and IC2)*

    IC1 is a setpoint that sets any circuit node to a selectable voltage.
    IC2 is a setpoint that sets any voltage *difference* to a selectable value.

    To place a setpoint: **CLICKL** on the *Selects a part to draw* toolbar button, **IC1** (or **IC2**), **Place**, **Drag** to desired location, **CLICKL** to set, **CLICKR** to abort. (**Edit**, **Flip** and **Edit**, **Rotate** as necessary.)

    To set the initial conditions: **DCLICKL** on the value attribute (presently 0 by default) to bring up the *Set Attribute Value* dialog box, enter the desired value (such as 4.4V), **OK**.

*   Method Two: *Assign initial condition to component (usually a capacitor)*

    DCLICKL on component's *symbol* to bring up the Part Name dialog box, **IC=**, fill in the Value box, **Save Attr** (**Change Display**, etc., if desired), **OK**.

---

10. Change the transient display back to 0 to 4ms, display the new waveforms, and compare with the results of Figure 12.6. Does the circuit approach steady state sooner?

        Yes   No

Marching waveforms

11. Delete the initial condition devices (IC), and place voltage markers on the input and output of the multiplier circuit of Figure 12.8.

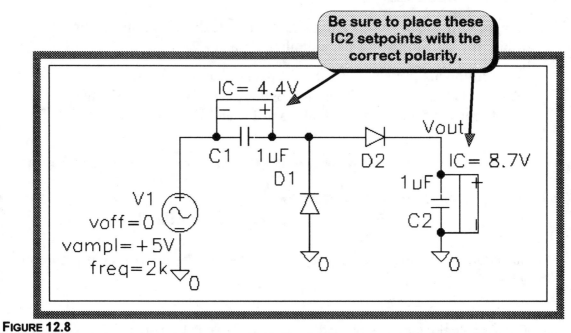

FIGURE 12.8

Component
initialization

12. To enable the marching feature: **Analysis, Probe Setup, Monitor Waveforms [auto update], OK**.

13. Run the simulation and note the waveforms generated.

14. Chances are that the waveforms did not march very smoothly. To improve the display: **Tools** (from Probe), **Options, CLICKL** on *Every %* to enable, change 10 to 1 (for 1%), **OK**. (The 1% entry means that a waveform segment will be added each 1% of the total calculation time.)

15. Run the simulation again and note the smoother waveform generation. (As the waveforms march, note the percent display at the top of the Probe window.)

16. When done, disable the marching feature because it may interfere with other analyses. (From Schematics, choose **Analysis, Probe Setup, Automatically Run Probe after Simulation, OK.**)

Advanced Activities

17. Using PSpice, do a *surge current* analysis of the multiplier circuit of Figure 12.5. Do the numbers indicate that a surge-protection resistor is needed?

EXERCISES

- Design a digital-based clipper (limiter) circuit that limits an input waveform to the range from 0 to +5V.

- By using the two back-to-back (mirror image) multipliers (doublers) of Figure 12.5, design a multiplier that increases the peak input voltage by a factor of four.

QUESTIONS AND PROBLEMS

1. What two components are necessary for clamping?

2. Show how to use a silicon diode (barrier = .7V) and a germanium diode (barrier = .3V) to create a clipper that limits an input waveform to the 0 to +1V range.

3. When voltage is multiplied, what happens to the current? Why?

4.   Quite often, clamping is unwanted.   Referring to the circuit shown in Figure 12.9, how does resistor R3 reduce the effects of clamping?

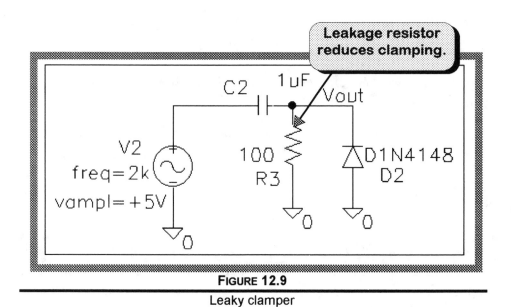

FIGURE 12.9

Leaky clamper

5.   Referring to Figure 12.5, why is capacitor C2 pumped up over time? (Why does it take an infinite number of cycles for C2 to reach full charge?)

CHAPTER 13

The Analog Switch
Crash Studies

OBJECTIVES

- To perform crash studies using a voltage-controlled switch.
- To use a diode to simulate the effects of safety devices.

DISCUSSION

This chapter's simulation study involves automotive safety. One of the most dangerous situations results from a quick stop (a crash). A crash is especially dangerous because of the great forces that can build up—even at moderate speeds. To model a sudden stop, we use the circuit of Figure 13.1.

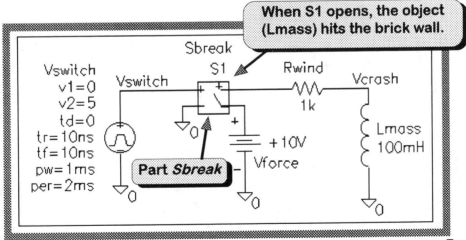

FIGURE 13.1

Analog computer circuit for crash studies

Component S1 is a voltage-controlled switch. When the switch closes, Vforce is applied to Lmass and the car builds up velocity (current) until all the Vforce is used to overcome wind resistance (Rwind × I). When top speed is reached, maximum kinetic energy is contained in Lmass ($1/2LI^2$). When the switch opens (a crash occurs), the velocity is suddenly forced to zero and the back EMF ($V = L\Delta I/\Delta t$) simulates the very large crash forces.

To counter the large forces developed in a crash, we must dissipate the energy over a longer period of time with the use of safety devices—such as seat belts and air bags. To model such safety devices, we use a diode to separate the speed-up (accelerate) portion of the simulation from the slow-down (crash) portion.

SIMULATION PRACTICE

1. Draw the test circuit of Figure 13.1 and enter all parameters and attributes. [Switch S1 is part *Sbreak* from library *Breakout.slb* .]

2. Run a transient solution and generate the curves of Figure 13.2.

   (a) Does the car reach steady state velocity prior to the crash?

      Yes   **No**

   (b) Which component *stores* energy prior to the crash?

      R   **L**

   (c) How large are the crash forces (back EMF voltage) and when do they occur?

3. Figure 13.2 has shown us what happens when an object is stopped suddenly, with no restraining devices. To simulate the effects of an air bag, add the resistor/diode circuit of Figure 13.3. The back EMF current now has a pathway through *Rbag* and the forces will be reduced because the energy will be dissipated over a longer period of time.

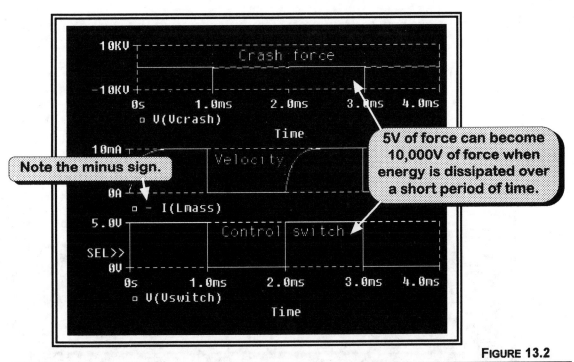

FIGURE 13.2

Crash study
results

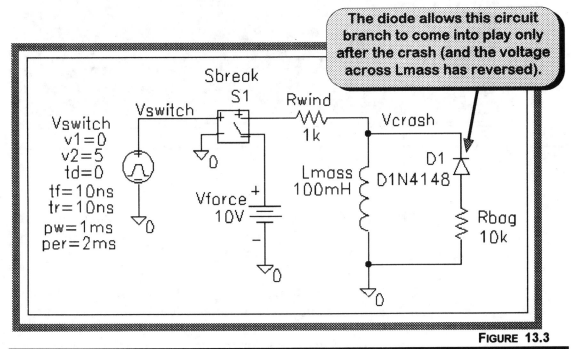

FIGURE 13.3

Simulating a
safety device

4.   Test our new restraining system by generating the curves of Figure 13.4.

(a) Are the crash forces greatly reduced?

Yes   **No**

(b) Is the crash force spike slightly wider?

Yes   **No**

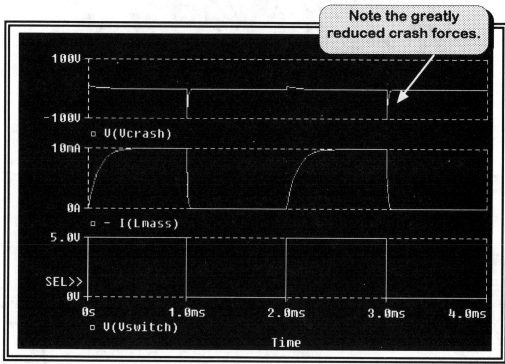

FIGURE 13.4

Restraining system curves

5.   To better interpret the forces that occur during the moment of crash, we would like to zoom in on just the *crash force* plot, leaving the *control switch* and *velocity* plots as they are.

One method is to uncouple (unsync) the crash force plot and give it an X-axis time range that is independent of the other plots.

Review *Probe Note 13.1* to uncouple the crash force plot, zoom in on the crash force spike, and generate the waveform set of Figure 13.5.

Probe Note 13.1
How do I uncouple individual plots of a multiple-plot graph?

When multiple plots are first generated, their X-axes are synchronized, and any X-axis action on one will affect them all.

To uncouple (unsync) a given plot: **CLICKL** on plot to select (place SEL>>), **Plot**, **Unsync Plot**. We are then free to use any Zoom or Plot technique on the uncoupled plot independent of all the others.

To resynchronize the plot to the others: **Plot**, **X-axis Settings**, **Auto Range**.

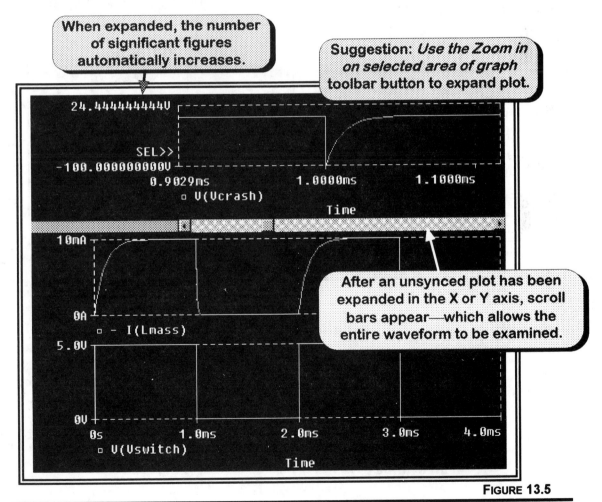

When expanded, the number of significant figures automatically increases.

Suggestion: *Use the Zoom in on selected area of graph* toolbar button to expand plot.

After an unsynced plot has been expanded in the X or Y axis, scroll bars appear—which allows the entire waveform to be examined.

FIGURE 13.5

Unsynced crash force plot

Watch Point

In many circuits, certain voltages may be critical. For example, let's say that the maximum safe crash force corresponds to –80V. During simulation, we wish to know if and when this value is exceeded. That is the job of a *watch point*.

6. Place a watch point (part WATCH1 from library *special.slb*) and **DCLICKL** to set attributes as shown in Figure 13.6.

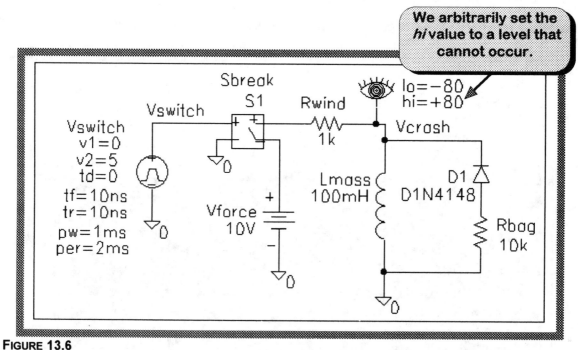

FIGURE 13.6

Setting a watch point

7. Run PSpice and note that simulation pauses, and a watch alarm is quickly issued in the PSpice window. In the space below, record the watch alarm time and the watch value (*V(Vcrash)*).

    Watch alarm time = _____

    Watch value (V(Vcrash)) = _____

8. We then allow the simulation to complete: **File** (from the PSpice dialog box), **Pause Simulation**.

9. Display V(Vcrash) and note the crash forces. Did the forces first exceed −80V at the time indicated in step 7?

    Yes   **No**

10. Because the watch alarm indicated a dangerous situation at 1ms, lower *Rbag* to 7k (to dissipate the stored kinetic energy faster) and repeat the simulation. Is the new design safe now?

    (a) Did the watch alarm stay silent?

        Yes   **No**

    (b) Are the crash forces less than −80V?

        Yes   **No**

Advanced Activities

11. Using the circuit of Figure 13.3, create the demonstration graph of Figure 13.7.

    > Figure 13.7 demonstrates all of the multiple-curve display methods available under *Probe*: *multiple windows*, *multiple plots*, *multiple Y-axes*, *unsynced plots*.
    >
    > Be aware that a darkened border refers to a selected window, SEL>> refers to a selected plot, and >> refers to a selected Y-axis. **CLICKL** on window, plot, or Y-axis, respectively, to select.

12. Based on the data presented by our demonstration graph:

    (a) Does the relationship between velocity and force obey Newton's second law (F = mΔV/Δt)?

        Yes   **No**

    (b) Using *V = LdI/dt*, solve for L. Does it equal $\approx$100mH?

        Yes   **No**

13. Repeat the crash studies using the open/close switches of Figure 13.8. (Switches U1 and U2 are parts *Sw_tClose* and *Sw_tOpen* from library *eval.slb*.)

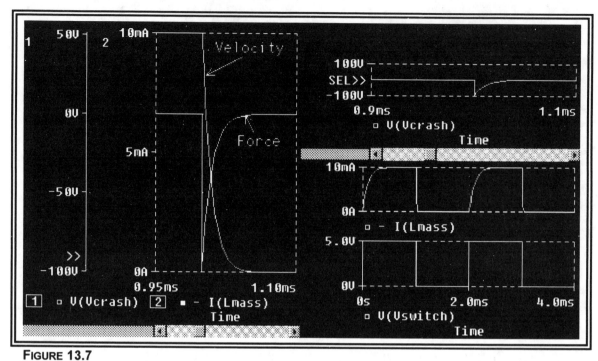

FIGURE 13.7

Multiple-plot
demonstration

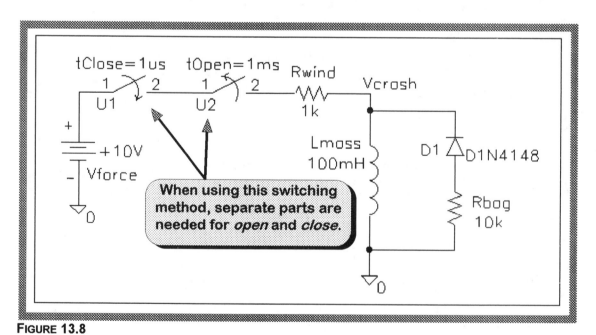

FIGURE 13.8

Crash study
using switches

14. In step 10, we found that lowering the value of *Rbag* reduced the maximum crash forces. Perform a study of this effect, and determine why there is a limit on how low we can take *Rbag*. (Hint: Lowering *Rbag* increases travel distance.)

To help your study, refer to the following equation, which gives the distance traveled by an applied force. Based on this equation, you may wish to plot graphs of *s(s(V(Vcrash)/100mH)))* or *s(I(Lmass))*.

$$\text{Distance} = \int \text{Velocity } dt = \iint \frac{\text{Force}}{\text{Mass}} \, dt dt$$

EXERCISE

- Perform a power/energy study of both crashes (with and without *Rbag*). How much energy was absorbed by *Rbag*? *Suggestion*: Use the "s" (integrate) operator to determine the area under a power curve —which equals energy.

QUESTIONS AND PROBLEMS

1. Based on the results of this chapter, does switch S1 bounce? How could bouncing be simulated? (<u>Hint</u>: We have total control over the opening and closing of the switch.)

2. When *Rbag* is not present (Figure 13.1), where does the inductor (kinetic) energy go when a crash occurs?

3. To make the restraining system more effective (lower the crash forces still more), should *Rbag* (presently 10kΩ) be increased or decreased?   Why? (Hint: See step 10.)

4. Referring to Figure 13.7, when the crash force is maximum, what is true about the current?   (Hint: $V = LdI/dt$.)

5. Which of the following equations demonstrates Newton's second law of motion [$F = ma$, where a (acceleration) = $dVelocity/dt$].

    (a) $V = LdI/dt$
    (b) $E = 1/2LI^2$
    (c) $Q = CV$

6. What does our crash study tell you about the dangers of back EMF (the voltage caused by the presence of an inductor in a circuit that opens suddenly)?

PART III
The Bipolar Transistor

In Part III, we move to bipolar transistors, one of the fundamental building blocks of electronics. The emphasis is on amplifiers and buffers.

In Part III we take another step in turning over the PSpice operations to the student. The process summaries will be used more sparingly, and it will be primarily the responsibility of the student to set up PSpice and generate the proper graphs. Just remember, to generate a Probe graph, you must answer the following two questions:

1. What sweep mode will I use?
2. What variables will I assign to the X- and Y-axes?

CHAPTER 14

Bipolar Transistor Characteristics
Collector Curves

OBJECTIVES

- To display collector and base curves for a *bipolar* transistor.
- To determine a transistor's *Beta* (β).
- To determine temperature effects.

DISCUSSION

The bipolar transistor of Figure 14.1 is a solid-state device with two PN junctions. Physically, it seems to be nothing more than two back-to-back diodes.

However, when the center P-region was made thin, and when it was *biased* as shown in Figure 14.1, it took on truly revolutionary properties: it became a *voltage-controlled current source* with a current gain (*Beta*) in the range of 25 to 1000.

It was an invention that changed the world.

VCIS

In simple terms, a bipolar transistor is useful in analog applications because it is a *voltage-controlled current source* (VCIS). That is, the input master voltage (V_{BE}) controls an output slave current (I_C)— regardless of the slave voltage (V_{CB} or V_{CE}).

Although these VCIS properties were not new (vacuum tubes have these properties), it was the very first time they appeared in an inexpensive solid state device.

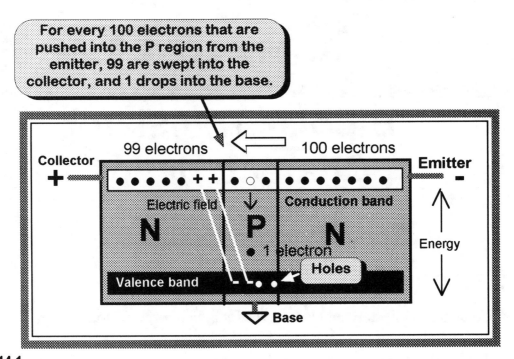

FIGURE 14.1

NPN transistor
physical configuration

Although it is not necessary to know *how* a transistor achieves its VCIS characteristics, observe the following from Figure 14.1:

- The slave (collector-base) circuit is a reverse-biased PN junction that acts as a charged capacitor with an electric field between its plates. Therefore, no output current (I_C) flows as a result of output voltage (V_{CB}). (The output current is independent of the output voltage.)

- The master (base-emitter) circuit is a forward-biased PN junction in which the input voltage (V_{BE}) pushes electrons into the P region conduction band. Held up briefly by quantum mechanical action, most of the electrons diffuse between the plates of the capacitor, are swept up by the strong electric field, and become collector current (I_C). Only a small percentage fall into the base's valence band and become base current (I_B).

When these two physical facts are put together, a transistor becomes a VCIS. (Give me an input voltage, and I will give you an output current—the output voltage doesn't matter.)

VCIS versus ICIS

Because the master circuit of a bipolar transistor is a forward-biased PN junction, the driving source must supply current to the transistor. Furthermore, the relationship between base current in and collector current out is quite linear. For these reasons, a bipolar transistor is also called a *current-controlled current source* (ICIS).

Transistor Beta (β)

To measure the effectiveness of any control device, we determine *output* divided by *input*. Using current as our input/output variables, the transistor of Figure 14.1 has a current gain (*Beta*) of 99/1 (I_C/I_R). Because *Beta* (β) typically lies in the 25 to 1000 range, and because $I_E = I_B + I_C$, β is also approximately equal to I_E/I_B.

Saturation

Should the voltage between the collector and emitter (V_{CE}) drop below approximately .3V, the resulting weak electric field between collector and base is no longer able to sweep 99% of the electrons into the collector. Instead the electrons fall into (and saturate) the base.

Therefore, the region from $V_{CE} = 0$ to approximately .3V is known as the *saturation* region. In the saturation region, the transistor is no longer a current source. (In the saturation region, I_C depends on V_C.)

When used in an analog application, we generally stay away from the saturation region; when used in a digital application, we generally make use of the saturation region.

NPN versus PNP

The test circuits of Figure 14.2 show the schematic symbols for both the NPN and PNP versions. The PNP transistor performs like the NPN, except that all voltages and currents are reversed. (Note the change in direction of the arrow between the base and emitter.)

To investigate the VCIS/ICIS characteristics of a bipolar transistor, we will generate collector (slave) curves. This is accomplished with the test circuits of Figure 14.2.

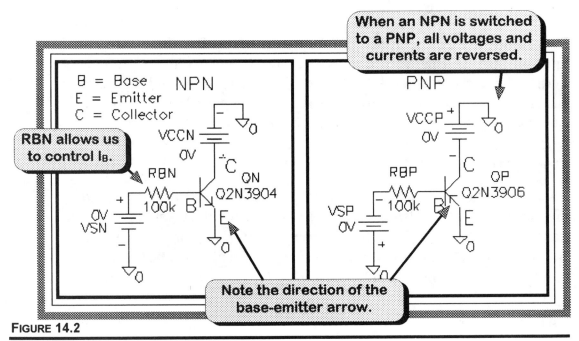

FIGURE 14.2

The bipolar
transistor

SIMULATION PRACTICE

Collector Curves (NPN)

1. Draw the NPN circuit of Figure 14.2 and set the attributes as shown. (Because both voltage sources will be swept, it is not necessary to change the DC default values of zero at this time.)

2. Using PSpice, generate the collector curves of Figure 14.3. (If necessary, refer to the *process summary* below.)

Process Summary for Collector Curves

- The <u>Main Sweep</u> variable is collector voltage (VCCN), generated with a linear DC Sweep from 0 to +10V in increments of .01V. The <u>Nested Sweep</u> variable is VSN from 0V to +10V in linear increments of 2V.

- The <u>X-axis</u> variable is V_VCCN (Main Sweep default), and the <u>Y-axis</u> variable is IC(QN) (collector current).

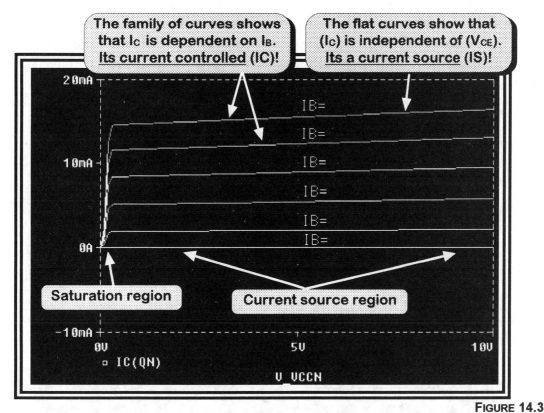

FIGURE 14.3

Collector curves

3. Add another Y-axis (or plot) to your graph and generate a set of six base current [IB(QN)] curves. Realizing that the six new current curves correspond one-to-one to the six voltage curves, fill in the corresponding "IB =" for each of the six curves of Figure 14.3 (use the margin and arrows, if necessary).

4. State in your own words how the graph of Figure 14.3 proves that a bipolar transistor (in the current source region) is an ICIS. (Hint: Does a smaller I_B control a larger I_C, and why is it important that the curves are flat?)

Collector impedance

5. Determine the AC collector impedance ($Z_C = \Delta V/\Delta I$) of the current-source region (flat portions) for curves 2, 4, and 6 (curve 1 is at the bottom, and curve 6 is at the top). (Suggestion: Use the 1/slope method, as demonstrated for curve 6 in Figure 14.4.)

Z_C (2) = _____ Z_C (4) = _____ Z_C (6) = _____

As we move from bottom to top (curves 1 to 6), does the collector impedance generally lower?

Yes   **No**

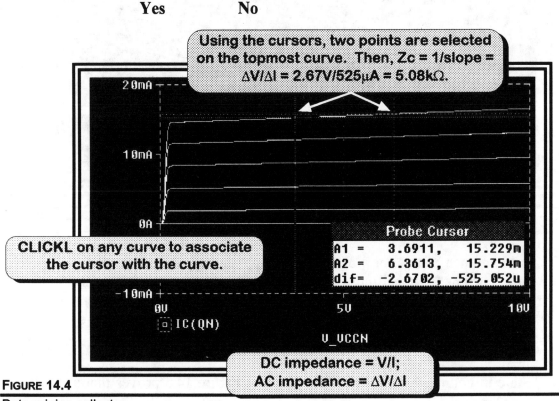

FIGURE 14.4
Determining collector impedance

6. Determine a *typical* value for *Beta* (I_C/I_B) in the current-source region for the same three curves (2, 4, and 6). (Remember: Use the *IB=* values generated in step 3.)

Beta (2) = _____   *Beta* (4) = _____   *Beta* (6) = _____

Is *Beta* fairly constant from one curve to the next?

Yes   **No**

Saturation

7. The region from V_C (V_{CCN}) = 0 to approximately .3V is known as the *saturation* region because the low collector/emitter voltage causes electrons to fall into (and saturate) the base, rather than being swept to the collector. In the saturation region, the transistor is no longer a current source.

    Expand the lower range of the curves (0 to .3V), and determine the value of *Beta* for any typical curve (such as curve four) at V_{CCN} = 300mV, 200mV, and 100mV.

	300mV	200mV	100mV
Beta			

8. Based on the results of step 7, does β decrease as we go from the current source region to deeper and deeper into the saturation region?

    Yes   **No**

Base (master) curves

9. The collector curves of Figure 14.3 do not *directly* show the VCIS transconductance relationship. (How does the input *voltage* affect the output *current*?) To see this relationship, generate the master curve of Figure 14.5. (If necessary, refer to the *process summary* below.)

    > **Process Summary for Master Bipolar Curve**
    >
    > - The DC <u>Main Sweep</u> variable is VSN, from 0 to +10V in increments of .01V. (The DC Nested Sweep is disabled and VCCN is set to +10V.)
    >
    > - The <u>X-axis</u> variable is V_{BE} [V(QN:b)], and the <u>Y-axis</u> variable is I_C [IC(QN)].

10. As expected, Figure 14.5 shows the characteristics of a forward-biased PN junction. Is it similar to the diode curve of Figure 10.5?

    Yes   **No**

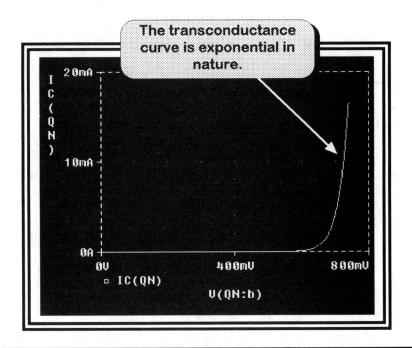

FIGURE 14.5

Collector current
versus base voltage

Temperature Effects

11. Of all the temperature-related variables of a bipolar transistor, *Beta* is the most sensitive.

   Re-create the graph of Figure 14.6, which shows how β changes with temperature. Note that the cursor is set at two **arbitrary** coordinates, showing a β of 122.9 at $-40.1°$ and 189.1 at $+40.1°$. (If necessary, refer to the *process summary* below.)

Process Summary for Temperature Effects of β

- The Main Sweep variable is temperature, using a linear DC Main Sweep from -50 to $+50$ in increments of $1°$. (The Nested Sweep is disabled; VCCN and VSN are both set to $+10V$.)

- The X-axis variable is temperature (Main Sweep default), and the Y-axis variable is I_C/I_B (*Beta*).

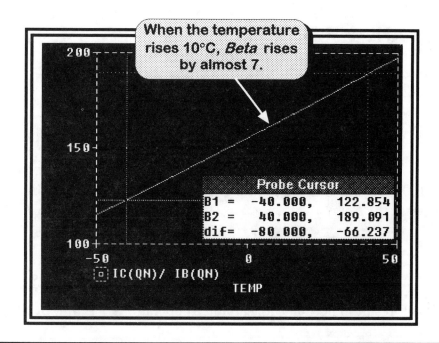

FIGURE 14.6

Beta as a function of temperature

12. Based on the results of step 11, *Beta* is quite dependent on temperature. As a quantitative measure of this dependency, determine the following:

$\Delta \beta / \Delta$**Temperature = slope =** _____

Advanced Activities

13. Generate a set of collector curves for the PNP circuit of Figure 14.2. Based on your results, what is the difference in operation between an NPN and PNP transistor?

EXERCISES

• Design a current source of 10mA using each of the following:

(a) a 3904 NPN transistor
(b) a 3906 PNP transistor

QUESTIONS AND PROBLEMS

1. What is a *current source*?

2. If for every 100 electrons that are pulled into the emitter, 98 go on to the collector, what is the *Beta*?

3. With the emitter grounded, what is the approximate minimum collector voltage that will result in normal (nonsaturated) operation?   (<u>Hint</u>: See Figure 14.3.)

4. For the circuits of Figure 14.2, place "base-emitter" or "collector" in the correct spaces below.

    VCIS means that the input _____ voltage controls the output _____ current, regardless of _____ voltage.

5. A transistor's *alpha* is equal to I_C / I_E.   If *Beta* for a given transistor is 200, what is *alpha*?

6. Based on the results of procedure step 5, what is a *typical* (average) value for Z_C (AC collector impedance in the current-source region)? Is there a difference between DC impedance and AC impedance?

7.   When the temperature rises, *Beta*

(a) goes up.
(b) goes down.

8.   When using the transistor schematic symbol, the arrow points in the direction of emitter

(a) electron flow.
(b) conventional flow.

9.   When a transistor enters saturation, V_C is approximately .3V higher than the emitter. However, V_B is .7V higher than the emitter. Does this mean that the collector can actually be lower in voltage than the base (by as much as .4V) and still receive 99% of the electrons entered from the emitter?   (Hint: Reformat Figure 14.3 so the X-axis is V_{CB}, rather than V_{CE}.)

CHAPTER 15

Bipolar Biasing
Stability and DC Sensitivity

OBJECTIVES

- To design and analyze several popular bipolar transistor biasing circuits.
- To compare the temperature stability characteristics of biasing circuits.
- To perform a DC sensitivity analysis on bias circuits.

Discussion

In analog applications, a bipolar transistor is primarily used as an amplifier or buffer. Because analog applications usually involve an AC signal, we must *bias* the transistor. (As we will see in Chapter 23, a bipolar transistor used in a digital application is a *switch* and does not generally require biasing.)

To bias a bipolar transistor is to use a DC voltage to place its *quiescent* (Q) *point* at an appropriate place in the master curve. When properly biased, the superimposed AC signal will have room to operate on both its positive and negative cycles. A typical Q point for the 3904 NPN bipolar transistor is shown in Figure 15.1.

Because of a transistor's sensitivity to voltage (beyond the .7V knee), Figure 15.1 shows that we usually establish the Q point by designing for the desired *current* (such as $I_C = 10mA$).

There are many trade-offs involved in the design of a bias circuit. Several of the most important are *cost, temperature stability, sensitivity to tolerances*, and *number of power supplies required*.

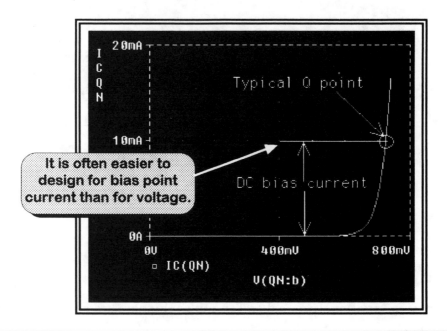

FIGURE 15.1

NPN transistor biasing
and Q points

STABILITY

Stability is a temperature problem. Will a circuit that operates properly at room temperature continue to operate properly when the temperature rises (and the value of *Beta* changes, for example)?

To perform a stability analysis, we sweep through a range of temperatures and examine Q-point values.

DC SENSITIVITY

Sensitivity is a tolerance problem. For example, we might use DC sensitivity analysis to tell us how the Q point voltage is affected by each resistor in the circuit. If we find that the Q point is very sensitive to a particular resistor, we might want to reduce that resistor's tolerance from 10% to 5%.

To perform a DC sensitivity analysis, we first select an output variable (such as Q point voltage). By performing a linear analysis of all devices about the bias point, the sensitivity of the output variable to all the device values and model parameters will be calculated and sent to the *output file*.

SIMULATION PRACTICE

Base Biasing

1. The simplest type of biasing for a bipolar transistor is the *base-biased* circuit of Figure 15.2. The following equations govern the DC values:

    *   **Beta** $= I_C / I_B = $ (approximately) I_E / I_B

    * $V_{CC} = .7V + I_B R_B$

    * $V_{CC} = V_C + I_C R_C$

    Assuming a *Beta* of 175, solve for the Q point by hand and fill in the following values. (C = "collector" and CEQ = "difference between collector and emitter.")

    $$I_C = \underline{\qquad} \qquad\qquad V_{CEQ} = \underline{\qquad}$$

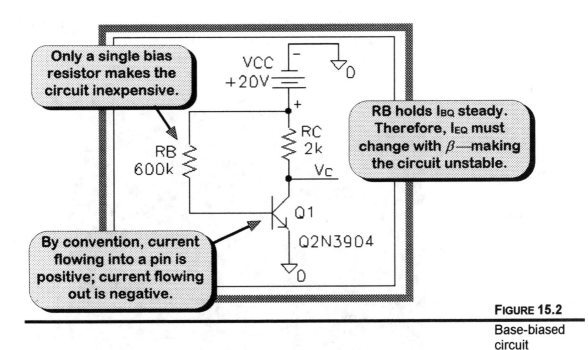

FIGURE 15.2

Base-biased circuit

2. Using PSpice, run a DC bias point solution (**iprobe** and **viewpoint**, or examine the output file) and determine the Q point values:

    $$I_C = \underline{\qquad} \qquad\qquad V_{CEQ} = \underline{\qquad}$$

3. Compare the theoretical values of step 1 with the experimental values of step 2. Are they approximately the same?

Yes **No**

Temperature Stability

4. Using just a single base resistor, the *base-biased* circuit is inexpensive—but is it stable? A good measure of stability is to answer the question, what happens to the Q point current (I_{CQ}) as the temperature changes? To determine Q point stability, generate the graph of Figure 15.3. (If necessary, refer to the *process summary* below.)

Process Summary for Base-Biased Stability

- The Main Sweep variable is temperature, generated by a DC Sweep from −50°C to +50°C in increments of 1°C. (The Nested Sweep variable is disabled.)

- The X-axis variable is temperature (Main Sweep default), and the Y-axis variable is collector current [IC(Q1)].

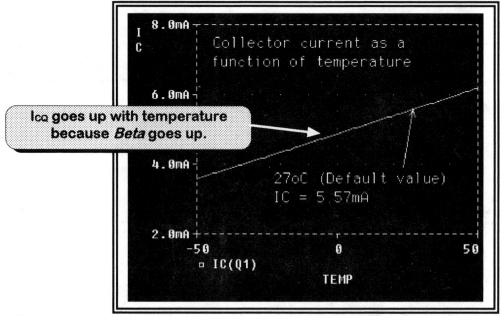

FIGURE 15.3

I_{CQ} as a function
of temperature

PSpice for Windows

5. Based on the results of step 4, it is clear that a base-biased circuit is not stable. As a quantitative measure of this instability, determine the slope of the curve.

$\Delta I_{CQ} / \Delta \text{Temperature} = \underline{\hspace{3cm}}$

Voltage-Divider Bias

6. The most popular biasing circuit is shown in Figure 15.4. It uses *voltage-divider* biasing to further improve stability. Following the same steps as with base biasing, determine each of the following:

- Using calculations: $I_{CQ} = \underline{\hspace{2cm}}$ $V_{CEQ} = \underline{\hspace{2cm}}$

- Using PSpice: $I_{CQ} = \underline{\hspace{2cm}}$ $V_{CEQ} = \underline{\hspace{2cm}}$

$\Delta I_{CQ} / \Delta \text{Temperature} = \underline{\hspace{2cm}}$

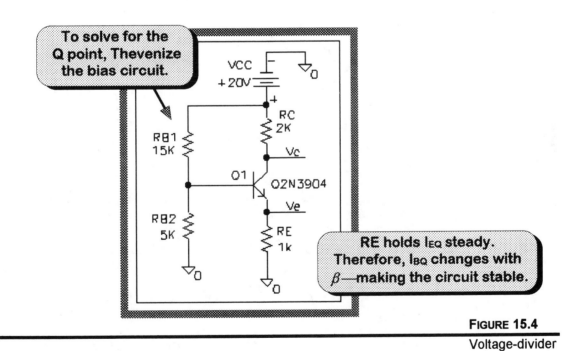

FIGURE 15.4

Voltage-divider bias

7. Based on the results so far, is voltage-divider biasing more stable than base-biasing?

        Yes   **No**

Collector-Feedback and Emitter Biasing

8. Two additional biasing circuits are the *collector-feedback* and *emitter* biasing circuits of Figure 15.5(a) and (b). Use PSpice to analyze both circuits for temperature stability and enter your results below:

- **Collector-feedback:** $\Delta I_{CQ} / \Delta\text{Temperature}$ = _____

- **Emitter biasing:** $\Delta I_{CQ} / \Delta\text{Temperature}$ = _____

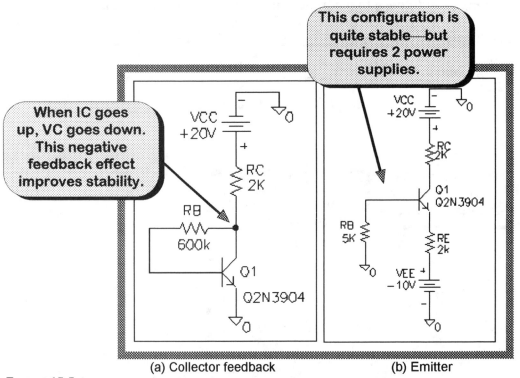

(a) Collector feedback   (b) Emitter

FIGURE 15.5

Additional bipolar
bias circuits
(a) Collector feedback
(b) Emitter

9. To better compare the temperature stability properties of the four bias circuits, plot all of them on a single graph (as shown in Figure 15.6).

> To combine data files: From Probe, **File**, **Append**, **DCLICKL** on desired data file, **Do not skip sections**. Repeat for each data file you wish to append.

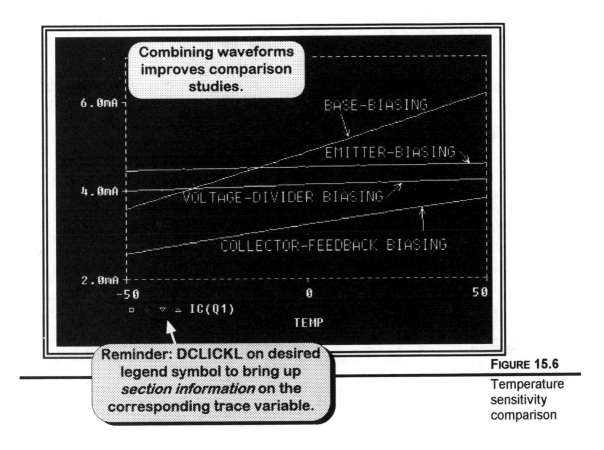

FIGURE 15.6

Temperature
sensitivity
comparison

10. Based on the results of Figure 15.6, what conclusions can you
     draw about the relative temperature stability of the four types of
     bias circuits?

DC Component Sensitivity

Remember: *Stability* is a temperature problem; *sensitivity* is a
tolerance problem.

11. Bring back the voltage-divider bias circuit of Figure 15.4.

12. Enable the *Sensitivity Analysis* mode, and open the dialog box of Figure 15.7 (**CLICKL** on the *Sets up the simulation analysis for active* toolbar button, **CLICKL** to enable, **Sensitivity**, and enter the desired sensitivity variable (such as V(Vc,Ve)), **OK, Close**).

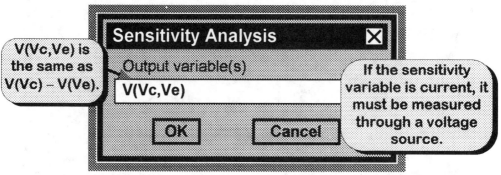

FIGURE 15.7

Sensitivity Analysis
dialog box

13. Analyze the circuit and examine the *DC Sensitivity Analysis* portion of the output file (Table 15.1). The top of the table indicates that all values refer to the Q point voltage [V(Vc,Ve)], the voltage difference between collector and emitter.

14. Next, we observe that the data (Table 15.1) is divided into two sections: resistor and voltage-source components at the top, and transistor parameters at the bottom.

    (a) How many R and V components affect V(Vc,Ve)? _____

    (b) How many transistor parameters affect V(Vc,Ve)? _____

15. To interpret the table, look at the first line. It tells us that, for every 1Ω change in the $2k\Omega$ value of R_C, V(Vc,Ve) will change by $-.00416V$. Or, for every 1% change in R_C (20Ω), V(Vc,Ve) will change by $-.0832V$.

    As an example, if R_C changes from $2k\Omega$ to $2.1k\Omega$, enter the expected change in V(Vc,Ve) below (Reminder: V(Vc,Ve) = V_{CEQ}):

    ΔV_{CEQ} **(from table) =** _____

DC SENSITIVITY ANALYSIS	TEMPERATURE =	27.000 DEG C	
DC SENSITIVITIES OF OUTPUT V(Vc,Ve)			
ELEMENT NAME	ELEMENT VALUE	ELEMENT SENSITIVITY (VOLTS/UNIT)	NORMALIZED SENSITIVITY (VOLTS/%)
R_RC	2.000E+03	−4.160E-03	−8.320E-02
R_RB1	1.500E+04	7.287E-04	1.093E-01
R_RB2	5.000E+03	−2.132E-03	−1.066E-01
R_RE	1.000E+03	7.994E-03	7.99E-02
V_VCC	2.000E+01	2.712E-01	5.424E-02
Q_Q1			
RB	1.000E+01	7.246E-05	7.246E-06
RC	1.000E+00	1.936E-05	1.936E-07
RE	0.000E+00	0.00E+00	0.000E+00
BF	4.164E+02	−2.989E-04	−1.244E-03
ISE	6.734E-15	2.904E+13	1.956E-03
BR	7.371E-01	1.597E-10	1.177E-12
ISC	0.000E+00	0.000E+00	0.000E+00
IS	6.734E-15	−3.421E+13	−2.304E-03
NE	1.259E+00	−3.346E+00	−4.213E-02
NC	2.000E+00	0.000E+00	0.000E+00
IKF	6.678E-02	−2.883E-01	−1.925E-04
IKR	0.000E+00	0.000E+00	0.000E+00
VAF	7.403E+01	4.211E-04	3.188E-04
VAR	0.000E+00	0.000E+00	0.000E+00

TABLE 15.1

DC sensitivity portion of output file

16. Using the method of your choice (viewpoint or output file), measure the DC collector/emitter voltage when R_RC = 2kΩ and again when R_RC = 2.1kΩ. Enter the results below. Do they agree with those of step 15?

    ΔV_{CEQ} **(from PSpice) =** _____

17. By examining the data of Table 15.1, the output Q point voltage [V(Vc,Ve)] is most sensitive to a *percent* change in which resistor? Circle your answer:

    R_C R_{B1} R_{B2} R_E

18. From Table 15.1, if the transistor's *maximum Beta* parameter (BF) changes by 10%, what change occurs in the output Q point voltage?

$$\Delta V_{CEQ} = \underline{\hspace{3cm}}$$

Advanced Activities

19. By changing the value of R_B, redesign the collector feedback circuit of Figure 15.5(a) to give *midpoint bias* operation ($V_C = 10V$).

20. Redesign any of the bias circuits of this experiment using a PNP (3906) transistor. (Hint: Following convention, draw the circuit upside down.)

EXERCISE

- Design a bias circuit giving an $I_C = 10mA$ and having maximum temperature stability. (Hint: What configuration is best?)

QUESTIONS AND PROBLEMS

1. What is the purpose of biasing a transistor? (Hint: What would be the result if the transistor were not biased?)

2. Based on the bipolar examples of this experiment, which of the following results in the most stable circuit? (R_B refers to the base resistors and R_E refers to the emitter resistor.)

    (a) R_B small and R_E large

    (b) R_B large and R_E small

3. When biasing bipolar transistors, why is it easier to design for bias *current* (and let the bias voltage "tag along")?

4. What is the major disadvantage of emitter biasing [Figure 15.5(b)]?

5. Describe the feedback process in the collector-feedback circuit of Figure 15.5(a).   (Why is collector-feedback biasing more stable than base-biasing, although both use the same number of bias resistors?)

6. To improve the design of the voltage-divider bias circuit of Figure 15.4, you might lower the tolerance of two of the four resistors (for example, from 10% to 5%).   Based on the results of the sensitivity analysis (Table 15.1), which two resistors would you select?

7. Why is voltage-divider biasing more stable than base-biasing?

CHAPTER 16

Bipolar Amplifier
Small-Signal

OBJECTIVES

- To analyze a common-emitter small-signal amplifier.
- To demonstrate the trade-off between linearity and gain.

DISCUSSION

The small-signal amplifier circuit of Figure 16.1 uses *voltage-divider* biasing for stability. Because the emitter is AC grounded, it is in the *common-emitter* configuration.

To better understand the action of the circuit, we apply the *superposition theorem* to divide its operation into two parts: a DC *equivalent circuit* [Figure 16.2(a)], and an AC *equivalent circuit* [Figure 16.2(b)]. The total voltage or current at any circuit point is the algebraic sum of the DC and AC values. (DC variables are usually labeled with capital letters, and AC variables with lowercase letters.)

- **DC equivalent circuit**   The purpose of the DC equivalent circuit is to *bias* the transistor to its Q point. To extract the DC equivalent circuit, we open all capacitors, remove all AC sources, display the collector as a current source, and show the base-emitter (BE) junction as a diode. We calculate the DC values as follows:

> "||" means
> "in parallel with."

DC *Beta* = 175 (assumed value)

$I_{EQ} \cong I_{CQ} = (V_{TH} - .7V) / (R_E + (R_{B1}\|R_{B2})/\beta)$
$(10V - .7V) / (2k\Omega + (10k\Omega\|20k\Omega)/175) = 4.65mA$

$V_{CEQ} = V_{CC} - I_{CQ}(R_C + R_E) = 30V - 4.65mA(2k\Omega + 2k\Omega) = 11.4V$

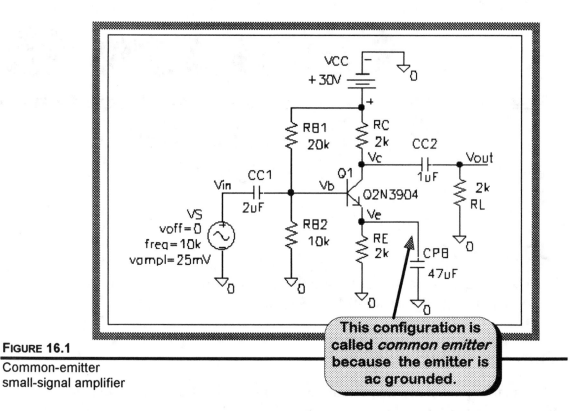

FIGURE 16.1

Common-emitter
small-signal amplifier

- **AC equivalent circuit** The purpose of the AC equivalent circuit is to amplify the signal.

    To extract the AC equivalent circuit of Figure 16.2(b), we short all capacitors and DC power supplies, turn the collector into a current source, and show the BE junction as a bulk resistor.

    The *approximate* AC values are as follows:

AC *Beta* = 175 (assumed to be the same as DC *Beta*)

Bulk resistance (re') ≈ 25mV / I_{EQ} = 25mV / 4.6mA = 5.4Ω

A (voltage gain) = R_C||R_L/re' = (2k || 2k) / 5.4Ω = 1k / 5.4Ω = 185

**Z_{IN} (input impedance) = R_{B1}||R_{B2}||(B × re') = 10k||20k||(175 × 5.4Ω)
= 900Ω**

Z_{OUT} (output impedance) = r_C||$Z_{CURRENT SOURCE}$ * = 2k||10k = 1.67k

* $Z_{CURRENT SOURCE}$ is from Chapter 12, and is assumed to be 10kΩ.

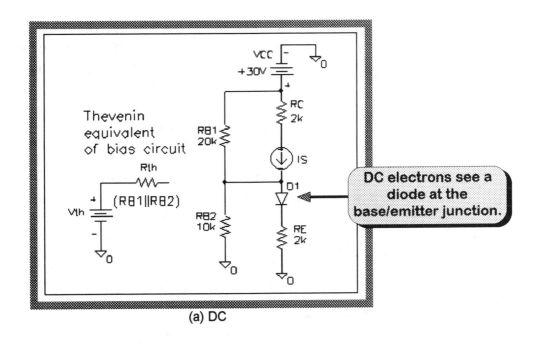

(a) DC

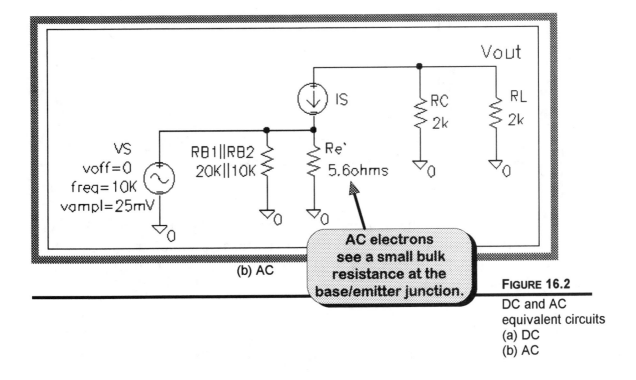

(b) AC

FIGURE 16.2

DC and AC
equivalent circuits
(a) DC
(b) AC

THE COUPLING AND BYPASS CAPACITORS

The coupling capacitors (CC1 and CC2) couple the AC in and out of the circuit without disturbing the DC biasing. The bypass capacitor (CBP) increases the voltage gain by shorting the AC signal to ground (bypassing RE). To perform their duties properly, the values of CC1, CC2, and CBP must be large enough to act as near shorts—but not too large because they can be expensive and bulky.

As an example, let's see how the value of CC1 was determined. The first step is to Thevenize the amplifier and generate the equivalent circuit of Figure 16.3. We also assume (arbitrarily) that the lowest frequency of interest is 1kHz.

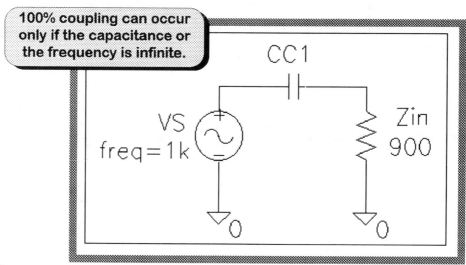

FIGURE 16.3

Equivalent circuit
to isolate CC1

Because the capacitive reactance (X_{CC1}) can never be zero (unless f or C is infinite), we must choose a reasonable value for X_{CC1}. With a Z_{IN} of 900Ω, we arbitrarily choose a value of 90 (1/10 of Z_{IN}). The equation then becomes:

$$X_{CC1} = 1/2\pi fC = 1/(2 \times 3.14 \times 1k \times CC1) = 90\Omega$$

Solving for CC1 yields approximately 2μF.

Values for the other two capacitors were determined in the same manner.

Experimentally Measuring Z_{IN} and Z_{OUT}

Referring to the Thevenized version of the amplifier (Figure 16.4), we experimentally determine Z_{IN} by dividing V_{IN} by I_{IN}. We determine Z_{OUT} by measuring V_{OUT} with and without a load. Without a load (RL = infinity), $V_{OUT} = V_{TH}$; with a load, V_{OUT} is less than V_{TH}. We then use algebra and Kirchhoff's laws to determine Z_{OUT}.

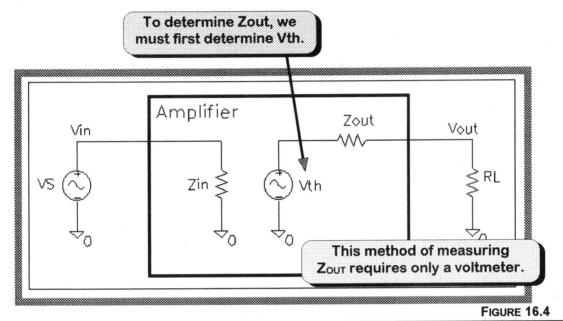

FIGURE 16.4

Thevenized amplifier showing Z_{IN} and Z_{OUT}

Time Domain Versus Frequency Domain

In this chapter, we use time-domain (transient) analysis to determine all amplifier characteristics—the type of analysis that might be done hands-on with an oscilloscope. In the next chapter, we will switch to frequency-mode analysis—the type of analysis that might be done hands-on with a spectrum analyzer. A complete analysis might include both.

Simulation Practice

1. Draw the circuit of Figure 16.1 and set the attributes as shown.

DC Analysis

2. Using PSpice, perform a DC bias-point analysis and record each of the values listed below.   (Remember: $V_{CEQ} = V_{CQ} - V_{EQ}$.)

    $I_{EQ} \cong I_{CQ} =$ _____ $V_{CEQ} =$ _____

3. Compare your experimental DC results from step 2 with the theoretical predictions made in the discussion. Are they *approximately* the same (within 10%)?

    Yes   **No**

AC Analysis

4. Using PSpice, perform a transient analysis and determine the following. (Note: *Use peak-to-peak* values for all voltages and currents to average out the effects of nonlinear distortion.)

    $A\ (v_{OUT}\ /\ v_{IN}) =$ _____

    AC *Beta* $= i_C\ /\ i_B =$ _____

    $Z_{IN} = v_{IN}\ /\ i_{IN} =$ _____

    $Z_{OUT} =$ _____ (See discussion on Z_{IN} and Z_{OUT}.)

    > Be sure to plot all variables separately and use peak-to-peak values.

5. Compare your experimental AC results from step 4 with the theoretical predictions made in the discussion. Are they *generally* the same (within 20%)? Comment on any significant differences.

6. In the discussion, we designed coupling capacitor CC1 to drop less than 10% of the 25mV input signal at 1kHz. Using PSpice, verify our design calculations. (Hint: Be sure to lower the frequency to 1kHz, and be sure to record only the ac component of the signal on the right plate of CC1.)

    Does CC1 drop less than 10% of the input signal?

    Yes   **No**

Linearity

7. Look at the amplifier's output signal. Is it distorted (*nonlinear*)?
   Use the following equation to give a quantitative measure of the
   distortion. (See Figure 16.5 for an example.)

$$\% \text{ distortion} = \frac{\text{Vpeak(difference)}}{\text{Vpeak(average)}} \times 100 = \underline{\hspace{2cm}}$$

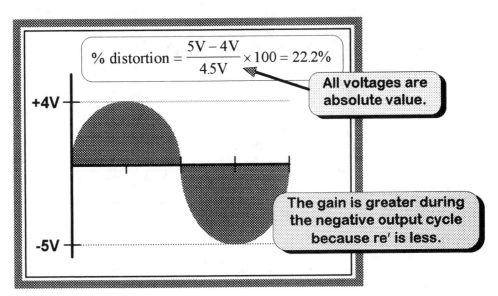

FIGURE 16.5

Example of
percent distortion
calculation

8. To reduce distortion (at the expense of gain), we add the 100Ω
   swamping resistor (R_S), as shown in Figure 16.6. (Note: We
   increase V_S to 250mV to compensate for the reduced gain.)

9. For the circuit of Figure 16.6, determine *theoretically* (by hand
   calculation) the big three: A, Z_{IN}, and Z_{OUT}.

   (a) $A = (R_C \| R_L) / (R_S + re') = \underline{\hspace{3cm}}$

   (b) $Z_{IN} = R_{B1} \| R_{B2} \| \beta (R_S + re') = \underline{\hspace{3cm}}$

   (c) $Z_{OUT} = R_C \| Z_{COLLECTOR} = \underline{\hspace{3cm}}$

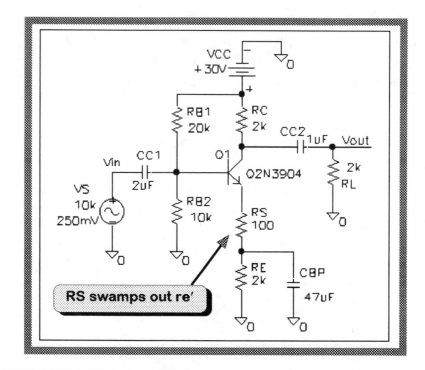

FIGURE 16.6

Swamped amplifier

10. Using PSpice, *experimentally* determine the big three.

    (a) **A** = _____

    (b) $\mathbf{Z_{IN}}$ = _____

    (c) $\mathbf{Z_{OUT}}$ = _____

11. Are the theoretical and experimental values *generally* the same? (Compare steps 9 and 10.)

    Yes   **No**

12. Generate an output waveform, and determine the swamped degree of distortion.

$$\% \text{ distortion} = \frac{\text{Vpeak(difference)}}{\text{Vpeak(average)}} \times 100 = \underline{\qquad}$$

13. Swamping produced what percent change in each of the following?

    (a) **Distortion reduced (%) =** _____

    (b) **Gain reduced (%) =** _____

Multiple Data Files in a Single Window

As we learned in the last chapter, the most direct way to compare waveforms from two separate circuits is to place both on the same window.

14. Display *Vout* for the swamped case.

15. To append *Vout* for the unswamped case: **File** (from Probe), **Append** (to bring up the *Append* dialog box), **CLICKL** on the file name for the unswamped case, **OK**, **Do Not Skip Sections**, and the combined graph of Figure 16.7 is generated.

The Initial Transient Solution

16. For the swamped case, plot V_C (the collector voltage) and examine its amplitude at TIME = 0. Is the amplitude the same as that listed in the INITIAL TRANSIENT SOLUTION of the output file?

    Yes   No

Advanced Activities

17. Create the *common-base* (base is AC grounded) circuit of Figure 16.8 by simply moving V_S from the base to the emitter. Measure A and Z_{IN}. Why did A remain the same, but Z_{IN} go way down? (The common-base configuration is often used in high-frequency applications because of its reduced input capacitance.)

18. Redesign the amplifier of Figure 16.6 using a PNP transistor. Are the major characteristics (A, Z_{IN}, Z_{OUT}, linearity) the same as those of the NPN transistor circuit?

19. For either of the amplifiers of this experiment (swamped or unswamped), determine *average* re' experimentally from the gain and the gain equation. Compare your result to the theoretical value (re' = 25mV/I_{EQ}).

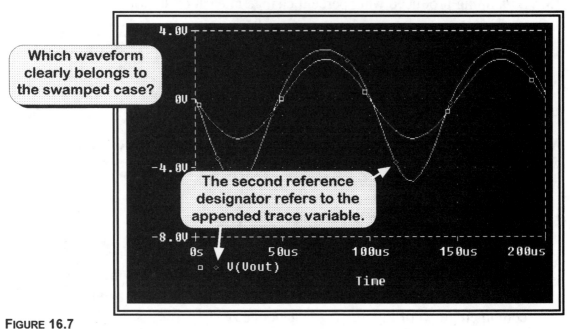

FIGURE 16.7

Combined data files

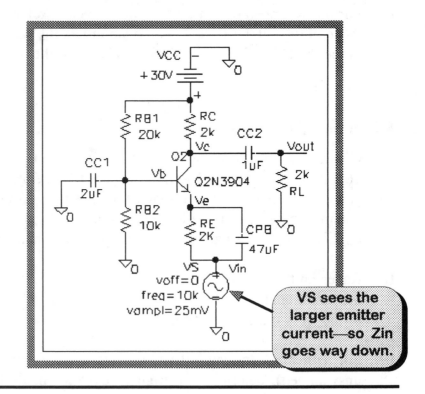

FIGURE 16.8

Common-base configuration

EXERCISE

• Design a highly stable, highly linear *two-stage* common-emitter amplifier with an overall gain of 100.

QUESTIONS AND PROBLEMS

1. To give an undistorted (linear) output signal, why is it important for the transistor to be a *current source*?

2. Referring to Figure 16.6, what is the purpose or function of each of the following components?

    (a) Capacitors CC1 and CC2

    (b) Capacitor CBP

    (c) Resistor RE

    (d) Resistor RS

3. Why is the circuit of Figure 16.1 stable but nonlinear?

4. Regarding the amplifier circuit of Figure 16.1, what is the phase relationship between input and output?

5. Referring to Figure 16.1, if the lowest frequency of interest were decreased from 1kHz to 100Hz, should we increase or decrease the values of the coupling and bypass capacitors?

6. What is the *power gain* of the circuit of Figure 16.6?   (<u>Hint</u>: Power gain = A × β.)

7. What would happen to the voltage gain of the swamped circuit of Figure 16.6 if the bypass capacitor (CBP) opened?

8. Ignoring capacitive effects, what is the only difference between the *common-emitter* and *common-base* configurations?   (Hint: How does Z_{IN} compare between the two?)

CHAPTER 17

Bipolar Buffer
Frequency-Domain Analysis

OBJECTIVES

- To analyze the *common collector* (*emitter follower*) buffer in the AC Sweep mode.
- To determine the A, Z_{IN}, Z_{OUT}, bandwidth, and linearity characteristics of a buffer.
- To perform parametric analysis on a model parameter.

DISCUSSION

A *buffer* is first and foremost an *isolation* circuit. It follows that its most important characteristics are high Z_{IN} and low Z_{OUT}. Additional properties usually include a voltage gain near unity, moderate power gain, and a high degree of linearity.

For example, turning to the Thevenized circuit of Figure 17.1, we used a buffer to isolate the load (R_L) from the source impedance ($RS(Z_{OUT})$), thereby greatly reducing the 50% voltage losses. As an added bonus, the buffer gives a positive power gain. In communication circuits, a buffer is often used to match impedances for maximum power transfer.

One popular circuit that achieves all the characteristics of a buffer is the *common-collector* (grounded collector) configuration of Figure 17.2. Note that the output is taken off the emitter rather than the collector. Because the output voltage is nearly equal to the input voltage, the circuit is also known as an *emitter follower* (the emitter voltage follows the base voltage). In short, the output is approximately equal to the input in both amplitude and phase.

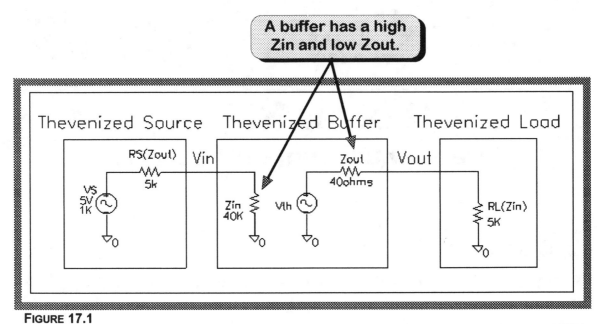

FIGURE 17.1

Thevenized buffer
circuit

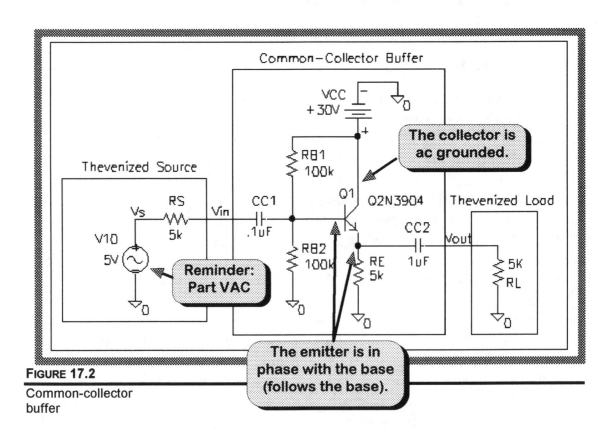

FIGURE 17.2

Common-collector
buffer

FREQUENCY-DOMAIN ANALYSIS

In the previous chapter, we analyzed a small-signal amplifier in the time domain using transient analysis. In this chapter, we analyze the buffer of Figure 17.2 by switching to the frequency domain and the *AC Sweep* mode.

A big advantage is that the properties of the circuit are displayed over a range of frequencies. For audio amplifiers, this is vital because the frequency spectrum must match that of human speech and hearing.

THEORY

A complete and accurate frequency domain theoretical analysis of the buffer of Figure 17.2 would involve elaborate equations of complex numbers. However, if we assume ideal *midband* characteristics, where all capacitors are short circuits, then the calculations are relatively simple.

The following equations determine the midband characteristics:

Midband calculations

$$A = V_{OUT}/V_{IN} = (i_e \times R_E \| R_L)/(i_e \times (R_L \| R_E + re')) = 5k\|5k/(5k\|5k + 8.3) = \underline{.997}$$

where $re' = 25mV / I_{EQ} = 25mV / 3mA = 8.3\Omega$

$$Z_{IN} = R_{B1}\|R_{B2}\|\beta(re' + R_E\|R_L) = 100k\|100k\|175(8.3 + 5k\|5k) = \underline{45k}$$

$$Z_{OUT} = ((R_S\|R_{B1}\|R_{B2})/\beta + re')\|R_E = ((5k\|100k\|100k)/175 + 8.3)\|5k = \underline{35\Omega}$$

$$G(\text{power gain}) = \frac{.5V_{OUT}^2 / R_L}{.5V_{IN}^2 / Z_{IN}} = Z_{IN} / R_L = 45k / 5k = \underline{9} = \underline{19.1dB}$$

As expected, voltage gain is nearly one, input impedance is high, output impedance is low, and a modest amount of power gain is provided.

Looking at the gain equation [A(buffer)] we see that the linear term (5k||5k) is much larger than the nonlinear term (8.3Ω), and therefore we predict a highly linear output waveform.

SIMULATION PRACTICE

Unless you are fortunate enough to have a *spectrum analyzer*, **the** activities of this chapter are best carried out under PSpice.

1. Draw the circuit of Figure 17.2 and set all attributes as shown.   (It is not necessary to draw the boxes around the three stages.)

2. Set up the AC Sweep analysis as follows:

    *   AC sweep type: Decade
    *   Sweep parameters: Pts/Decade: 100
                                       Start Freq.: 10Hz
                                       End Freq.: 100GHz

Voltage Gain, Power Gain, and Bandwidth

3. Simulate the circuit and generate the voltage gain plot of Figure 17.3.

Because all magnitude values are peak, they can be plotted in combination form (such as *Vout/Vin*).

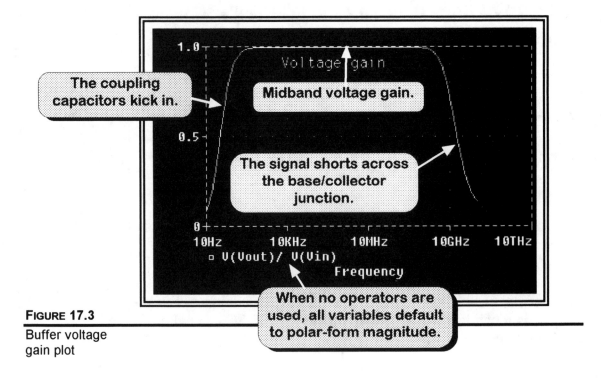

FIGURE 17.3

Buffer voltage
gain plot

4. Viewing the results, give an approximate value for the midband voltage gain.

    Midband voltage gain = _____

5. *Bandwidth* refers to the midband range of frequencies —specifically, the difference between the low- and high-frequency points where the gain drops 3dB (70.7%) of its peak midband value. Using this rule, what is the approximate bandwidth of the buffer?

    Bandwidth = _____

6. Use the equation shown below to add a plot of *real* power gain. The result is shown in Figure 17.4.   (Real power = VIcos(θ).)

> The output V and I are in phase across a resistor, so no cos( ) term is needed.

$$\text{Power gain (real)} = \frac{V(V_{OUT}) \times I(RL)}{V(V_{IN}) \times I(RS) \times \cos(6.28 / 360 \times P(V(V_{IN}) / I(RS))}$$

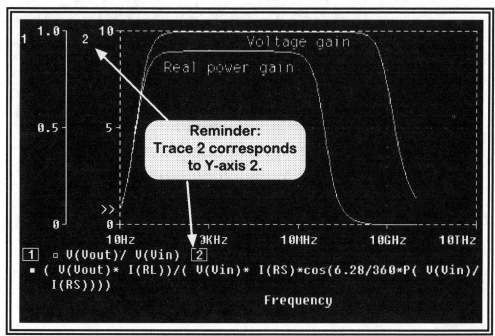

FIGURE 17.4

Adding power gain

7. What is the approximate midband real power gain?

   Midband power gain = _____

8. Add a plot of phase change (between input and output) to your graph—as shown in Figure 17.5 ("d" = degrees).

9. What is the approximate midband phase shift between input and output? (Round off to the nearest degree.)

   Phase shift (midband) = _____

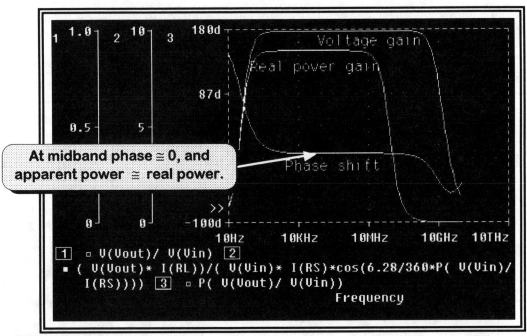

FIGURE 17.5

Adding phase

Z_{IN} and Z_{OUT}

10. To determine Z_{IN}, display a plot of $V_{IN}/I(R_S)$—as shown in Figure 17.6. (Because three Y-axes are the maximum allowed, first delete one or all of the present curves from Figure 17.5.)

11. What is the approximate midband Z_{IN}?

    Z_{IN} (midband) = _____

12. To measure Z_{OUT}, we move the source voltage from input to output, as shown in Figure 17.7.

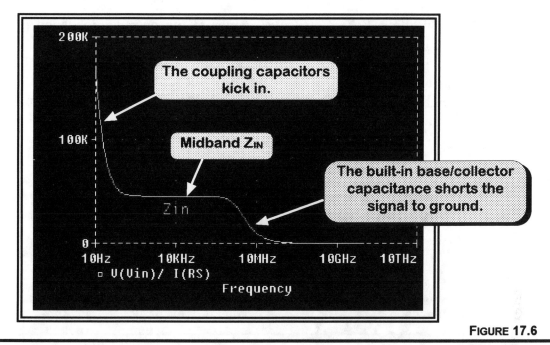

FIGURE 17.6

Plot of Z_{in}

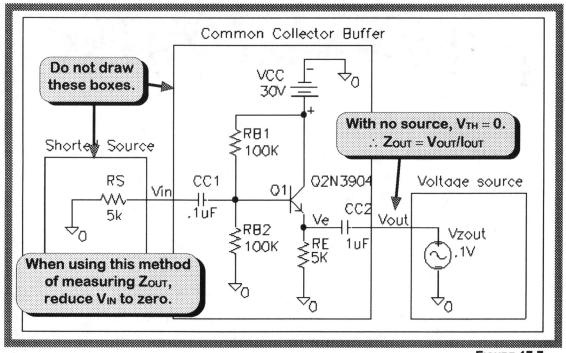

FIGURE 17.7

Determining Z_{OUT}

13. By plotting *V(Vout)/I(Vzout)*, generate the output impedance plot of Figure 17.8 and report the midband Z_{OUT}.

> The midband Z_{OUT} looks zero only because it is swamped by its high value at low frequencies. The cursor shows the actual value.

Z_{OUT} **(midband)** = _____

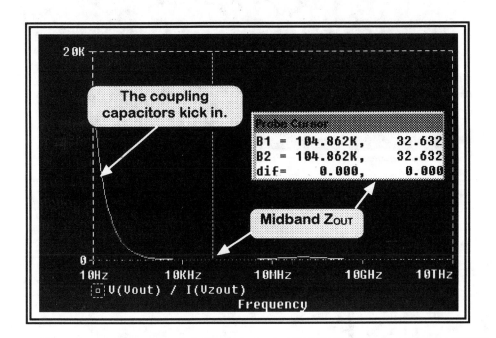

FIGURE 17.8

Plot of Z_{OUT}

14. Compare the midband PSpice results for A, G, Z_{IN}, and Z_{OUT} with the theoretical calculations of the discussion. Are they *approximately* the same?

    Yes   **No**

Bode Plot

15. When reporting frequency-domain gain, it is common practice for both axes to be logarithmic, and for the Y-axis to be plotted in *decibels* using the equation *A(dB) = 20 × logA(reg)*. Such a log-log plot is called a *Bode* plot.

    Return to the configuration of Figure 17.2, and use the *DB* operator to generate the Bode plot of Figure 17.9.

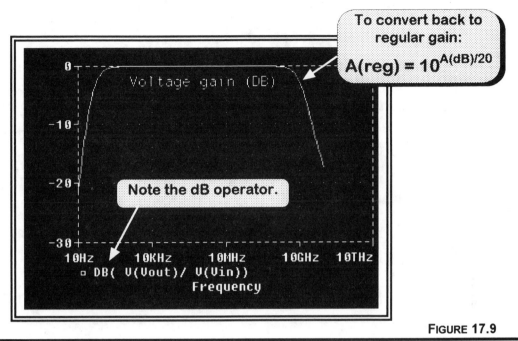

FIGURE 17.9

Voltage gain
in decibels

16. When switching to dB, 70.7% translates to −3dB.   Using the two "3dB down" points, again measure the bandwidth.   (How do the results compare with step 5?)

   Bandwidth = _____

17. This time, replace VAC with VSIN and enter appropriate amplitude, offset, and frequency attributes.   Select the transient mode, generate V_{OUT}, and determine the amplitude distortion from the following equation. [Frequency (harmonic) distortion techniques are the subject of Chapter 25.]

$$\% \text{ distortion} = \frac{\text{Vpeak(difference)}}{\text{Vpeak(average)}} \times 100 = \underline{\hspace{2cm}}$$

18. Based on all the previous results, does the circuit of Figure 17.2 have all the characteristics of a buffer?

   Yes   **No**

Advanced Activities

Parametric Analysis of Model Parameters

Looking at the theoretical calculations in the discussion, Z_{IN} is highly dependent on *Beta*. To show this dependency, we will generate a family of Z_{IN} curves for a variety of *Beta* values. In the 3904 model, parameter *Bf* is the *ideal maximum forward Beta*.

19. For the buffer circuit of Figure 17.2, bring up the parametric dialog box and fill in as listed below. (The AC analysis parameters remain the same.)

• Sweep Var. Type: **Model Parameter**	• Param. Name: **Bf**
• Sweep Type: **Linear**	• Start Value: **100**
• Model Type: **NPN**	• End Value: **1000**
• Model Name: **Q2N3904**	• Increment: **100**

20. Run PSpice and generate the expanded Z_{IN} family of curves of Figure 17.10. (If problems occur with the model name, change it to a custom name of your choice.)

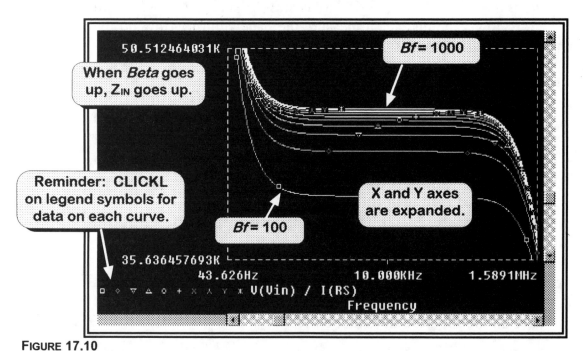

FIGURE 17.10

Family of Z_{IN} curves for various values of *Bf*

21. Based on the results of Figure 17.10, by what approximate percentage did Z_{in} increase when the *maximum Beta* increased from 100 to 1000?

     % change in Z_{IN} = _____

The Darlington Buffer

22. Draw the buffer circuit of Figure 17.11, which uses a Darlington pair to greatly increase its effective β ($\beta_{total} = \beta 1 \times \beta 2$).

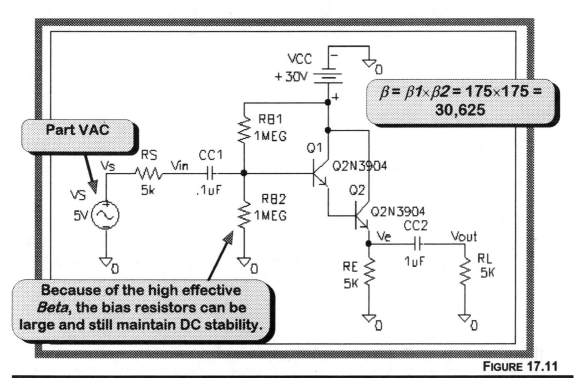

FIGURE 17.11

The Darlington buffer

23. Using AC analysis, measure midband Z_{IN} and Z_{OUT} for the Darlington buffer and compare to the non-Darlington values of steps 11 and 13.

Darlington	**Non-Darlington**
Z_{IN} = _____	Z_{IN} = _____
Z_{OUT} = _____	Z_{OUT} = _____

PSpice for Windows

24. Based on step 23, does a Darlington buffer increase the isolation properties of a buffer?

    Yes   **No**

25. For the Darlington pair buffer of Figure 17.11, determine the amount of quiescent (DC) power dissipated in each transistor (Q1 and Q2). Which transistor is likely to require a heat sink?

26. The low-frequency breakpoints shown in Figure 17.3 result from the two RC lead/lag networks involving capacitors CC1 and CC2. By Thevenizing the input and output circuits, calculate (by hand) the two breakpoints and compare with Figure 17.3.

EXERCISES

- Perform a complete analysis of the amplifier/buffer of Figure 17.12, including such items as A(overall), G, Z_{IN}, Z_{OUT}, bandwidth, distortion, power and energy. (How does the buffer stage protect the gain of the amplifier stage?)

- Using transient and parametric analysis, investigate the properties of the *buffered voltage regulator* of Figure 17.13. (How low can we take R_L before the system comes out of regulation? Compare your answer to the results of Chapter 11.)

QUESTIONS AND PROBLEMS

1. In the following statement, fill in each blank with "collector" or "emitter":

   To achieve voltage gain, we tap the output voltage off the _____, and to achieve buffering action, we tap the output voltage off the _____.

2. Why are the buffer circuits of this experiment called *emitter followers*? (What is the relationship between input and output voltage amplitude and phase?)

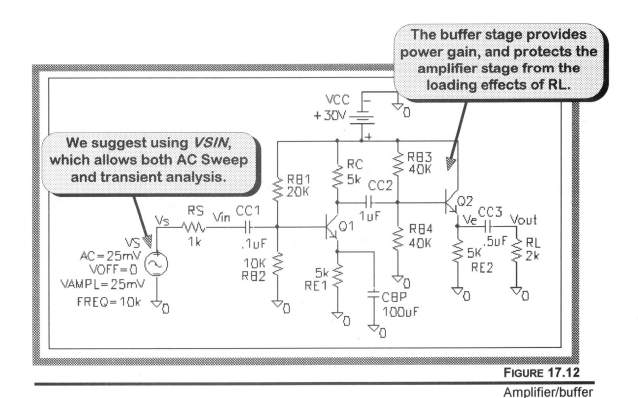

FIGURE 17.12

Amplifier/buffer

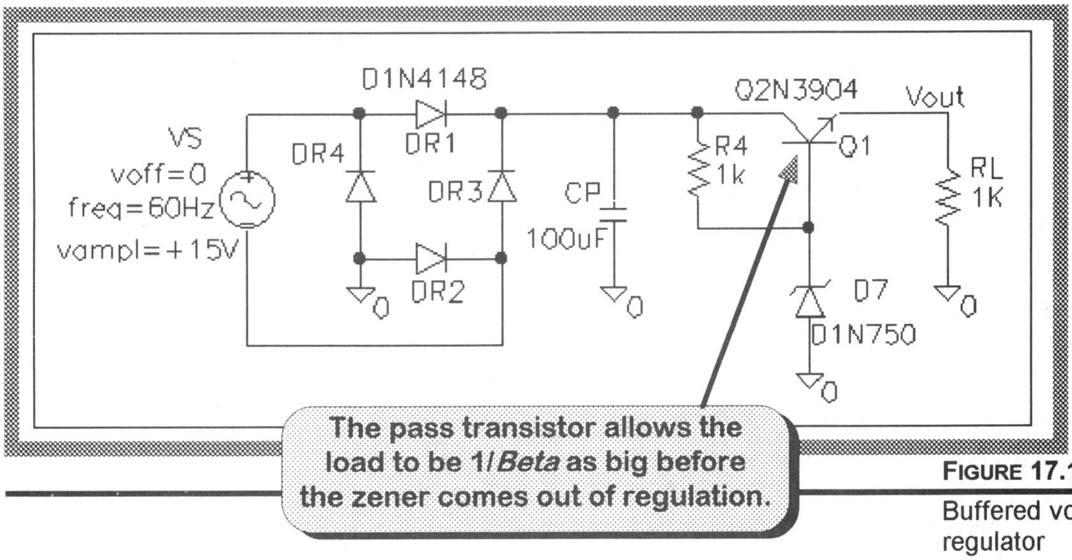

FIGURE 17.13

Buffered voltage regulator

3. For every 10,000 electrons that enter the emitter of a Darlington pair, how many electrons leave the base?   (Assume $\beta = 175$ for each transistor.)

4. By using the words "high," "low," or "medium" in the following spaces, contrast the amplifier of Figure 16.1 with the buffer of this chapter.

	Amplifier	Buffer
A	_____	_____
Z_{IN}	_____	_____
Z_{OUT}	_____	_____
Linearity	_____	_____

5. Why are all the buffer circuits of this experiment highly linear?   Would they remain highly linear if the load were reduced to 25Ω?   Why?

6. Referring to Figure 17.1, for maximum transfer of voltage from left to right (source to load), which of the following should exist?

   (a) Z_{IN} low, Z_{OUT} low
   (b) Z_{IN} low, Z_{OUT} high
   (c) Z_{IN} high, Z_{OUT} low
   (d) Z_{IN} high, Z_{OUT} high

PSpice for Windows

7. Referring to Figure 17.14, why is the input impedance at the base equal to 100kΩ? Why is the output impedance at the emitter equal to 10Ω? (Assume that re' is zero.)

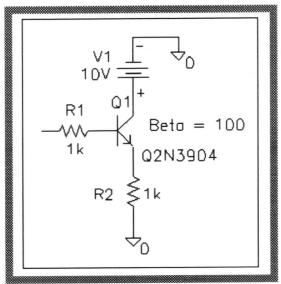

FIGURE 17.14 Transistor circuit

8. Referring to Figure 17.6, why does Z_{IN} go up at low frequencies and down at high frequencies?

9. Contrast and compare the two methods of measuring Z_{OUT} introduced in Chapters 16 and 17. (Hint: Refer to Figures 16.4 and 17.7.)

CHAPTER 18

Amplifier Power
Class A Operation

OBJECTIVES

- To design a Class A amplifier.
- To generate a load line.
- To determine power factors.

DISCUSSION

Unlike the small-signal amplifier of Chapter 16, the Class A amplifier of Figure 18.1 is designed for large voltage and current applications (note the small resistor values). Therefore, power is an important consideration. Because we have access to a split power supply, we choose emitter biasing.

In particular, our design must provide the following:

- The maximum possible unclipped output voltage.
- The ability to handle the heat dissipated in the transistor.

THE LOAD LINE

Our primary Class A design aid is known as a *load line*. As shown by Figure 18.2, we first locate the Q point, then we draw a line through the Q point whose inverse slope is equal to the total AC load.

When an AC signal is present, the operating point moves back and forth along the load line about the Q *point*. The two endpoints are called $I_{C(SAT)}$ and $V_{CE(OFF)}$. If the circuit is well designed, the Q point is *centered* and we generate the largest possible output signal without clipping.

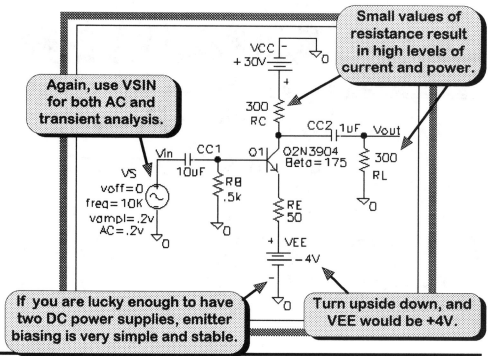

FIGURE 18.1

Initial Class A
amplifier design

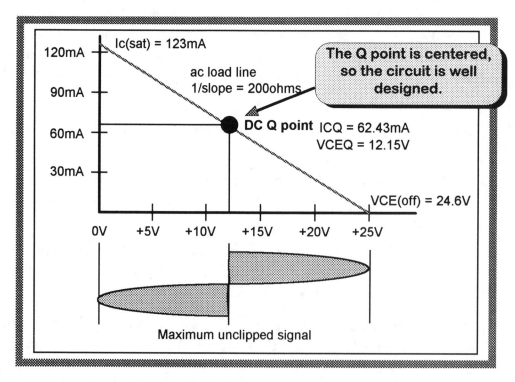

FIGURE 18.2

The load line

The values shown on Figure 18.2 were calculated as listed below. (The saturation and cutoff values are easily determined from the geometry of similar triangles.)

> As before, we base all calculations on midband operation in which all capacitors are assumed to be dead shorts.

$I_{EQ} = I_{CQ} = (4V - .7V) / (50\Omega + .5k\Omega/175) = \underline{62.43mA}$

$V_{CEQ} = V_{CQ} - V_{EQ} = (30V - 62.43mA \times 300) - (-4V + 62.43mA \times 50)$
$= 11.27V - (-.88V) = \underline{12.15V}$

rl (ac load) $= R_C \| R_L + R_E = 300\Omega \| 300\Omega + 50\Omega = \underline{200\Omega}$

Based on Figure 18.2, we predict a well-designed circuit (with a nearly centered Q point). We further predict a *compliance* (maximum unclipped signal) of approximately 12.15V. (However, this is not the compliance of the true output signal across R_L because R_E absorbs 25% of the load voltage. Therefore, we predict that the output voltage compliance across R_L is 75% of 12.15V, or 9.11V.)

POWER CONSIDERATIONS

- The *load power* (P_L) is the average AC power developed across resistor R_L (the true load) when driven at its maximum unclipped level. For a compliance of 9.11V:

$P_L = .5 \times V_{OUT}^2 / R_L = .5 \times 9.11^2 / 300\Omega = \underline{138mW}$

- The *source power* (P_S) is the average power supplied by the DC power supplies.

$P_S = (V_{CC} + V_{EE}) \times I_C(average) = (30V + 4V) \times 62.43mA = \underline{2.1W}$

- The *dissipated power* (P_D) is the worst case average power deposited into the transistor. Because *AC* voltage and current are out of phase within the transistor, the worst case dissipated power is the quiescent *DC* power.

$P_D = V_{CEQ} \times I_{CQ} = 12.4V \times 62.43mA = \underline{774mW}$

- The *efficiency* (η) is determined by dividing the maximum load power by the source power.

$\eta = P_L/P_S \times 100 = 138mW/2.1W \times 100 = \underline{6.6\%}$

In this chapter, we verify all of these predictions using PSpice. During our experimental activities, a major consideration will be: Should we use *transient* or *AC* analysis?

SIMULATION PRACTICE

1. Draw the circuit of Figure 18.1.

2. To determine the maximum unclipped output signal, we select transient analysis. We will input a sine wave of gradually increasing magnitude and note when clipping occurs on the output. Before generating a reverse damped sine wave, first review *Schematics Note 18.1*.

Schematics Note 18.1
How do I generate a damped sine wave?

VSIN uses the following formula to generate a sine wave:

$$V_{OUT} = V_{OFF} + V_{AMPL} \times \sin\{2\pi \times [\text{freq} \times (\text{time} - \text{td}) + \text{phase}/360]\} \times e^{-(\text{time - td})\times\text{df}}$$

A true damped sine wave (amplitude decreases with time) is created from positive values of df (*damping factor*), and a reversed damped sine wave (increases with time) is created from negative values of df. To generate a damped sine wave, bring up VSIN's *Part Name* dialog box (**DCLICKL** on VSIN symbol) and enter a df value along with the usual parameters.

As an example, let's create an increasing sine wave that starts from 200mV and rises to approximately 10V in 10 cycles of a 10kHz waveform. For this case, df is calculated as follows:

$$e^{-(1ms \times df)} = 10V/.2V = 50 \qquad\qquad df \cong -4000$$

3. Using a reverse damped sine wave, generate the input/output waveforms of Figure 18.3. (<u>Hint</u>: Use Vampl = .2V and df = −4000, as determined in *Schematics Note 18.1*.)

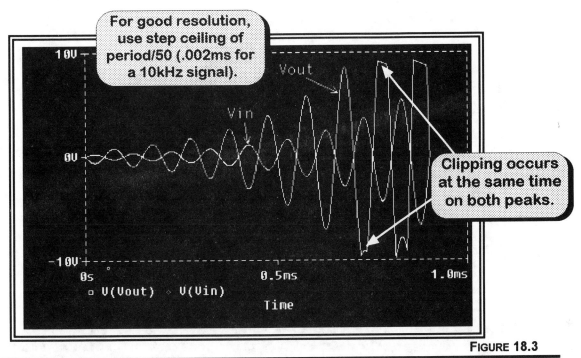

FIGURE 18.3

Looking for clipping

4. Do the waveforms of Figure 18.3 verify that the circuit is well designed? (Does the output signal clip on both ends at approximately the same time, indicating the Q point is approximately centered?)

   Yes   **No**

5. Is the output signal compliance (maximum unclipped output signal) approximately 9V, as predicted?

   Yes   **No**

Power

Because we are interested in power over a range of input signal *amplitudes*, we remain with a transient analysis.

6. Erase the amplitude waveforms of Figure 18.3, and use the power equations developed in the discussion to generate the *instantaneous* power waveforms of Figure 18.4.

PSpice for Windows

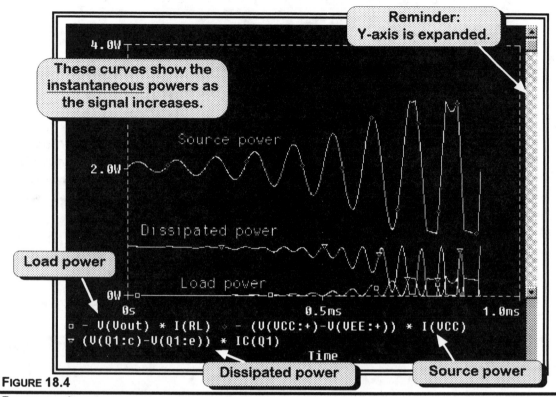

FIGURE 18.4

Power graphs

7. Based on the power curves of Figure 18.4, estimate each of the following. (Hint: Average <u>load</u> power at any point is one-half the peak power.)

   - P_{LOAD} **(average at maximum unclipped point)** = _____

   - $P_{DISSIPATED}$ **(worst case)** = _____

   - P_{SOURCE} **(average)** = _____

   - η **(efficiency)** = $P_L / P_S \times 100$ = _____%

8. Do the experimental values of step 7 approximately equal the theoretical values calculated in the discussion?

       Yes   **No**

9. Using frequency domain analysis, generate a Bode plot and determine the voltage bandwidth of the amplifier of Figure 18.1.

    Bandwidth = _____

Advanced Activities

10. Generate the real-time load line of Figure 18.5. (<u>Hint</u>: Start with the same damped sine wave Probe data as the other plots, but be sure to redefine the X-axis.) Can you tell approximately where the Q point is by the thickness and intensity of the curve? Compare the result to the predicted load line of Figure 18.2.

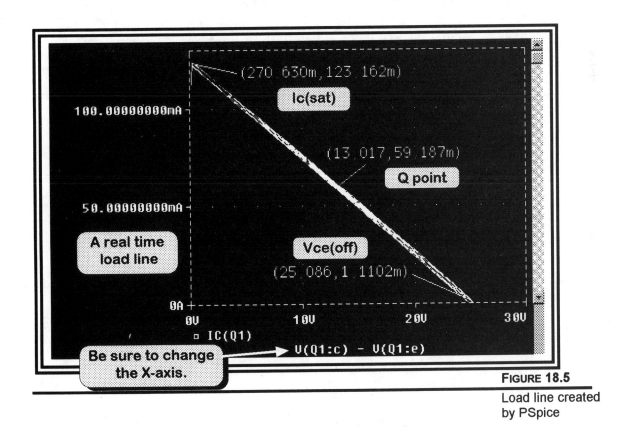

FIGURE 18.5

Load line created by PSpice

EXERCISE

*   Check the audio amplifier of Chapter 17 (Figure 17.12) for Class A operation. If necessary, make changes to bring it into Class A operation.

PSpice for Windows

QUESTIONS AND PROBLEMS

1. How does a Class A amplifier differ from a small-signal amplifier?

2. If the Q point is centered, the output signal clips

    (a) at the positive peaks first.
    (b) at the negative peaks first
    (c) at both positive and negative peaks at the same time.

3. Would you say that the efficiency of a Class A amplifier is high or low?

4. For a sine wave across the load resistor (R_L), the average current and voltage are zero.   Why is the average *power* not equal to zero?

5. Why does the worst case dissipated power (power lost in the transistor) occur when the *AC* signal input is zero?

6. Why do *power* amplifiers use smaller resistors than *small-signal* amplifiers?

7. Referring to the load line of Figure 18.5, why is the thickness and intensity of the load line greatest about the Q point?

8. What is the difference between *power* and *energy*?

9. Why is a load line straight (linear)?

10. If the load (R$_L$) is increased, would the load line slope of Figure 18.5 increase or decrease?

CHAPTER 19

Amplifier Efficiency
Class B and C

OBJECTIVES

- To design and analyze class B and C amplifiers.
- To compare the efficiency of Class A, B, and C amplifiers.

DISCUSSION

The Class A amplifier of Chapter 18 suffers from notoriously poor efficiency. To greatly increase efficiency, we switch to the Class B and C amplifier/buffer designs of this chapter.

- The Class B circuit of Figure 19.1 employs two transistors in a push/pull configuration. Because we have the luxury of a split power supply, no coupling capacitors are required. The circuit is called Class B because each transistor is on (conducts) for approximately 50% of each cycle. The upper (NPN) transistor conducts during the positive half cycles and the lower (PNP) conducts during the negative half cycles.

  The Class B configuration is usually employed as a buffer and power amplifier in the common-collector (emitter-follower) configuration. A Class B buffer can yield more than 70% efficiency because very little power is wasted in biasing the circuit.

- The Class C circuit of Figure 19.2 is the most efficient of all. When in operation, it simulates the action of a hammer and a bell. A biased clipper is the hammer, and a tank circuit is the bell.

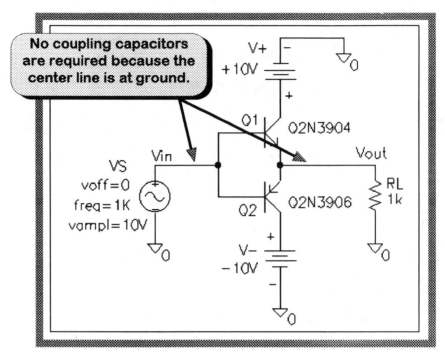

FIGURE 19.1

Class B operation

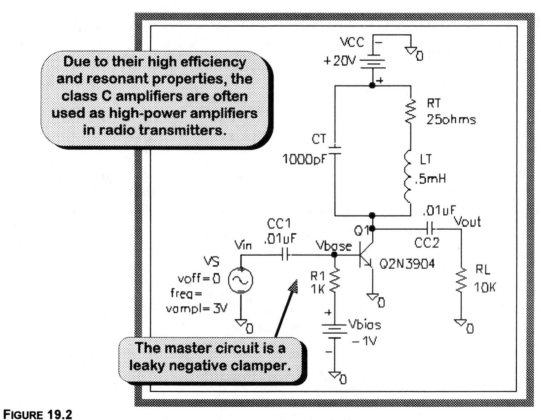

FIGURE 19.2

Class C operation

PSpice for Windows

At the top of each input cycle, the transistor saturates, the collector is grounded, and the capacitor is suddenly charged (the hammer hits the bell). The transistor then goes into cutoff for the rest of one or more cycles and the capacitor and inductor trade energy (the bell rings). The amplifier is called Class C because the transistor is on for much less than 50% of each cycle.

A Class C amplifier typically yields more than 90% efficiency because almost no power is lost in biasing the circuit or is dissipated in the transistor. Because of its high efficiency and the use of a resonant tank circuit, the Class C amplifier is typically used as a common-emitter radio-frequency amplifier for frequencies above 1MHz.

SIMULATION PRACTICE

Class B Buffer

1. Draw the Class B buffer of Figure 19.1 and set the attributes as shown.

2. Using PSpice, generate the transient output waveform and determine the voltage gain.

    Class B voltage gain (A) = _____

    Is the voltage gain what you would expect of a buffer?

    Yes   No

3. Expand the output waveform (*Zoom in on selected area of graph* toolbar button) at the 1.5ms point where it crosses the 0V axis (Figure 19.3). This is called *cross-over distortion*, and it is caused by the barrier potential of the two transistors. (While the input signal is between plus and minus .7V, the output signal is zero.)

4. To overcome cross-over distortion, add the *trickle-bias* circuit of Figure 19.4. The circuit makes use of the familiar barrier potential characteristics of diodes to bias each transistor just beyond its knee.

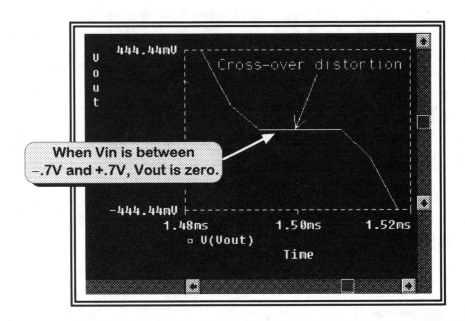

FIGURE 19.3

Cross-over distortion

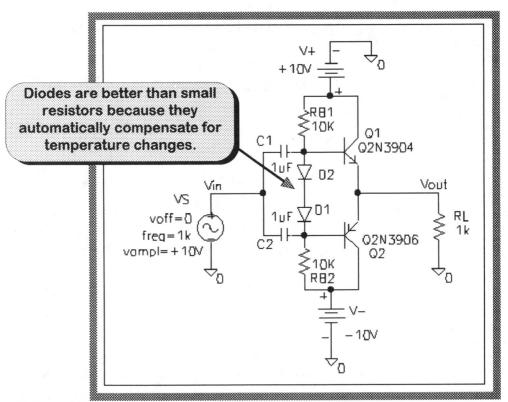

FIGURE 19.4

Adding trickle bias

5. Generate new output waveforms. Is the cross-over distortion gone?

    Yes   **No**

Efficiency

6. Efficiency is equal to *average* load power divided by *average* source power (reported as a percentage).

    For the trickle bias circuit of Figure 19.4, use the following midband equations to generate the *instantaneous* load and source power curves of Figure 19.5.   (The minus signs are necessary because source and emitter currents are negative.)

    - **P(load) = −V(V$_{OUT}$) × I(R$_L$)**

    - **P(source) = −(V(V+:+) × I(V+) + V(V−:+) × I(V−))**

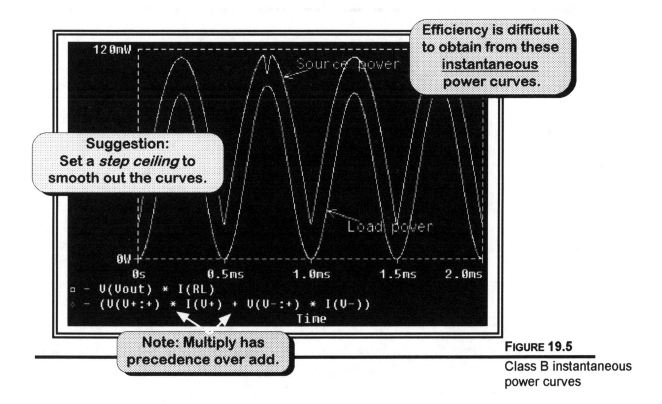

FIGURE 19.5

Class B instantaneous power curves

7. From the curves of Figure 19.5, we could obtain average power through mathematical analysis.   Instead, use the AVG (average) operator to generate the running average curves of Figure 19.6.

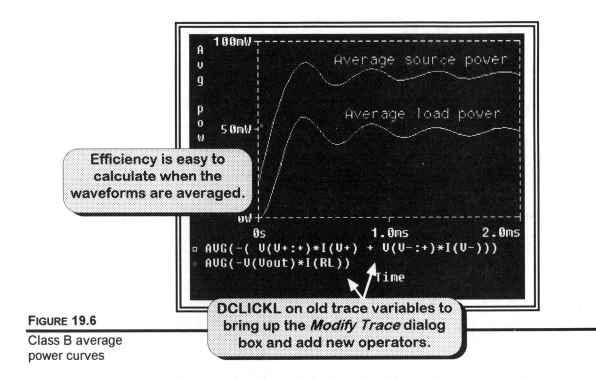

FIGURE 19.6

Class B average
power curves

8. Use your cursor to determine the steady-state average source and load power (the values near the right-hand side of the graph).

Average load power   = _____

Average source power = _____

9. From the results of step 8, determine experimental efficiency. (How does it compare with the <u>maximum</u> value mentioned in the discussion?)

$$\eta \text{ (efficiency)} = \frac{\textbf{Average load power}}{\textbf{Average source power}} \times 100 = \underline{\hspace{2cm}} \%$$

Class C Amplifier

10. Draw the circuit of Figure 19.2 and set the attributes as shown. (The frequency value of V_S will be set later.)

11. Determine the resonant frequency of the tank circuit.

$$F(\text{resonant}) = \frac{1}{2\pi\sqrt{LC}} = \underline{\hspace{3cm}}$$

12. Set the frequency value of V_S to approximately one-tenth of the resonant frequency.

13. Generate the input, base voltage, and output waveforms of Figure 19.7.

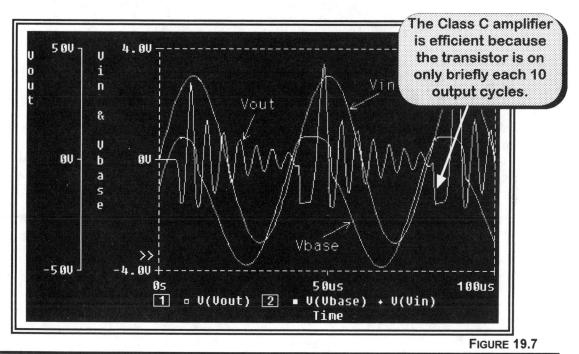

FIGURE 19.7

Class C input and output waveforms

14. (a) Is the base voltage negatively clamped?

    Yes   **No**

    (b) Is the output waveform a damped sine wave at the resonant frequency?

    Yes   **No**

15. As time permits, change the value of the input frequency and note the result.

Advanced Activities

16. Perform an energy analysis of the Class C amplifier and *estimate* its efficiency.

EXERCISE

- Using PSpice results, compare the overall efficiency of the audio amplifier of Figure 19.8 (using a Class B output stage) with the overall efficiency of the audio amplifier of Figure 17.12 (using a conventional output stage). Note that the amplifier uses a single power supply and is able to drive an 8Ω speaker.

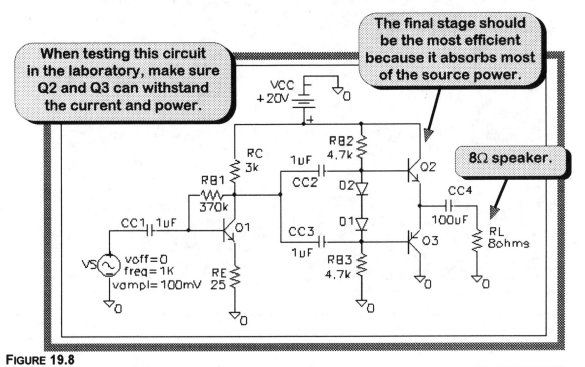

FIGURE 19.8

Audio amplifier

QUESTIONS AND PROBLEMS

1.   Referring to the biased Class B buffer stage of Figure 19.8, what provides power to the circuit during the half cycle when the upper NPN transistor is biased off?   (Hint: What circuit component stores energy?)

2.   Why does the trickle-bias circuit of Figure 19.4 consume very little power?

3.   Assuming that the transistors of Figure 19.1 have a *Beta* of 175, what is the approximate power gain?

4.   The input circuit to the base of a Class C amplifier is

   (a) a positive clamper.
   (b) a negative clamper.

5.   Viewing the Class C waveforms of Figure 19.7, what causes the output waveform to decay between hits?

6.   Why is the efficiency of a Class C amplifier so high?   (Hint: Why does most of the source energy pass on to RL?)

7.   For each of the amplifier classes listed below, approximately what percentage of the time is a given transistor on?

   Class A _____

   Class B _____

   Class C _____

8. Why is a Class C amplifier used to power the final stage of a radio or television transmitter?

9. Why is the trickle bias circuit of Figure 19.4 often called a *current mirror*?

PART IV
The Field-Effect Transistor

In Part IV, we move from the bipolar to the field-effect transistor (FET). As in Part III, we concentrate primarily on amplifiers and buffers.

We will see how the FET's inherent high input impedance and vastly different transconductance properties influence its characteristics.

CHAPTER 20

Field-Effect Transistor Characteristics
Drain Curves

OBJECTIVES

- To display FET master and slave curves.
- To determine a FET's input and output impedance.
- To determine the effects of temperature on a FET.

DISCUSSION

Like the bipolar transistor, a *field-effect transistor* (FET) is also a *voltage-controlled current source* (VCIS). That is, an input voltage controls an output current, regardless of the output voltage. However, the way the FET achieves its VCIS characteristics is vastly different.

The FET comes in a number of different types. The JFET (*junction field-effect transistor*) of Figure 20.1 was developed first. It achieves its VCIS characteristics as follows: As the positive drain/source voltage increases, it pulls on electrons, creating a drain current in the N region. However, because of the reverse-biased PN junction between gate and drain, it also creates a positively charged *depletion region* that squeezes the drain current.

In normal operation, when the *drain voltage* is above a certain threshold (*pinchoff*), this pulling and squeezing cancel—*and the drain becomes a current source* (current independent of voltage). However, the *input* gate/source voltage is not subject to cancellation (it squeezes only) and therefore *does* control the current.

In summary, the input gate/source (master) voltage controls the output drain (slave) current, regardless of the drain/source voltage—making the FET a *voltage-controlled current source* (VCIS).

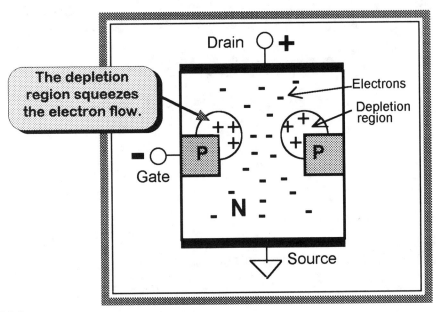

FIGURE 20.1

JFET internal
operation

THE BIPOLAR VERSUS THE JFET

If both the bipolar transistor and FET are simply VCISs, then how do they differ? The most important differences are the JFET's extremely high input impedance and its vastly different input/output (transconductance) characteristics. These two differences give the JFET an edge when used in certain applications.

TEST CIRCUIT

The test circuit of Figure 20.2 shows an N-channel JFET. The JFET also comes in the P-channel version, but may not be available in the PSpice evaluation library (*eval.lib*). The P-channel is identical in operation to the N-channel, except all voltages and currents are reversed.

TRANSCONDUCTANCE

When operated as a VCIS, the output of a FET is drain current (I_D), and the input is gate/source voltage (V_{GS}).   This ratio ($\Delta I_D/\Delta V_{DS}$) is called the transistor's *transconductance* (g_M) and is given in units of μSeimens (μS). A typical value for transconductance is 4000μS (or 1/250 Ω).

As before, one of the best ways to investigate the VCIS characteristics of a JFET is by generating drain and gate/source curves. This is done with the test circuit of Figure 20.2.

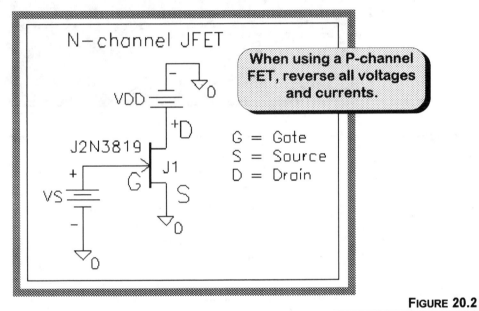

FIGURE 20.2

N-channel JFET
test circuit

SIMULATION PRACTICE

1. Draw the circuit of Figure 20.2 and set the attributes as shown. (V_S and V_{DD} will be swept and therefore need not be assigned bias point values at this time.)

Drain Curves

2. Using the DC Sweep mode, generate the set of FET drain curves of Figure 20.3. (Hint: V_{DD} is the main sweep and V_S is the nested sweep.)

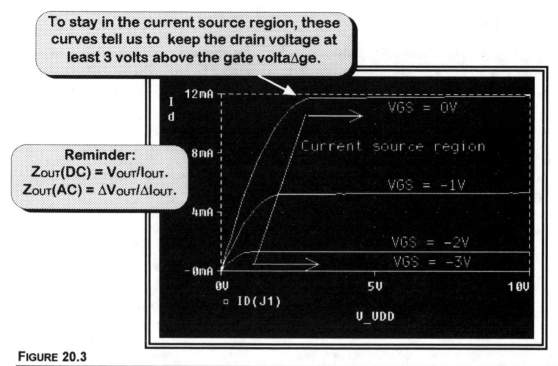

FIGURE 20.3

Drain curves for
JFET

---

3.   By taking measurements, answer the following:

(a)   What is the maximum possible current (known as I_{DSS})? What input voltage (V_{GS}) produces I_{DSS}?

$I_{DSS} =$ _____ V_{GS} at $I_{DSS} =$ _____

(b)   What gate/source voltage causes *pinchoff* ($I_D = 0$)?   This value is called V_{GSOFF}.

$V_{GSOFF} =$ _____

(c)   Determine a typical value for output (drain) AC impedance. (Hint: Measure 1/slope for a typical point in the current source region, or use the "d" operator.)

$Z_{OUT} =$ _____

The Gate/Source Curve

4.   By taking values from Figure 20.3 (all in the current-source region), draw a *transconductance* curve on the graph of Figure 20.4.

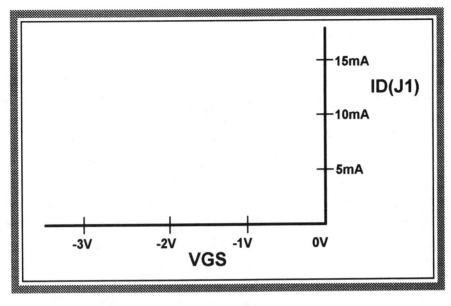

FIGURE 20.4

Transconductance curve

5. Using PSpice, generate the transconductance curve of Figure 20.5 *directly*, and compare to the *indirect* method of Figure 20.4. (<u>Hint</u>: Set V_{DD} to +10V and do a DC sweep of V_S.)

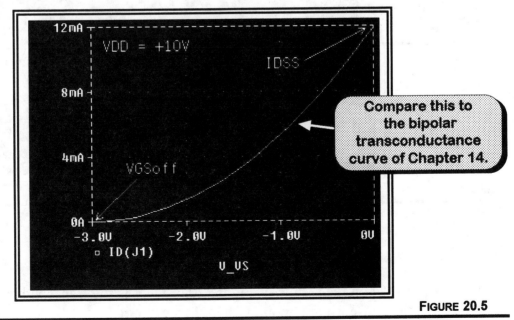

FIGURE 20.5

JFET transconductance curve

6. The master curve of Figure 20.5 is a *parabola* that obeys the following equation:

$$I_D = I_{DSS} (1 - V_{GS}/V_{GSOFF})^2$$

As an example of the use of this equation, at what V_{GS} does I_D = 1/2 I_{DSS} (a good Q point location)? Does your value agree with Figure 20.5? (Hint: Use values from step 3.)

V_{GS} (at 1/2 I_{DSS}) = _____

7. Transconductance is the *slope* of the curve (where slope = $\Delta I_D/\Delta V_{GS}$). Using the differentiate ("d") operator, add a curve of transconductance to the graph of Figure 20.5. (The result is shown in Figure 20.6.)

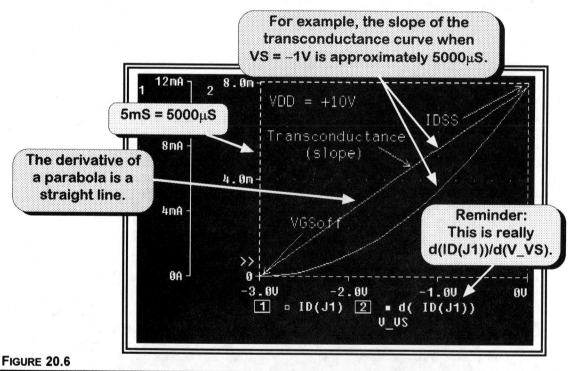

FIGURE 20.6

Adding a graph
of slope

8. Based on the results of Figure 20.6, what is the transconductance at the half-current Q point (where I_D = 1/2 I_{DSS})?

Transconductance at half-current (μS) = _____

9. Add a third Y-axis to the graph of Figure 20.6 and plot input impedance [V(J1:g)/IG(J1)]. Record below the value for Z_{IN} at the half-current Q point. (*Note*: "T" = *tera* = 10^{+12}.)

   Z_{IN} **(Q point) = _____**

   Based on your results, would you say that a JFET has a naturally high input impedance?

   Yes   No

Master Curve Temperature Effects

10. To determine how temperature affects the master (transconductance) curve of Figure 20.5, re-create the graph of Figure 20.7. (Make temperature a nested DC sweep from −50°C to +50°C in increments of 25°C.)

11. Based on the results of step 10, answer the following: When the temperature increases from 0°C (32°F) to +25°C (103°F), IDSS changes by what percent?

   % change in I_{DSS} = _____

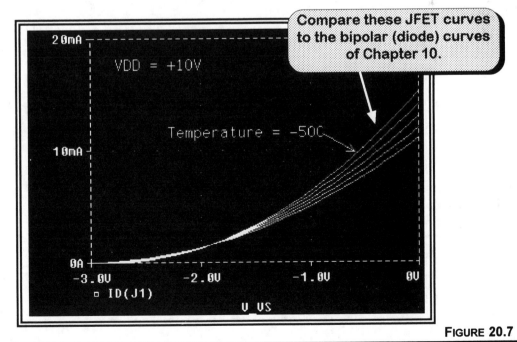

FIGURE 20.7

JFET temperature effects

Advanced Activities

12. Figure 20.8 is a master curve of the irf150 power E-MOSFET (enhancement-MOSFET).   Draw the test circuit, and complete the study by generating the slave (drain) curves. Sketch the resulting drain curves in Figure 20.9.

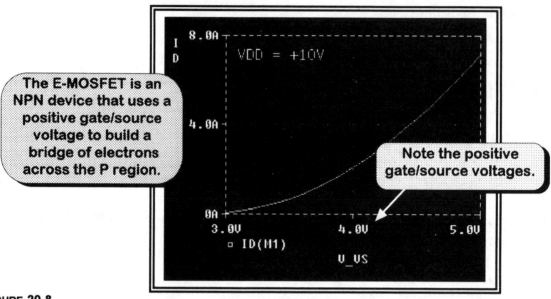

FIGURE 20.8

Master curve for
irf150 E-MOSFET

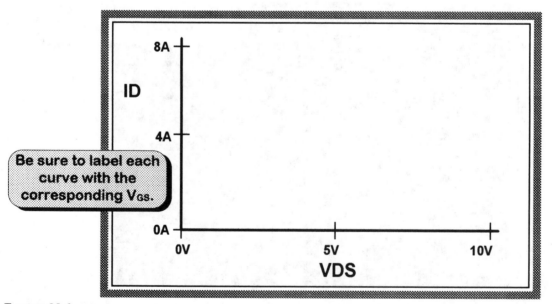

FIGURE 20.9

Drain (slave) curves for
irf150 power MOSFET

PSpice for Windows

EXERCISES

- The CMOS (*complementary-symmetry metal-oxide semiconductor*) circuit of Figure 20.10 is the most popular technology used by the digital IC industry. It uses an irf150 (N-channel E-MOSFET) and an irf9140 (P-channel E-MOSFET) in a totempole configuration. It is popular because of its extremely low power consumption.

(a) Generate the typical input/output waveforms of Figure 20.11. (Why is the simple CMOS unit also called an *inverter*?)

(b) To perform an energy analysis of the CMOS circuit, first generate the source <u>power</u> waveforms of Figure 20.12 (top plot). Then use the *s* (integrate) and *ABS* (absolute value) operators to plot the <u>energy</u> graph of Figure 20.12 (bottom plot).

   Is it safe to say that the CMOS configuration consumes very little energy?

   Yes   **No**

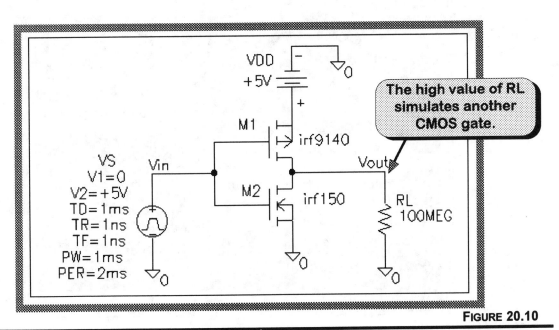

FIGURE 20.10

The CMOS inverter

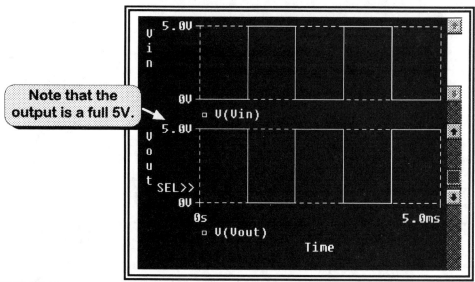

FIGURE 20.11

The CMOS inverter:
Test waveforms

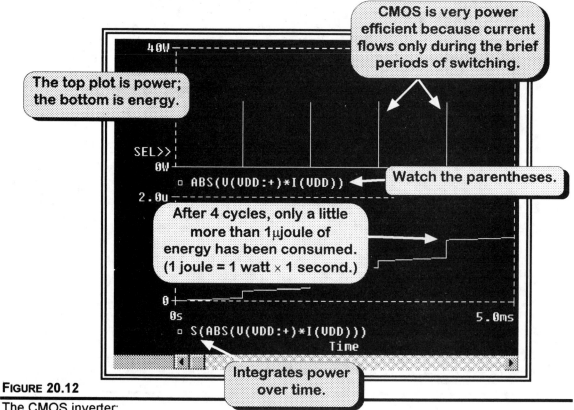

FIGURE 20.12

The CMOS inverter:
Power and energy
test waveforms

- Referring to Figure 20.3, we see that a FET's ohmic region (to the left of the current-source region) acts as a *voltage-variable resistor* for small voltages. Using the test circuit of Figure 20.13(a), generate the curves of Figure 20.13(b). (Hint: Use a *Vcontrol* variable list of 0, −2.8, −2.9, −2.95, −3.)

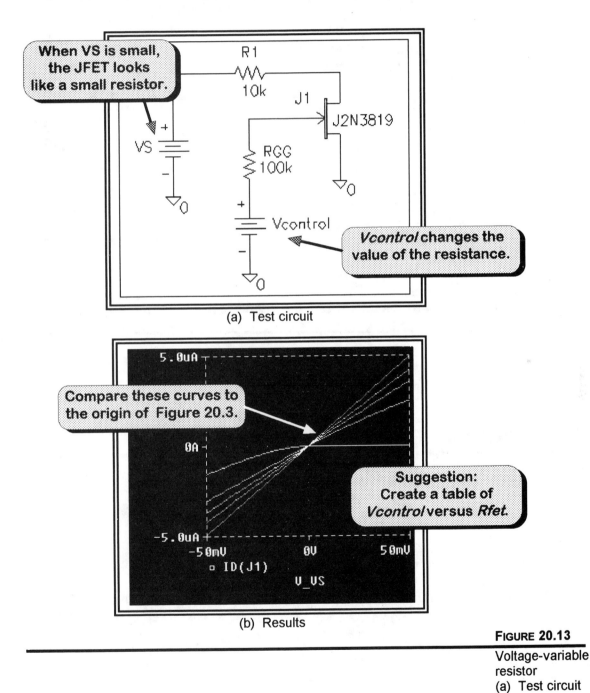

(a) Test circuit

(b) Results

FIGURE 20.13

Voltage-variable resistor
(a) Test circuit
(b) Results

PSpice for Windows

- Draw the E-MOSFET circuit of Figure 20.14, and display Vin1, Vin2, and Vout. Based on the results, what is the purpose of the circuit? (Hint: It is a basic digital gate.)

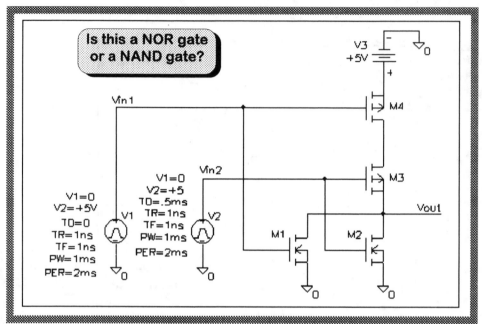

FIGURE 20.14

CMOS digital
gate

QUESTIONS AND PROBLEMS

1. Why is the input impedance of a JFET so high?

2. Why is a JFET (when biased as in Figure 20.1) a VCIS (rather than an ICIS)?

3. Which of the following typically has the highest *transconductance* (output current <u>change</u> divided by input voltage <u>change</u>)?

    (a) Bipolar transistor
    (b) FET

4. Write "bipolar" or "JFET" before each statement.

    _____ Normally off, requires voltage to turn on.

    _____ Normally on, requires voltage to turn off.

5. The transconductance of a JFET is highest

    (a) at low values of drain current.
    (b) at high values of drain current.

6. What do the NPN transistor and E-MOSFET have in common?   (<u>Hint</u>: Compare the master curves of each.)

7. A transconductance of 4000μS is equivalent to what in inverse ohms?

CHAPTER 21

FET Biasing
Stability

OBJECTIVES

- To design and analyze several popular FET biasing circuits.
- To determine how temperature affects stability.

DISCUSSION

We bias a FET for the same reason we bias a bipolar transistor: to place its quiescent (Q) point at an appropriate place in the master curve.

Based on the JFET master graph of Figure 21.1 (reproduced from Chapter 20), biasing requires a negative DC voltage across its gate/source junction. When properly biased, the superimposed AC signal will have room to operate on both its positive and negative cycles.

As with the bipolar transistor, we can choose from a variety of JFET biasing circuits. The major considerations are simplicity, stability, and flexibility.

SIMULATION PRACTICE

Self-Bias

1. The simplest type of JFET biasing is the *self-biased* circuit of Figure 21.2. (We use the word *self* because rising current through RS automatically places a positive bias voltage at the source, while the gate voltage remains zero.) Draw the circuit and set the attributes as shown. (The value of RS is determined later.)

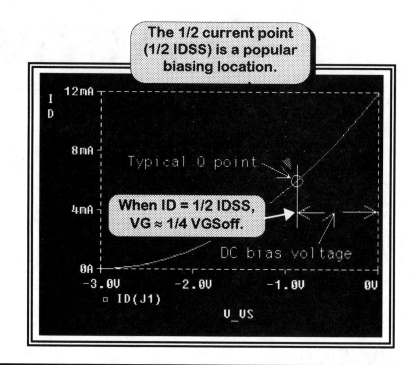

FIGURE 21.1

JFET biasing and
Q point

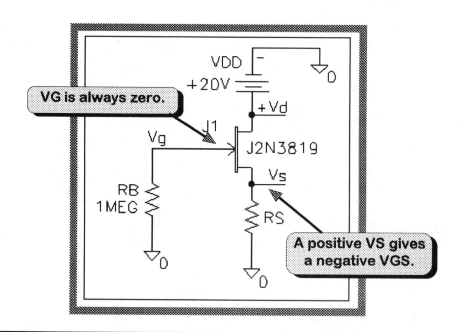

FIGURE 21.2

Self-biasing

2.   By again solving the following equations (as we did in Chapter 20), determine the gate/source quiescent voltage (V_{GS}) that places the Q point at the half-current biasing point (when $I_D = 1/2\ I_{DSS}$).

   $I_{DSS} = 12mA$ (from Figure 21.1)

   $V_{GSOFF} = -3V$ (from Figure 21.1)

   $I_D = I_{DSS} (1 - V_{GS}/V_{GSOFF})^2$

   V_{GS} (for half-current biasing) = _____

3.   Is the half-current value for V_{GS} calculated in step 2 close to that indicated by Figure 21.1?   (If not, redo your calculations.)

   Yes   No

4.   From the value of V_{GS} (at half-current) determined in step 2, use Ohm's law to calculate the value of R_S required to give this half-current Q point.   (Hint: V_G is approximately zero.)

   R_S (half-current bias point) = _____

5.   Set R_S to the value determined in step 4.   Using PSpice, perform a bias point analysis and record the Q point values below.   Are the actual values approximately equal to the expected values of step 2? (Hint: $R_S \approx 150\Omega$.)

   I_{DQ} = _____ V_{GSQ} = _____

Temperature Effects

6.   To determine temperature stability, we will see how the drain current [ID(J1)] changes with temperature.   Generate the graph of Figure 21.3 and determine the following:

   $\Delta I_D\ /\ \Delta Temperature$ = _____

Voltage-Divider Bias

7.   To improve stability, we turn to the *voltage-divider* bias circuit of Figure 21.4.   Use Ohm's law to determine the value of R_S required to place the Q point at the half-current point. (Hint: Vsource will be more positive than Vgate by the half-current DC bias voltage.)

   R_S (half-current point) = _____

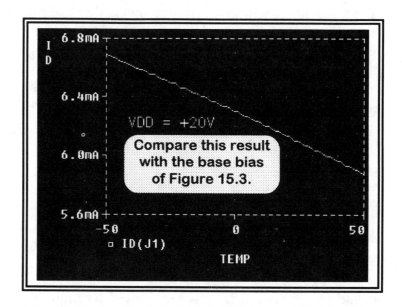

FIGURE 21.3

Self-bias temperature stability

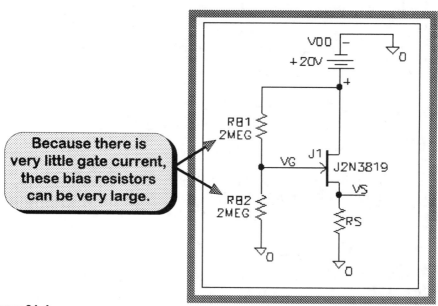

FIGURE 21.4

Voltage-divider bias

8. Set R_S to the value determined in step 7. Using PSpice, perform a bias point analysis and record the Q point values. Are the actual values approximately equal to the expected values? (<u>Hint</u>: RS ≈ 1.8k.)

    I_{DQ} = _____ V_{DSQ} = _____

9. Perform a temperature analysis of voltage-divider bias (similar to step 6) and report the following:

    ΔI_{DQ} / Δ**Temperature** = _____

10. To better compare the temperature stability of both bias circuits (base and voltage-divider), show both curves on a single graph as shown in Figure 21.5 (from Probe, **File**, **Append**, etc.).

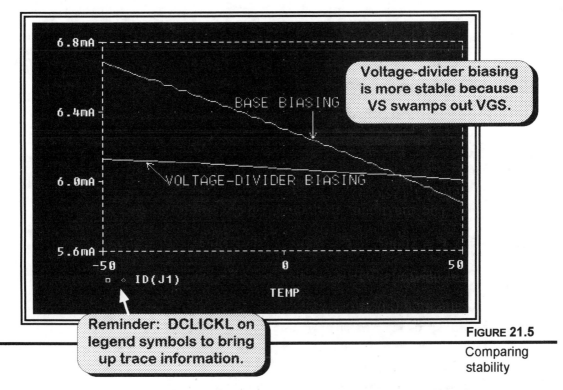

FIGURE 21.5

Comparing stability

11. Based on Figure 21.5, give one reason why voltage-divider biasing is superior to self-biasing.

Advanced Activities

12. Based on the graphical data of the previous chapter (Figure 20.8), determine the value of R_D that will give the E-MOSFET drain-feedback biasing circuit of Figure 21.6 a bias current of 4A. Check your results using PSpice.   (<u>Hint</u>: Assume that $I_{RG} = 0$.)

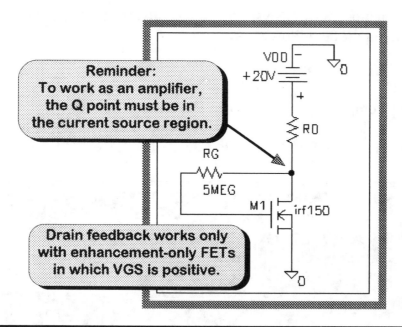

FIGURE 21.6

Drain feedback
biasing of
E-MOSFET

EXERCISE

• Perform a sensitivity analysis on the voltage-divider bias circuit of Figure 21.4. The Q-point is most sensitive to which resistor?   (If necessary, see Chapter 15.)

QUESTIONS AND PROBLEMS

1. Referring to Figure 21.1, when the current is at the half-current point (6mA), the voltage is *approximately* at the

    (a) quarter-voltage point (−3/4V).
    (b) half-voltage point (−1-1/2V).

2. Why is the biasing technique of Figure 21.2 called "self-biasing"?

3. Based on the transconductance curve of Figure 21.1, what gate voltage will place the JFET in Figure 21.7 at the half-current point?

    V$_G$ (half-current) = _____

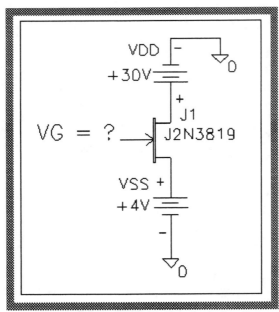

FIGURE 21.7 JFET biasing test circuit

4. Referring to the voltage-divider biasing circuit of Figure 21.4, why can we be quite sure that the gate voltage is very close to 10V?

5. Can we use the drain feedback biasing method of Figure 21.6 on a JFET? Why or why not?   (<u>Hint</u>: With a JFET, can V_G ever equal V_D?)

CHAPTER 22

FET Amplifiers and Buffers
Input Impedance

OBJECTIVES

- To design, analyze, and compare JFET amplifiers and buffers.
- To determine FET circuit input and output impedance.

DISCUSSION

Amplifiers and buffers made with JFETs are similar in design and function to those made with bipolar transistors. The major difference is that FET circuits offer a much higher input impedance, and the differences in transconductance characteristics lead to differences in gain and linearity.

SIMULATION PRACTICE

Amplifier

1. Draw the JFET amplifier of Figure 22.1 and set the attributes as shown. (Note that the amplifier is biased by the same half-current self-biasing circuit analyzed in the previous chapter.)

2. Using PSpice, run a bias point solution. Examine the output file, and mark the Q point on the transconductance curve of Figure 22.2. Is the Q point at the expected half-current point? (Figure 22.2 is a copy of Figure 20.6 and need not be generated by the student.)

    Yes   **No**

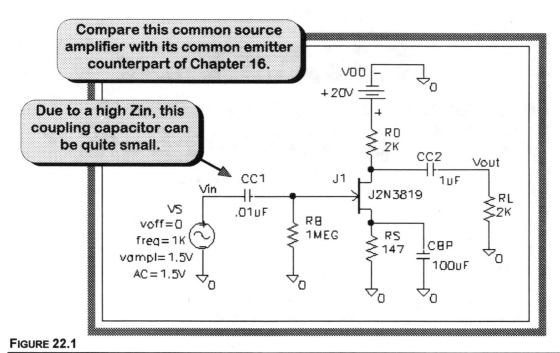

FIGURE 22.1

JFET amplifier
using self-biasing

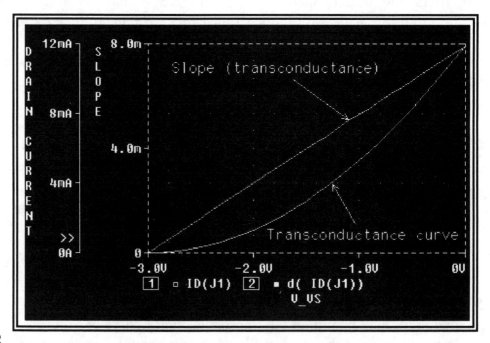

FIGURE 22.2

JFET
transconductance
curve

PSpice for Windows

3. *Transconductance* is the slope of the transconductance curve.

    Based on Figure 22.2, what is the transconductance (g_m) at the Q point?   (Your answer should be the same as Chapter 20, step 8.)

    g_m (at Q point) = _____ μSiemens

4. Using the value of g_m from step 3, calculate by hand the big three. [Hint: As an approximation, assume the ideal value of infinity for both Z_{IN}(FET) and Z_{OUT}(FET).]

A	=	$R_L \| R_D \times g_m$	=	_____
Z_{IN}	=	$R_B \| Z_{IN}$(FET)	=	_____
Z_{OUT}	=	$R_D \| Z_{OUT}$(FET)	=	_____

5. Using either the transient or AC mode, determine the big three with PSpice and compare these results to the theoretical results of step 4.

A (midband)	=	_____
Z_{IN} (midband)	=	_____
Z_{OUT} (midband)	=	_____

6. Using AC Sweep mode, determine the amplifier's bandwidth.

    BW = _____

7. Using the transient mode, generate V_{OUT} and note the distortion. As a quantitative measure of the distortion, determine the following. (Reminder: Frequency-based harmonic distortion is the subject of Chapter 25.)

$$\% \text{ distortion} = \frac{\text{Vpeak(difference)}}{\text{Vpeak(average)}} \times 100 = \text{_____}$$

Buffer

8.   Draw the JFET buffer circuit of Figure 22.3 and set the attributes as shown.

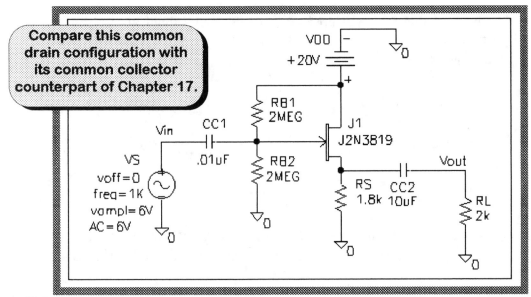

FIGURE 22.3

JFET buffer

9.   Using the following equations, calculate by hand the big three. (Because we are still using half-current biasing, g_m at the Q point is the same as determined in step 3.)

A	=	$\dfrac{RL\|RS}{RL\|RS + 1/g_m}$	=	_____
Z_{IN}	=	$RB1\|RB2\|Z_{IN}(FET)$	=	_____
Z_{OUT}	=	$RS\|1/g_m$	=	_____

10. Using PSpice (transient or AC mode), determine the big three. Compare your answer to the theoretical results of step 9.

A (midband)	=	_____
Z_{IN} (midband)	=	_____
Z_{OUT} (midband)	=	_____

11. Using AC Sweep mode, determine the buffer's low-frequency cutoff. (The high-frequency cutoff is well beyond 100THz, where $T = 10^{12}$.)

    $f_{CUTOFF} =$ _____

12. Based on the transient output waveform, determine the degree of distortion from the following equation:

$$\% \text{ distortion} = \frac{\text{Vpeak(difference)}}{\text{Vpeak(average)}} \times 100 = \underline{\hspace{2cm}}$$

13. Based on the results so far, compare the characteristics of the JFET amplifier/buffer of this chapter with their bipolar counterparts of Chapters 16 and 17. (What one has the greatest gain? The greatest Z_{IN}? The least distortion?)

Advanced Activities

14. Based on the results of Figure 22.2, develop an equation for transconductance (g_m) in terms of V_{GS}, V_{GSOFF}, and a constant. (<u>Hint</u>: The equation is linear.)

EXERCISES

- Analyze the circuit of Figure 22.4 and predict the waveforms at the gate and drain of the FET. (<u>Hint</u>: The circuit is called a "chopper.") Generate the waveforms using PSpice and compare them to your predictions.

- Perform a complete analysis of the three-stage amplifier of Figure 22.5. Why would the design be appropriate for a hand-held battery-powered megaphone? Why is the front-end stage a JFET amplifier, the middle stage a bipolar amplifier, and the final stage a class B buffer? What is the voltage gain, power gain, efficiency, bandwidth, etc. of the circuit?

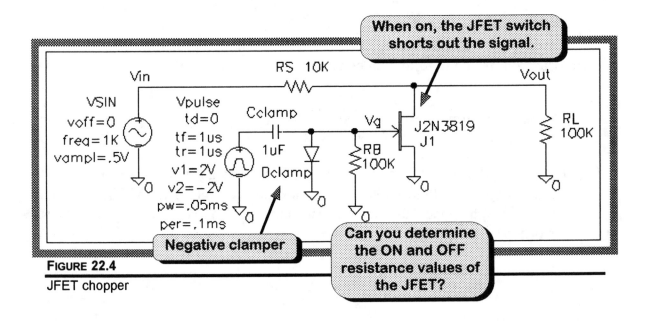

FIGURE 22.4

JFET chopper

QUESTIONS AND PROBLEMS

1. Why is the voltage gain (A) of a FET amplifier generally less than that of a bipolar amplifier?

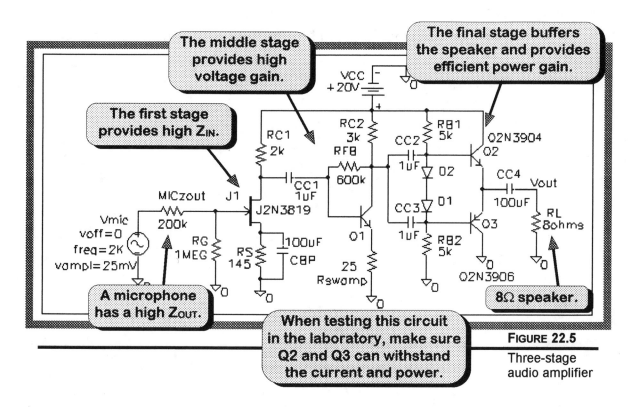

The middle stage provides high voltage gain.

The final stage buffers the speaker and provides efficient power gain.

The first stage provides high Z_{IN}.

A microphone has a high Z_{OUT}.

When testing this circuit in the laboratory, make sure Q2 and Q3 can withstand the current and power.

8Ω speaker.

FIGURE 22.5

Three-stage audio amplifier

2. Referring to Figures 22.1 and 22.2, why would the voltage gain go up if the value of R_S is decreased?

3. Referring to Figure 22.1, what allows resistor R_B to be so large? What advantage is there to having a large value of R_B?

4. Why is the power gain of a FET circuit very large?

5.   What is the major difference between bipolar and FET amplifiers and buffers?

PART V
Special Solid-State Studies

In Part V we examine several special applications of solid-state devices. We will find that the transistor can be used as a switch for digital applications, and that a special four-layer device can act as a latch.

CHAPTER 23

The Transistor As a Switch
Frequency of Operation

OBJECTIVES

- To design and analyze the bipolar transistor and FET when they are used as switches.
- To test methods of increasing the frequency of operation.

DISCUSSION

Most of the previous chapters have concentrated on the transistor as used in analog (linear) applications. The other side of the coin is digital (nonlinear) applications. In a digital application, the transistor is a switch that operates between high and low states.

- When the bipolar transistor is used as a switch, the high and low states usually correspond to saturation and cutoff.

- When the FET is used as a switch, the high and low states usually correspond to I_{DSS} (maximum current) and V_{GSOFF} (no current).

SWITCHING SPEED

An important consideration in digital circuits is the time it takes to switch between states. The faster the switching speed, the higher the frequency of operation. For the bipolar transistor, we define the terms of Figure 23.1 as follows:

- t_S (*storage time*) is the time required to come out of saturation (0% to 10%).

- t_R (*rise time)* is the time required to make the transition from saturation to cutoff (10% to 90%).

- t_D (*delay time*) is the time required to come out of cutoff (100% to 90%).

- t_F (*fall time*) is the time required to make the transition from cutoff to saturation (90% to 10%).

For the 3904 transistor, the spec sheet lists these terms as follows:

$$t_S = 200ns \qquad t_R = 35ns \qquad t_D = 35ns \qquad t_F = 50ns$$

The maximum frequency of operation $[1/(t_D + t_R + t_S + t_F)]$ is therefore 3.125MHz.

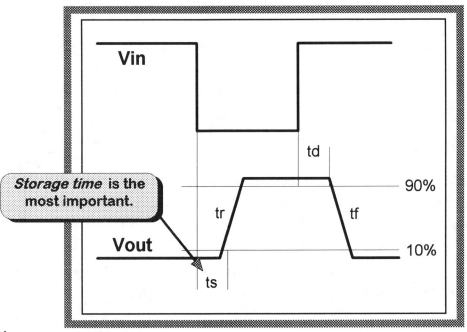

FIGURE 23.1

Switching time definitions

SIMULATION PRACTICE

The Bipolar Switch

1. Draw the basic transistor switch of Figure 23.2. (Note: The values of R_B and R_C were chosen to match the spec sheet test conditions of $I_CMAX = 10mA$ and $I_BMAX = 1mA$.)

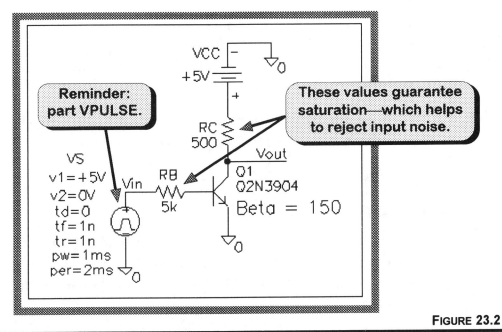

FIGURE 23.2

Basic bipolar
transistor switch

2.   Run PSpice and generate the waveforms of Figure 23.3. (Because of
     a slight overshoot, you may have to adjust the Y-axes for a 0 to 5V
     range.)

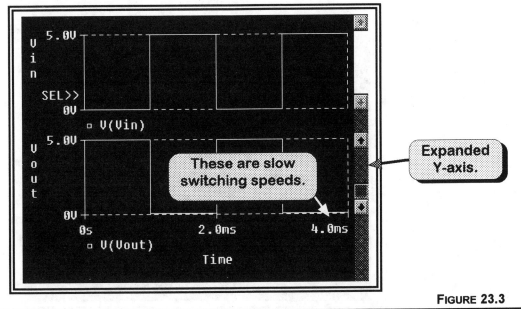

FIGURE 23.3

Bipolar switch
waveforms

3. Based on the waveforms of Figure 23.3, why is the switch also called an *inverter*?

4. Judging from the waveforms of Figure 23.3, does the transistor operate properly between saturation and cutoff?

    Yes   **No**

BJT Switching Time

5. Looking at the waveforms of Figure 23.3, it appears the output changes instantly with the input. However, increase the frequency by a factor of 1000 (pw = 1μs, per = 2μs), and generate the curves of Figure 23.4.

6. Using the cursor, determine values for each of the following and compare them to the spec sheet values listed earlier in the discussion. (<u>Note</u>: Because our test conditions are not precisely the same as the spec sheet test conditions, do not expect close correlation between the PSpice results and the spec sheet results.)

    t_S = _____ t_R = _____ t_D = _____ t_F = _____

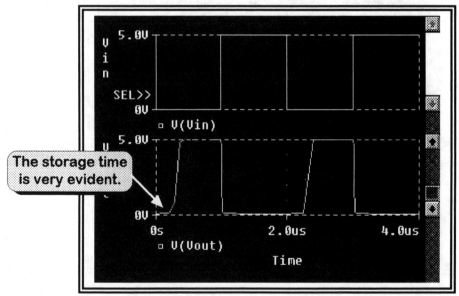

FIGURE 23.4

High-speed waveforms
showing delays

PSpice for Windows

7. To reduce the switching times [especially the storage (t_S) and delay (t_D) times], add the *speedup capacitor* of Figure 23.5. (The speedup capacitor bypasses resistor R_B during *changes*, thereby allowing electrons to move more quickly into and out of the base.)

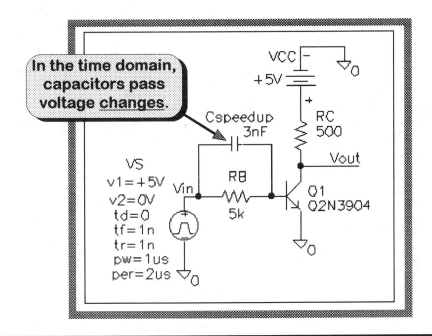

FIGURE 23.5

Adding a speedup capacitor

8. Generate new waveforms and note the storage, delay, and transition times. Were they greatly reduced?

    Yes   No

Advanced Activities

9. Using the equation developed in the discussion, analyze the waveforms generated by step 8 (expand the rise and fall sections) and determine the highest frequency of operation. By increasing the frequency in steps, verify your findings using PSpice.

10. By generating waveforms, compare the base current between the regular and speedup switches (Figures 23.2 and 23.5). Comment on the results.

11. Draw the JFET switch of Figure 23.6, determine an appropriate value of R_D, and generate input/output waveforms. (Hint: Refer to Figure 20.3 and note that the transistor is driven between the top and bottom curves as V_{GS} alternates between 0 and $-3V$.)

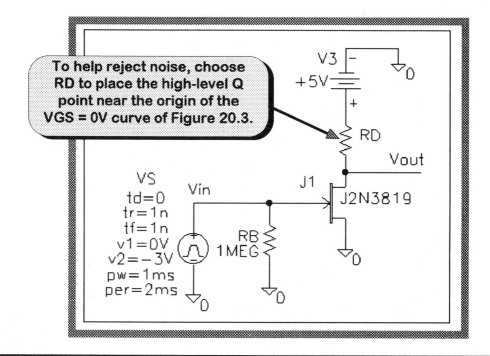

FIGURE 23.6

JFET switch

EXERCISES

- Using PSpice, determine the maximum frequency of operation of the CMOS inverter of Figure 23.7. (Could this basic inverter be part of a 250MEGHz Pentium microprocessor?)

- Determine the input/output characteristics and maximum frequency of operation of the TTL (*transistor-transistor logic*) inverter of Figure 23.8. Place speedup capacitors about R1, R2, and R4 and again determine the maximum frequency of operation.

- The ECL (*emitter-coupled logic*) switch (inverter) shown in Figure 23.9 increases the switching speed by avoiding saturation. Explain how the circuit works. Using PSpice, determine its characteristics and maximum frequency of operation. (Does it avoid saturation?)

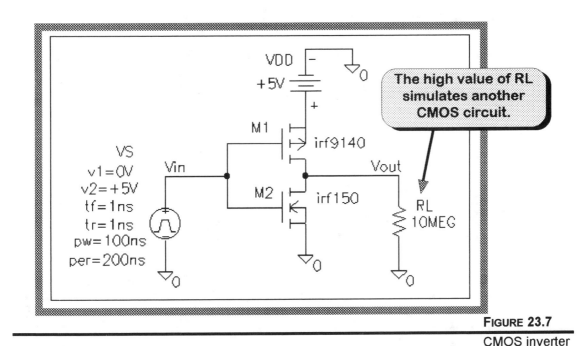

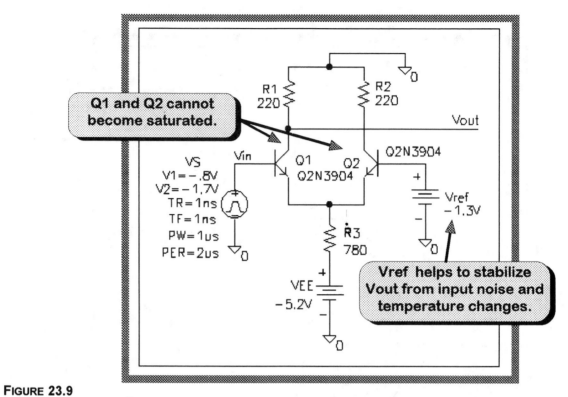

FIGURE 23.9

ECL inverter
circuit

QUESTIONS AND PROBLEMS

1. When the transistor of Figure 23.2 enters saturation, what happens to the following?   (Enter "up" or "down" after each term.)

    (a) V_{CE} goes _____
    (b) *Beta* goes _____
    (c) I_C goes _____

2. Electrons that have saturated the base are swept out of the base during:

    t_S t_R t_D t_F

3. Why does the speedup capacitor of Figure 23.5 reduce the delay (t_D) and storage (t_S) times?

4. On the load line graph in Figure 23.10, circle the area in which analog (linear) circuits normally operate, and box the areas in which digital circuits normally operate (except when in transition).

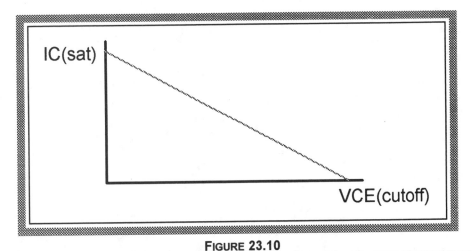

FIGURE 23.10
Analog/digital operating
region comparison

5. Referring to Figure 23.2, how does driving the transistor into saturation help to reject input noise? (Hint: When VS = 4V, is the transistor still in saturation?)

6. Prove that neither transistor of Figure 23.9 can ever be in saturation. (Hint: What is the worst case state when V_{CE} of Q1 is minimum?)

CHAPTER 24

Thyristors
The Silicon-Control Rectifier

OBJECTIVES

- To determine the on and off characteristics of the SCR.
- To use the SCR in the design of an efficient power controller.

DISCUSSION

Thyristors are used for special switching applications. The most common thyristor is the *silicon-control rectifier* (SCR), a device that uses positive feedback to act as a latch. When turned on, it tends to stay on; when turned off, it tends to stay off.

Turning to Figure 24.1(a), an SCR is a four-layer PNPN device. As shown by the equivalent circuit of Figure 24.1(b), it acts as overlapping NPN and PNP transistors. Because the collector of one transistor feeds the base of the other, both transistors must be on or both must be off. (It is impossible for one transistor to be on and the other off, except during the brief time when they are changing state.)

The schematic symbol for the SCR is given in Figure 24.1(c). (Because the SCR is made up of PSpice primitives, it is a *subcircuit* and therefore carries the "X" designator.)

We will use the test circuit of Figure 24.2 to demonstrate the SCR's characteristics.

- The SCR is turned on by a threshold combination of anode (A) voltage and gate (G) current.

- The SCR is turned off when the forward anode-to-cathode current drops below the *holding current* (I_H).

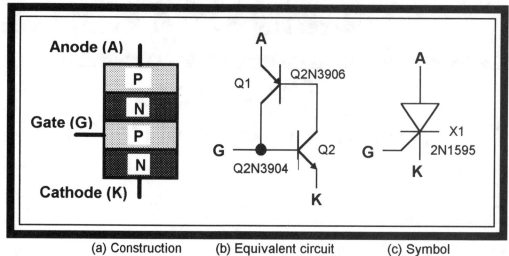

FIGURE 24.1

The SCR
(a) Construction
(b) Equivalent circuit
(c) Symbol

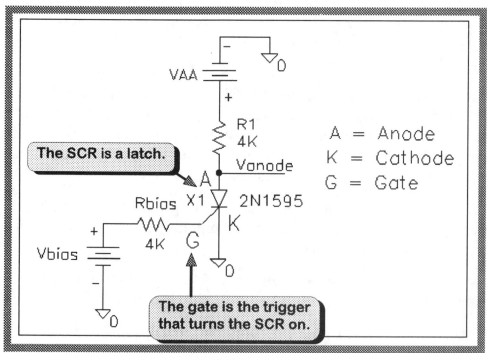

FIGURE 24.2

SCR test circuit

PSpice for Windows

Simulation Practice

1. Draw the test circuit of Figure 24.2 and set the attributes as shown. (Because both V_{BIAS} and V_{AA} will be swept, DC bias point values need not be assigned at this time.)

SCR Operating Curves

2. Generate the SCR *operating curves* of Figure 24.3. (Refer to the *process summary* below.)

> ### Process Summary for Generating SCR Operating Curves
>
> - The <u>Main Sweep</u> variable is V_{AA}, generated by a DC Main Sweep from 0 to 55V in increments of 1V. The <u>Nested Sweep</u> variable is Vbias, generated by a DC Nested Sweep of value list 8.35, 8.5, and 8.75.
>
> - The <u>X-axis</u> variable is SCR anode voltage [V(Vanode)], and the <u>Y-axis</u> is negative anode current [−I(R1)]. A second Y-axis is gate current [I(Rbias)].

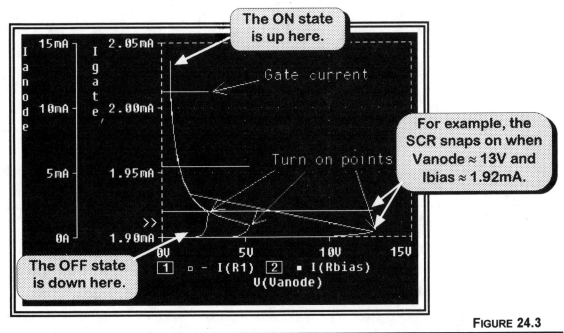

FIGURE 24.3

SCR operating curves

PSpice for Windows

3. List below the three pairs of anode voltages [V(Vanode)] and gate currents [I(Rbias)] shown in Figure 24.3 that will turn on the SCR.

V(Vanode)	I(Rbias)
Pair 1:	
Pair 2:	
Pair 3:	

Power Controller

4. Draw the circuit of Figure 24.4, which shows the SCR used as a *power controller*. (Resistor *Rcontrol* varies the percentage of time that the SCR is on.)

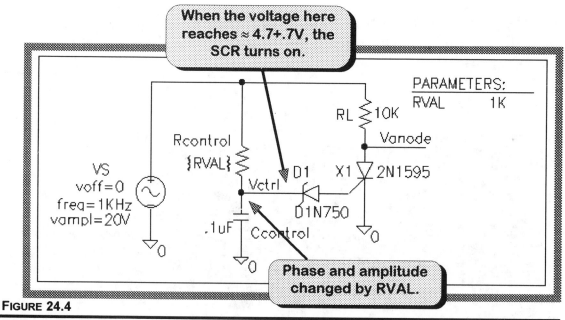

FIGURE 24.4

SCR power control

5. By sweeping *Rcontrol* as a parameter (100Ω, 2kΩ, and 5kΩ), generate the plots of Figure 24.5. In each case, circle the area when the SCR is on. (Note the use of the "@" operator.)

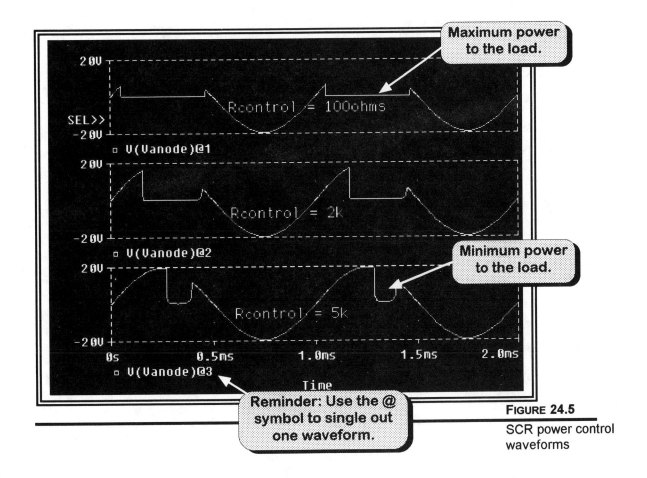

FIGURE 24.5

SCR power control
waveforms

6. Based on Figure 24.5, what value of Rcontrol delivers the greatest
    power to the load?   (Circle your answer.)

    100Ω   **2kΩ**   **5kΩ**

7. To the power control waveforms of Figure 24.5, add graphs of
    control voltage [V(Vctrl)@1, etc.] and note the trigger (turn on)
    points.   Is the phase change between plots apparent?

    Yes   **No**

Advanced Activities

8. For the Rcontrol = 100Ω case, determine the approximate holding
    current.   (<u>Hint</u>: What is the current when the SCR *starts* to turn
    off?)

EXERCISES

- Substitute the SCR equivalent circuit of Figure 24.1(b) and re-generate the curves of Figure 24.5. Is the equivalent circuit similar in function to the SCR?

- A *triac* is a latching device that consists of two back-to-back SCRs to achieve full-wave control. Using the 2N5444 triac, redesign the power control circuit of Figure 24.4, and compare your results with those of Figure 24.5.

QUESTIONS AND PROBLEMS

1. How do you turn an SCR on, and how do you turn it off?

2. Referring to Figure 24.1(b):

    (a) Explain how positive feedback comes into play during switching.

    (b) Why are the transistors either both on or both off?

3. Based on Figure 24.3, if the gate current is 1.94mA, approximately what anode voltage would turn on the SCR?

4.   Why is the SCR an efficient method of controlling power?   (Hint: Is any power wasted in a resistor?)

5.   Looking at the two symbols in Figure 24.6, what is the difference between the SCR and the triac?

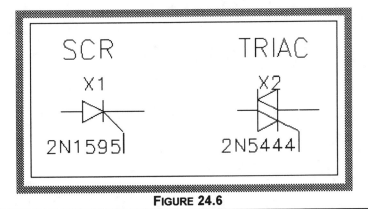

FIGURE 24.6

SCR and TRIAC
comparison

6.   Referring to Figure 24.4, when the SCR is on, how much power is delivered to the load?

PART VI

Special Processes

In Part VI we introduce a number of special processes available under PSpice. These include *harmonic distortion, noise analysis, Monte Carlo analysis, worst case analysis, performance analysis, behavioral modeling, optimization,* and *hierarchy.*

    We will find that PSpice instantly presents results that would take many hours using hand analysis and calculation on actual circuits.

CHAPTER 25

Harmonic Distortion
Fourier Analysis

OBJECTIVES

- To show how nonlinear circuit elements lead to harmonic distortion.
- To determine total harmonic distortion in an amplifier.

DISCUSSION

As we have seen previously, transistors are inherently *nonlinear* devices because their transconductance curves (Figure 25.1) are not straight lines. When used in amplifiers, this leads to *nonlinear distortion* (Figure 25.2).

Generally, nonlinear distortion is unwanted, and in this chapter we will seek the means to reduce it. However, in Chapter 33, we will find that harmonic distortion is not only useful—but vital!

Although the distortion in the time domain is clear, in many cases it is more convenient and instructive to view the distortion in the frequency domain (the *harmonic* distortion). The process of converting from the time domain to the frequency domain is known as *Fourier analysis*, and is the subject of this chapter.

For continuous signals, we use the *continuous Fourier transform* (CFT) shown here:

Frequency-to-time

$$A(t) = \int_{-\infty}^{+\infty} A(f)e^{j2\pi ft}\,df$$

Time-to-frequency

$$A(f) = \int_{-\infty}^{+\infty} A(t)e^{-j2\pi ft}\,dt$$

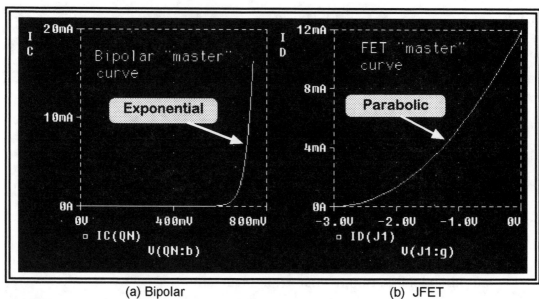

FIGURE 25.1

Transconductance curves
(a) Bipolar
(b) JFET

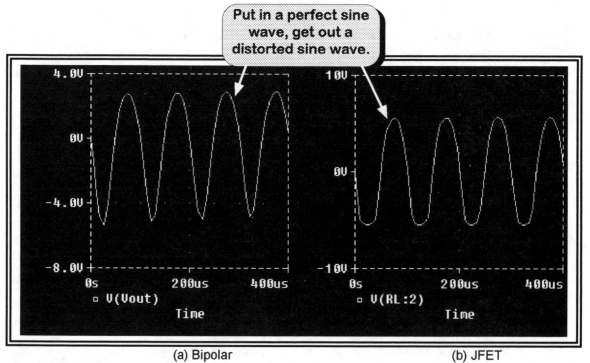

FIGURE 25.2

Output waveforms
(a) Bipolar
(b) JFET

PSpice for Windows

When the waveform is sampled or analyzed on a digital computer, we must adopt the *discrete Fourier transform* (DFT):

$$a(t) = \sum_{f=0}^{N-1} A(f)e^{i2\pi ft/N} \qquad A(f) = \frac{1}{N}\sum_{t=0}^{N-1} a(t)e^{-i2\pi ft/N}$$

If the time-domain waveform is repetitive, a great simplification results: The Fourier frequency components are harmonically related (multiples of the fundamental frequency). This means that the discrete Fourier transform can be performed by *fast Fourier transform* (FFT) techniques, resulting in a great reduction in calculation time.

Because all waveforms are assumed to be repetitive, PSpice offers the following two types of Fourier analyses:

- A DFT performed by PSpice on the last complete cycle of a specified voltage or current, with detailed harmonics tabulated in the output file.

- A FFT performed by Probe on any transient expression and displayed as a graph.

SIMULATION PRACTICE

1. Bring back the amplifier circuit shown in Figure 25.3 (first developed in Chapter 16).

The Discrete Fourier Transform (DFT)

<u>Reminder</u>: The results of a DFT are sent only to the output file, and are not sent to Probe for graphing.

2. Bring up the Transient dialog box and fill it in as shown in Figure 25.4. (We sweep from 0 to .4ms to provide four complete cycles of the 10kHz input signal.) The Fourier Analysis section tells the system to perform a DFT on V_{OUT}, using a center frequency of 10kHz (the input frequency), and to generate four harmonics for tabulation in the output file.

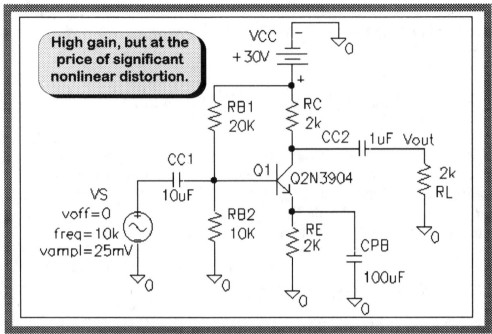

FIGURE 25.3

Bipolar amplifier
circuit

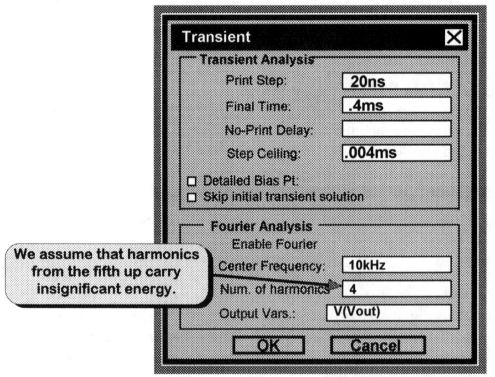

FIGURE 25.4

Transient dialog
box

PSpice for Windows

3. Run PSpice, bring up the output file (**Analysis, Examine Output**), and scroll to the Fourier data summarized by Table 25.1. (Leave the Probe window open for future use.)

FOURIER COMPONENTS OF TRANSIENT RESPONSE V(Vout)
DC COMPONENT = −2.893282E−01

HARMONIC FREQ. NO.	(HZ)	FOURIER COMPONENT	NORMALIZED COMPONENT	PHASE (DEG)	NORMALIZED PHASE (DEG)
1	1.000E+4	3.822E+00	1.000E+00	−1.782E+02	0.000E+00
2	2.000E+4	6.956E−01	1.820E−01	9.471E+01	2.729E+02
3	3.000E+4	5.561E−02	1.455E−02	1.149E+01	1.897E+02
4	4.000E+4	4.858E−03	1.271E−03	1.541E+02	3.323E+02

TOTAL HARMONIC DISTORTION = 1.825817E+01 PERCENT

To obtain each normalized component, divide each Fourier component by 3.822.

To obtain each normalized phase, add 178.2° to each regular phase.

TABLE 25.1

Detailed frequency, amplitude, and phase of each harmonic

4. Based on the results of Table 25.1, which harmonic components carry significant energy (greater than 1% of the total)?

    1   2   3   4

5. The *total harmonic distortion* shown in Table 25.1 is calculated by taking the square root of the sum of the squares of the harmonic components and reporting the result as a percentage of the fundamental component.

   The following equation uses values from Table 25.1. Using your calculator, verify the value determined by PSpice (18.26%).

$$\frac{(.6956^2 + .0556^2 + .0048^2)^{1/2}}{3.822} \times 100 = \underline{\hspace{2cm}}$$

The Fast Fourier Transform (FFT)

<u>Reminder</u>: The results of a FFT appear only as a Probe graph, and are not sent to the output file.

6. Bring the default (time domain) Probe graph window to the forefront and display V(Vout).

Fast Fourier transform

7. To convert to the frequency domain (take the Fourier transform), **CLICKL** on the *Display the Fourier transform of all Analog traces in the selected plot* toolbar button and generate the graph of Figure 25.5. (Expand the X-axis as necessary.)

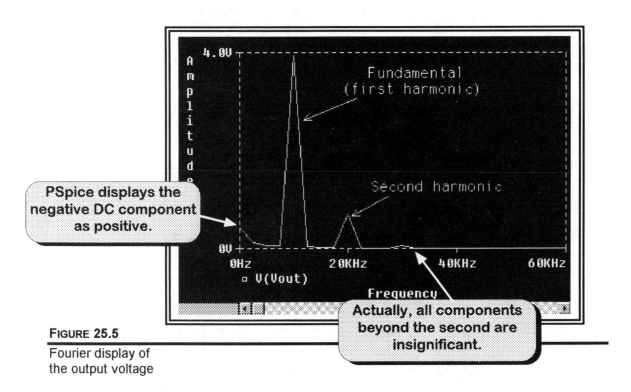

FIGURE 25.5

Fourier display of
the output voltage

8. Looking at the graph, *approximately* how many harmonics are visible (including the DC component)? How many carry significant energy?

       Number of visible harmonics = _____

       Number carrying significant energy = _____

9. Does the FFT-generated graph of Figure 25.5 generally give the same results as the DFT-generated data of Table 25.1? (<u>Hint</u>: Measure the amplitude of the DC and harmonic components and compare them to Table 25.1. Ignore the minus sign on the DFT DC component.)

    Yes   **No**

10. If you wish, perform a FFT on any other available voltage or current.

11. Add a 25Ω swamping resistor to the amplifier of Figure 25.3, and increase V_{in} to 100mV.   (If necessary, review Chapter 16.)

    (a) Using the DFT method, what is the *total harmonic distortion* (THD) and by what percentage is it reduced from the unswamped case?

    THD (unswamped) = __18.26%__

    THD (swamped) = _____

    Percent reduction = _____

    (b) Using the FFT method, display the output's Fourier components and compare them to the unswamped case. Are all harmonics (but the first) greatly reduced in amplitude?

    Yes   **No**

Advanced Activities

12. Perform a complete harmonic analysis of the JFET amplifier of Figure 25.6.

    (a) Are the third and fourth harmonics now significant?

    Yes   **No**

    (b) Compared to the bipolar case (unswamped), is the THD greater?

    Yes   **No**

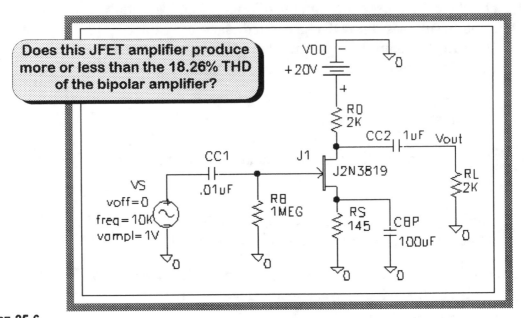

FIGURE 25.6

JFET amplifier

So far we have gone from the time-domain to the frequency-domain. To reverse the procedure, we should be able to take frequency and phase data from Table 25.1, superimpose the sine wave components, and re-create the original time-domain curves.

---

13. Using the data from Table 25.1, we generate the superposition equation shown below for the DC and first two harmonics. (Harmonic components 3 and 4 are not significant.)

$$-.289 + 3.82*sin(6.28*10k*Time - 178.2*6.28/360)$$
$$+ .695*sin(6.28*20k*Time + 94.7*6.28/360)$$

Using PSpice, display the corresponding <u>time-domain</u> curve. (**CLICKL** on the *Add trace(s) to the selected plot* toolbar button and enter the equation into the *Trace Command Box*.)

Does the resulting trace resemble the original waveform of Figure 25.2(a)?

        Yes   **No**

14. Using the techniques of your choice, determine how the resolution of the FFT depends on the *number* of cycles and *which* cycles are evaluated. Summarize your results. (To restrict the FFT evaluation to any portion of the time-domain waveform available: **Plot, X-axis Settings, Restricted** [under *Use Data*], fill in as desired, **OK**.)

EXERCISES

- Determine the total harmonic distortion of the audio amplifier of Figure 22.5. How would you improve (lower) the distortion value?

- Determine the total harmonic distortion of a square wave of various rise and fall times. Is there any relationship between rise/fall times and significant harmonic components?

QUESTIONS AND PROBLEMS

1. Why does a transistor cause harmonic distortion? Why *doesn't* a resistor cause harmonic distortion?

2. Under what conditions are the frequency components of a waveform harmonically related (multiples of the fundamental frequency)?

3. Based on the harmonic content of the first four harmonics (Table 25.1), were we justified in limiting the analysis to four harmonics?   Would we be justified in limiting the analysis to two harmonics?

4. Why does a buffer normally have a smaller total harmonic distortion than an amplifier?   (Hint: Does a buffer have built-in swamping?)

5. Referring to Figure 25.2(a), why is the DC component negative (as indicated by Table 25.1)?

6. Comparing Table 25.1 and Figure 25.5, does it appear that the FFT displays the DC component as an absolute number?

7. Looking at Table 25.1, how is the *normalized component* value obtained from the *Fourier component* value?

8. From step 13, we have a good idea how a Fourier transform generates a time-domain curve from frequency-domain data (component waveforms are superimposed). Explain how the opposite takes place. That is, how does a Fourier transform take a time-domain waveform and generate a frequency-domain curve? (<u>Hint</u>: Could we use test sine waves of different frequencies and phase and look for net constructive or destructive interference?)

CHAPTER 26

Noise Analysis
Signal-to-Noise Ratio

OBJECTIVES

- To perform a noise analysis on an amplifier.
- To determine the *signal-to-noise ratio*.

DISCUSSION

The noise-generating devices in a circuit are the resistors and the semiconductor devices. A *noise* analysis tells the designer how the noise from all such devices will affect an output signal.

Once we know the noise, we can easily generate the *signal-to-noise ratio* at the output node—a term that will tell us how important the noise is in relation to the output signal.

Noise analysis can be done only in conjunction with an AC analysis. The noise function generates a noise density spectrum for each device over a range of frequencies and performs an RMS sum at the specified output node. Also reported is the equivalent noise from a specified input source that would cause the same output noise value if injected into a noiseless circuit.

SIMULATION PRACTICE

1. Draw (or bring back from Chapter 16) the amplifier circuit of Figure 26.1.

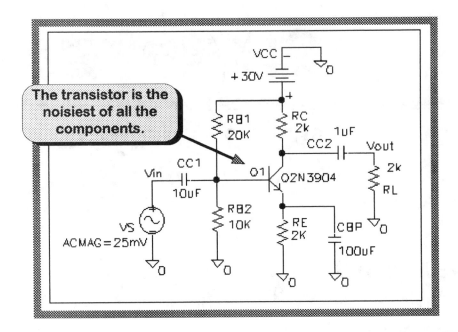

FIGURE 26.1

Amplifier test
circuit

2. Bring up the *AC Sweep and Noise Analysis* dialog box and fill it in as shown in Figure 26.2.

    *   *Output Voltage* [V(Vout)] gives the node at which the AC noise is to be determined.

    *   *I/V Source* (VS) is the independent voltage or current source at which the equivalent input noise will be calculated.

    *   *Interval* (100) causes a detailed table to be printed to the output file for every hundredth frequency. (If no value is specified, no tables will be generated.)

3. Run the analysis and generate the *noise density* (volts/root Hz) plots of Figure 26.3. (Note: Volts/root Hz = volts/Hz$^{1/2}$.)

    *   Y-axis 1 shows ONOISE (output noise density)—the RMS summed noise (volts/root Hz) at the output node [V(Vout)].

    *   Y-axis 2 shows INOISE (input noise density)—the equivalent RMS input noise (volts/root Hz) at V_{IN} (V_S).

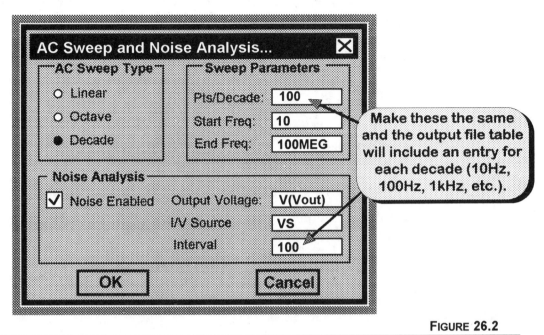

FIGURE 26.2

AC Sweep and
Noise Analysis
dialog box

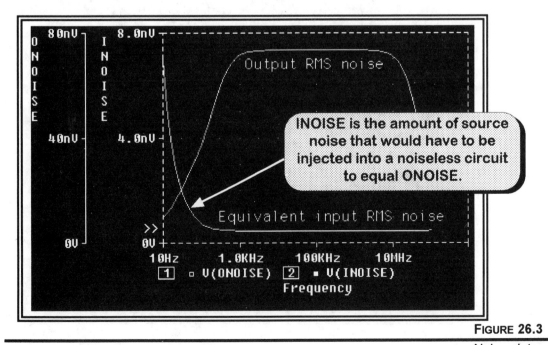

FIGURE 26.3

Noise plots

4. Based on the results (Figure 26.3), what is the output noise density at the midband frequency of 100kHz? At this same frequency, what is the equivalent noise density at the input (V_S)?

    VRMS/Hz(Onoise) at 100kHz = _____

    VRMS/Hz(Inoise) at 100kHz = _____

5. As shown in Figure 26.4, add a second plot and display the input and output *signal* voltages.

    What is the *signal-to-noise* ratio (SNR) at 100kHz? (What is the ratio of output signal voltage to output noise voltage density expressed in both regular and dB format?)

    Signal-to-noise ratio at 100kHz (regular) = _____

    Signal-to-noise ratio at 100kHz (dB) = _____

    $$SNR(dB) = 20\log_{10}SNR(reg)$$

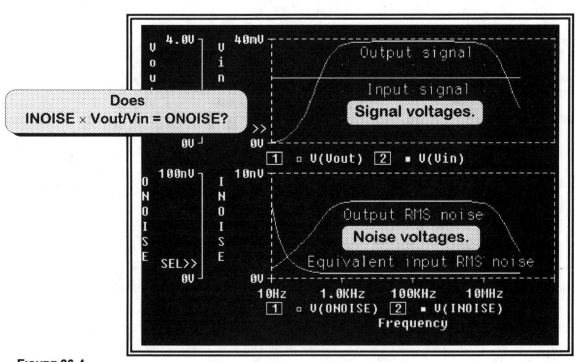

FIGURE 26.4

Comparing signal-
to-noise ratios

6.   Examine the *noise analysis* section of the output file. Per our instructions (Figure 26.2), was a separate noise analysis tabulated in detail for each decade of frequencies from 10Hz to 100MEGHz?

Yes   No

7.   Table 26.1 shows the noise analysis section in the output file for 100kHz.

(a) Does most of the noise come from the transistor?

Yes   No

(b) Which resistor or resistors contribute the greatest noise?

(c) Is the *equivalent input noise at VS* (4.699E–10 V/RT HZ) times the transfer function gain (156.3) equal to the *total output noise voltage* (7.346E–8 V/RT HZ)?

Yes   No

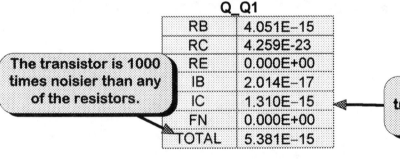

```
****  NOISE ANALYSIS        TEMPERATURE =  27.000 DEG C
      ***********************************************************
               FREQUENCY =  1.000E+05 HZ
      ****  TRANSISTOR SQUARED NOISE VOLTAGES (SQ V/HZ)
                          Q_Q1
```

	Q_Q1
RB	4.051E–15
RC	4.259E–23
RE	0.000E+00
IB	2.014E–17
IC	1.310E–15
FN	0.000E+00
TOTAL	5.381E–15

The transistor is 1000 times noisier than any of the resistors.

Don't confuse the transistor parameters with the resistors.

```
      ****  RESISTOR SQUARED NOISE VOLTAGES (SQ V/HZ)
            R_RC      R_RB1    R_RL      R_RB2    R_RE
   TOTAL   7.470E–18 5.130E–22 7.470E–18 1.026E–21 5.134E–23
   ****  TOTAL OUTPUT NOISE VOLTAGE     = 5.396E–15 SQ V/HZ
                                        = 7.346E–08 V/RT HZ
               TRANSFER FUNCTION VALUE:
            V(Vout)/V_VS          = 1.563E+02
      EQUIVALENT INPUT NOISE AT V_VS = 4.699E–10 V/RT HZ
```

TABLE 26.1

Noise analysis
at 100kHz

Advanced Activities

8. Increase the temperature to 100°C (212°F) and again determine the total noise at 100kHz. (How does it compare to the noise at the default temperature of 27°C?)

   Total V/RT HZ (noise) at 100kHz and 27°C = _7.346E-08_

   Total V/RT HZ (noise) at 100kHz and 100°C = _____

EXERCISE

- Perform a noise analysis on the audio amplifier of Figure 22.5. At 100kHz, how does the signal-to-noise ratio (dB) compare to that of the single-stage amplifier of this chapter (Figure 26.1)?

QUESTIONS AND PROBLEMS

1. Perform a root-mean-square (RMS) of the numbers below:

   RMS of 7, 2, –4, 8, 12 = _____

2. What causes noise in a resistor?

3. Based on Figure 26.3, what is the noise bandwidth of the amplifier circuit of Figure 26.1?

4. Referring to Figure 26.3, why does the equivalent input RMS noise rise significantly at lower frequencies?   (Hint: What role do the capacitors play?)

5. Determine the voltage gain of the amplifier of Figure 26.1 using each of the following methods and compare to the *TRANSFER FUNCTION VALUE* (156.3) of Table 26.1.

   (a) The ratio of resistors method ([rc‖rl]/re', where re' = 25mV/I_{EQ}).

   (b) Directly from Figure 26.4 (midband).

   (c) Using PSpice in the transient mode.

6. If it turns out that the signal-to-noise ratio of the amplifier of Figure 26.1 is too low (too much noise), what would be the most logical step to increase the ratio?   (<u>Hint</u>: Referring to Table 26.1, does the transistor give the greatest noise component?)

7. Referring to Table 26.1, how is 7.346E−08 V/RT HZ obtained from 5.396E−15 SQ V/HZ?

8. Based on the results of procedure step 8, why does the total noise voltage go up as the temperature goes down?

9.   Referring to Figure 26.4, does ONOISE = INOISE × Vout/Vin?

CHAPTER 27

Monte Carlo Analysis
Tolerances

OBJECTIVES

- To assign tolerance values to components.
- To perform a Monte Carlo analysis on an amplifier.

DISCUSSION

In past chapters, all the components in the amplifier of Figure 27.1 were assumed to be constants. For example, all the resistors had *exactly* the values indicated by their color code—and they never changed. In this chapter, all resistors will be assigned *tolerances*, which specify how they might vary from their nominal value.

To determine the effects of such tolerance variations, PSpice offers *Monte Carlo* analysis.

MONTE CARLO

During a Monte Carlo analysis, PSpice performs several runs of a DC, AC, or transient analysis, each time varying component values randomly within the tolerance range. This random nature gives the process its "Monte Carlo" tag. The first run is always the nominal run, using the component's face value, with no tolerance variations.

For simple parts (such as resistors), tolerance values are easily set as attributes; for more complex parts (such as transistors), tolerance values are set within the model definition. Output data is sent to *Probe* for graphical display and to the *output file* for tabular display.

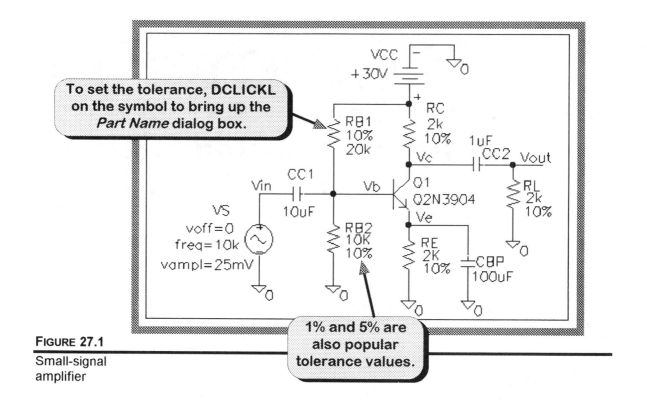

FIGURE 27.1

Small-signal
amplifier

In this chapter, we will first perform a Monte Carlo analysis with only the resistors given tolerances. We will then add a tolerance value to a transistor parameter.

SIMULATION PRACTICE

1. Draw the circuit of Figure 27.1 (from Chapter 16) and set all attributes as shown (including the 10% tolerances for all resistors).

Perform the Monte Carlo Analysis

2. Set up the system for transient analysis from 0 to .2ms. (Suggestion: Set the *Step ceiling* to .001ms.)

3. **CLICKL** on the *Sets up the simulation analysis for active* toolbar button, bring up the *Monte Carlo/Worst Case* dialog box of Figure 27.2, and fill in as shown.

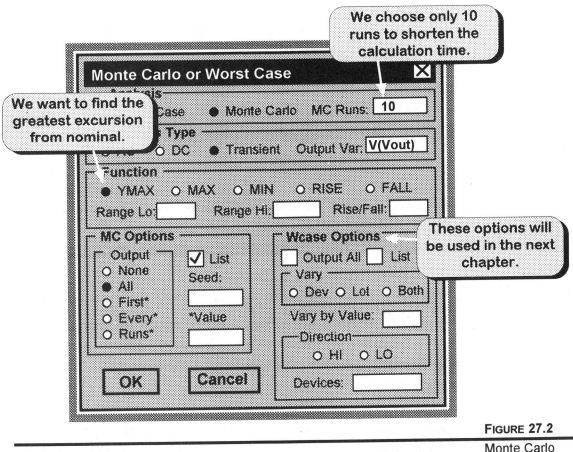

FIGURE 27.2

Monte Carlo
dialog box

- <u>Output var</u>: V(Vout) specifies the node at which the waveforms will be generated.

- <u>Function</u>: Specifies the function to be performed on the output variable waveform for each run. The results affect both the output file and the graphical presentation under *Probe*.

  YMAX finds the greatest difference from the nominal run, MAX and MIN find the maximum and minimum value, RISE and FALL find the first occurrence of the waveform crossing above or below the threshold value in the *rise/fall* field, and the *Range Lo:* and *Range HI:* boxes restrict the range over which a function will be evaluated. Only one function may be selected at a time.

- <u>MC Options</u> controls the runs. *None* causes only the nominal run to be produced, *All* causes all runs, *First* causes only the first *n* runs (*n* is placed in the *value* box), *Every* causes only every *n*th run, *Runs* causes only the runs listed in the "Value:" box, *List* prints to the output file the model parameter values used for each component during that run, and *Seed* defines the seed value for the random number generator (the default is 17533).

4. Run the Transient/Monte Carlo analysis and note the 10 runs performed in the PSpice run-time display box. When the *Available Sections* dialog box comes up, note that **ALL** (all runs) is selected by default. After **OK**, the Probe graph appears with the default X-axis assigned the time range specified in the transient analysis setup.

5. Add the output variable and generate the graph of Figure 27.3. Note the 10 different waveforms that result from the statistical variation of all the resistors. (The first waveform designator listed is the nominal waveform in which all resistors are at their face value.)

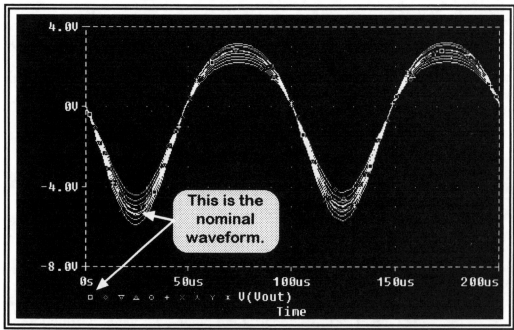

FIGURE 27.3

Monte Carlo
output waveform

PSpice for Windows

6. Looking at the results (Figure 27.3), what is the *approximate* percent variation between the lowest and highest peak values compared to the average peak value (all at 75μs)?

$$\% \text{ variation} = \frac{V_{PEAK}(\text{difference})}{V_{PEAK}(\text{average})} \times 100 = \underline{\hspace{3cm}}$$

Average = (high + low)/2

The Output File

7. During a Monte Carlo analysis, a great deal of data is written to the output file. Examine the output file and find the INITIAL TRANSIENT SOLUTION. For example, Table 27.1 shows the initial transient data for the nominal and arbitrary run (pass) three.

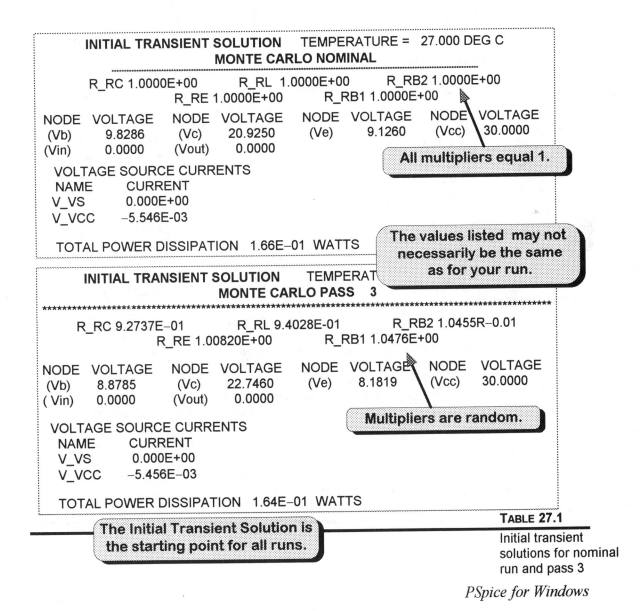

INITIAL TRANSIENT SOLUTION   TEMPERATURE = 27.000 DEG C
MONTE CARLO NOMINAL

R_RC 1.0000E+00   R_RL 1.0000E+00   R_RB2 1.0000E+00
R_RE 1.0000E+00   R_RB1 1.0000E+00

NODE	VOLTAGE	NODE	VOLTAGE	NODE	VOLTAGE	NODE	VOLTAGE
(Vb)	9.8286	(Vc)	20.9250	(Ve)	9.1260	(Vcc)	30.0000
(Vin)	0.0000	(Vout)	0.0000				

All multipliers equal 1.

VOLTAGE SOURCE CURRENTS
NAME   CURRENT
V_VS   0.000E+00
V_VCC   –5.546E-03

TOTAL POWER DISSIPATION 1.66E–01 WATTS

The values listed may not necessarily be the same as for your run.

INITIAL TRANSIENT SOLUTION   TEMPERAT
MONTE CARLO PASS   3

R_RC 9.2737E–01   R_RL 9.4028E-01   R_RB2 1.0455R–0.01
R_RE 1.00820E+00   R_RB1 1.0476E+00

NODE	VOLTAGE	NODE	VOLTAGE	NODE	VOLTAGE	NODE	VOLTAGE
(Vb)	8.8785	(Vc)	22.7460	(Ve)	8.1819	(Vcc)	30.0000
(Vin)	0.0000	(Vout)	0.0000				

Multipliers are random.

VOLTAGE SOURCE CURRENTS
NAME   CURRENT
V_VS   0.000E+00
V_VCC   –5.456E-03

TOTAL POWER DISSIPATION 1.64E–01 WATTS

The Initial Transient Solution is the starting point for all runs.

TABLE 27.1

Initial transient solutions for nominal run and pass 3

PSpice for Windows

8. Refer to Table 27.1. Pass 3 produced what percent change in the initial transient collector voltage (Vc) from nominal?

   % change in Vc from nominal = _____

9. Next, find the "sorted deviations" section of the output file (Table 27.2). In this table, all data is for node V(Vout) based on transient runs from TIME = 0 to 200μs, with all resistor values randomly varied within their tolerance range prior to each run.

   The data listed for each run is in response to the YMAX function. For each run *past the nominal* (2 through 10), the maximum V(Vout) amplitude deviation from the nominal waveform is found and listed in order of magnitude as an absolute number, a percent of nominal, and a standard deviation (sigma). Also listed is the time that the maximum deviation occurred and whether the deviation was lower or higher than nominal.

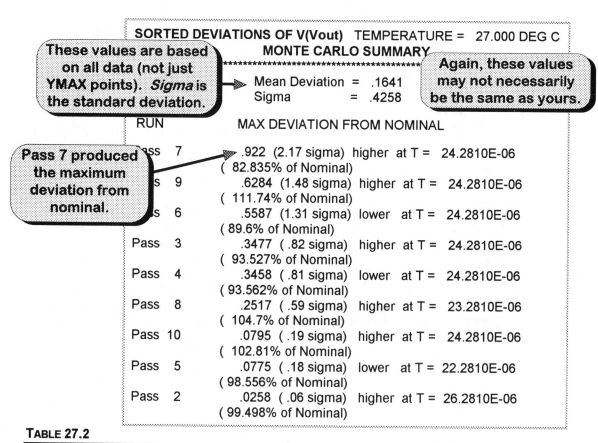

SORTED DEVIATIONS OF V(Vout)   TEMPERATURE = 27.000 DEG C
MONTE CARLO SUMMARY
****

These values are based on all data (not just YMAX points). *Sigma* is the standard deviation.

Again, these values may not necessarily be the same as yours.

Mean Deviation = .1641
Sigma   = .4258

RUN	MAX DEVIATION FROM NOMINAL
Pass 7	.922 (2.17 sigma) higher at T = 24.2810E-06 (82.835% of Nominal)
Pass 9	.6284 (1.48 sigma) higher at T = 24.2810E-06 (111.74% of Nominal)
Pass 6	.5587 (1.31 sigma) lower at T = 24.2810E-06 (89.6% of Nominal)
Pass 3	.3477 (.82 sigma) higher at T = 24.2810E-06 (93.527% of Nominal)
Pass 4	.3458 (.81 sigma) lower at T = 24.2810E-06 (93.562% of Nominal)
Pass 8	.2517 (.59 sigma) higher at T = 23.2810E-06 (104.7% of Nominal)
Pass 10	.0795 (.19 sigma) higher at T = 24.2810E-06 (102.81% of Nominal)
Pass 5	.0775 (.18 sigma) lower at T = 22.2810E-06 (98.556% of Nominal)
Pass 2	.0258 (.06 sigma) higher at T = 26.2810E-06 (99.498% of Nominal)

Pass 7 produced the maximum deviation from nominal.

TABLE 27.2

YMAX function results

PSpice for Windows

10. Based on your *sorted deviations* data, what was the greatest deviation in V_{OUT} from nominal and when did it occur?

    Greatest deviation from nominal = _____ Volts

    Found at time = _____μs during run _____

11. To verify the table, zoom in on the waveform set at the time indicated by step 10 ($\approx$ 25μs?) and generate curves such as those in Figure 27.4.

    Assign the cursors to the nominal and *run* curves indicated by step 10. Is the *greatest deviation* from nominal approximately the same as suggested by the cursor values?

            Yes   No

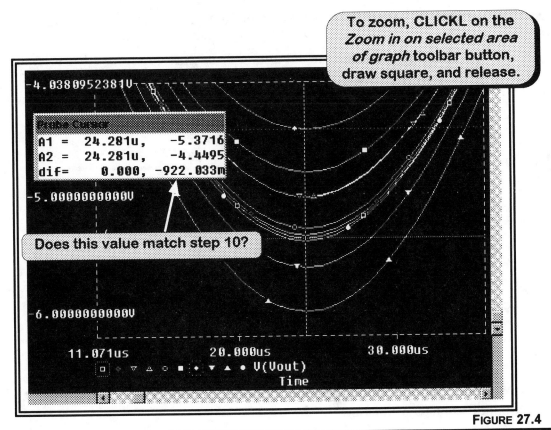

FIGURE 27.4

Zooming in on the maximum deviation

Advanced Activities

12. Assign the capacitors 10% tolerance values and compare the results with previous data. (Remove or keep the tolerances on the resistors as you wish.)

13. Assign transistor parameter *Bf* (maximum forward ideal *Beta*) a 50% tolerance as follows: select Q1, **Edit**, **Model**, **Edit Instance Model[Text]**, add *DEV=50%* after *Bf=416.4*, **OK**. (Remove or keep the tolerances on the resistors and capacitors as you wish.)

    Generate a new waveform set and a new *Sorted Deviation* table, and compare to the previous results.

EXERCISE

- Referring to Figure 27.1, change all resistors from low-cost (10% tolerance) to precision (1% tolerance) and perform another Monte Carlo analysis. How do the two cases compare? (If you are comparing the results to Figure 27.3, be sure to remove the tolerance values from the capacitors and transistor.)

QUESTIONS AND PROBLEMS

1. When running a Monte Carlo analysis, exactly what is randomized?

2. Which *function* would you use to determine the first occurrence of the waveform crossing above the threshold value for each run?

3. How would you repeat a Monte Carlo analysis using a different sequence of random parameter values?

4. When doing a Monte Carlo analysis, the first run is always the _____ run.

5. Define each of the following terms:

    (a) Initial transient.

    (b) Nominal.

6. During an initial transient solution (Table 27.1), why are Vin and Vout equal to zero? (Hint: What is the value of the sine wave at TIME = 0, and what are the states of all capacitors and inductors?)

CHAPTER 28

Worst Case Analysis
AC Sensitivity

OBJECTIVES

- To perform a sensitivity analysis on an amplifier.
- To perform a worst case analysis on an amplifier.

DISCUSSION

Although both Monte Carlo and worst case analysis make use of component tolerances and involve a number of runs, they are quite different. Monte Carlo analysis, covered in the last chapter, varies component values in a random manner as the runs are made; worst case analysis does not use random variations at all.

Instead, worst case analysis involves a two-step process. First, we perform a *sensitivity* analysis, in which model parameters are varied one at a time for each device, with a DC, AC, or transient analysis run for each variation.

When the sensitivity analysis is done, PSpice uses the corresponding data to perform one final worst case run, with each parameter set up or down by its *full* tolerance in such a way as to produce the greatest output signal or the greatest deviation from nominal (or other result, depending on the function chosen).

SIMULATION PRACTICE

1. Bring back the amplifier in Figure 28.1 (reproduced from Chapter 27).

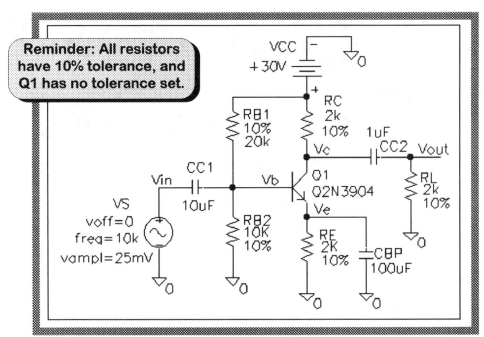

FIGURE 28.1

Amplifier ready for
worst case analysis

2. Bring back the *Monte Carlo or Worst Case* dialog box of Figure 28.2.

3. Switch to a worst case analysis (**Worst Case**), set *Analysis Type* to **Transient** and *Output Var* to V(Vout), and set *Function* to **MAX** (to generate the maximum amplitude worst case output waveform).

   Next, fill in the *Wcase Options* box as follows:

   • **Output All** to send data from all sensitivity runs to the output file. If not enabled, then only the nominal and final (worst case) runs generate output.

   • Under *Vary*, set **Dev** to activate only the device tolerances.

   > **Dev** is appropriate for discrete circuits in which devices vary independently. **Lot** is appropriate for integrated circuits, in which all devices vary as a group. For a more accurate worst case analysis, we should first perform an analysis with **Lot** selected, manually adjust the resistor values as specified, then perform another analysis with **Dev** selected. If **Both** is selected, all resistors are set up or down by the *same* (lot + dev) amount, and the result is difficult to interpret. (Device *Rbreak* is required to set the lot tolerance.)

- Under *Direction*, set **Hi** to specify which direction the worst case run is to go—relative to the nominal. (If *function* is YMAX or MAX, the default is HI; if MIN, the default is LO; if RISE_EDGE or FALL_EDGE, set to HI or LO as desired.)

- Leave the *Devices* box blank so all devices will be included in the analysis. (When devices are listed by model name, these are the only components included in the analysis.)

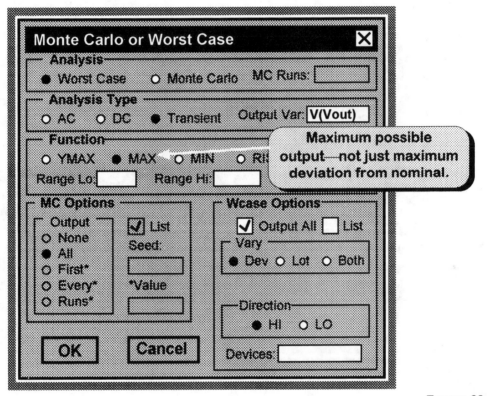

FIGURE 28.2

Monte Carlo or Worst Case dialog box

4. Exit the *Monte Carlo* or *Worst Case* dialog box (**OK**) and return to the *Analysis Setup* menu.

5. Be sure to enable both the *Monte Carlo/Worst Case* and *Transient* analyses. For the *Transient* analysis, set the *final time* to .2ms and the *step ceiling* to .001ms. Return to Schematics (**OK, Close**).

6. Run the *Transient/Worst Case* analysis and wait for the *Available Sections* box to appear. Since *All* is selected by default, **OK** to exit the box and generate the initial graph.

> Note: ...MINAL means the *nominal* waveform, ...L DEVICES means the waveform for *all devices*, and the other options specify waveforms to be generated for individual devices.

7. Add the output trace [V(Vout)] to generate the individual parameter and final (worst case) output waveforms of Figure 28.3.

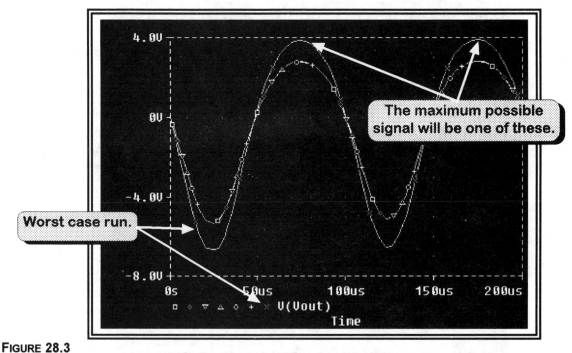

FIGURE 28.3

Worst case
waveform set

8. Referring to Figure 28.3, note that seven waveforms were drawn. In order of generation and listing, they are as follows:

     1 nominal waveform
     5 sensitivity waveforms for each resistor
     1 final worst case waveform

Zoom area

9. If you wish, zoom in on the six closely clustered nominal and sensitivity waveforms and verify that there are actually six *separate* waveforms.

10. Due to the MAX function, the worst case waveform (legend symbol ×) includes the maximum possible amplitude. Does this waveform show any evidence of clipping, on either the positive or negative peaks? (Hint: Carefully observe the waveform at 25μs.)

    Yes   **No**

Output File

11. Scan through the output file and locate the INITIAL TRANSIENT solution generated for the nominal case and each of the five resistors. This represents the starting point (TIME = 0) for each of the six sensitivity runs.

12. Scan further into the output file and locate the SENSITIVITY SUMMARY of Table 28.1, created using data from the six transient sensitivity runs—each from TIME = 0 to TIME = 200μs.

    As directed by the MAX function, each of the five resistors is increased in value one at a time for each run, and the maximum corresponding output voltage is located. The data is then compared to the nominal run, and the five resistors are ranked from most positive to most negative according to their sensitivity (their effect on the magnitude of the maximum output signal).

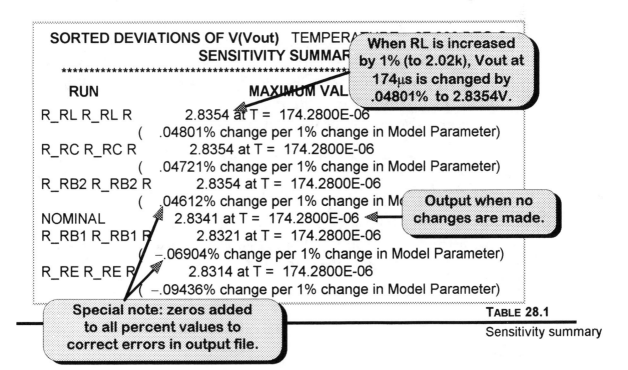

TABLE 28.1

Sensitivity summary

13. Based on Table 28.1:

(a) Which three resistors should be *increased* in order to increase the maximum output signal?

     _____   _____   _____

(b) Which two resistors should be *decreased* in order to increase the maximum output signal?

     _____   _____

(c) If the load resistor (R_RL) were increased by 10%, by what percentage would the maximum output voltage increase?

     % increase = _____

(d) If you desired to reduce the chance of clipping at minimal cost by changing just one resistor's tolerance from 10% to 1%, which resistor would you choose? (Circle your answer.)

     RC   RB1   RL   RB2   RE

     Why did you choose this resistor?

14. Continue to scan through the output file and locate the UPDATED MODEL PARAMETERS data of Table 28.2—which shows how all resistor values are increased or decreased by their full tolerance amount (10%) during the final worst case run.   (1.1 and .9 are scaling factors for the nominal values.)

     Does the data support your answers to step 13 (a) and (b)?

     Yes   No

15. When all tolerances are set as listed in Table 28.2, the system performs the final worst case run, and the summary data of Table 28.3 are written to the output file.

     As shown, is it true that 137.32% of 2.8341 = 3.8918?

     Yes   No

```
UPDATED MODEL PARAMETERS    TEMPERATURE = 27.000 DEG
              WORST CASE ALL DEVICES
****************************************************************

   DEVICE        MODEL        PARAMETER      NEW VALUE
    R_RL          R_RL            R         1.1 (Increased)
    R_RB2         R_RB2           R         1.1 (Increased)
    R_RB1         R_RB1           R          .9 (Decreased)
    R_RE          R_RE            R          .9 (Decreased)
    R_RC          R_RC            R         1.1 (Increased)
```

.9 = decrease by 10%.
1.1 = increase by 10%.

TABLE 28.2

Worst case parameter changes

```
SORTED DEVIATIONS OF V(Vout)   TEMPERATURE =  27.000 DEG C
              WORST  CASE SUMMARY
****************************************************************

        RUN              MAXIMUM VALUE
    ALL DEVICES          3.8918 at T =  175.0000E-06
                         (137.32% of Nominal)

    NOMINAL              2.8341 at T =  174.2800E-06
```

Absolute maximum worst case value.

TABLE 28.3

Worst case summary

16. Return to Probe and check the worst case maximum waveform at 175μs. Does it equal 3.8918V, as predicted by Table 28.3?

Yes   **No**

Advanced Activities

17. Assign transistor parameter *Bf* a 50% DEV tolerance and compare the outcome to the previous results. (Select, **Edit**, **Model**, **Edit Instance Model (text)**, set *Bf=416.4, DEV=50%*.)

18. Assign the three capacitors of Figure 28.1 10% tolerance values and compare the outcome to the previous results.

19. Repeat the worst case analysis using the YMAX function (instead of the MAX function). Explain the differences. (Hint: YMAX finds the greatest *difference* from nominal; MAX finds the greatest amplitude, without regard to nominal.)

EXERCISE

- Perform a *complete* worst case analysis on the audio amplifier of Figure 22.5. Set tolerances for the resistors, and include capacitor and transistor tolerances if you wish. Vary the function from YMAX to FALL. (Compare the results when using 10% and 1% resistors and capacitors.)

QUESTIONS AND PROBLEMS

1. Which of the following analyses generate random numbers?
    (a) Monte Carlo
    (b) Sensitivity
    (c) Worst case

2. When performing a worst case analysis, why must a sensitivity analysis be done first?

3. Based on the sensitivity data of Table 28.1, the output voltage is *least* sensitive to which resistor?

4. Based on Table 28.1, by what percent would V_{out} change if RC changed by 20%?

5. Based on Figure 28.3, why is there a potential problem with the amplifier design of Figure 28.1?   If so, what could you do to solve the problem?

6. Pick any two resistors from Table 28.2 and (based on the amplifier design of Figure 28.1) explain why their increased or decreased values resulted in a larger maximum output voltage.

7. Based entirely on the sensitivity data of Table 28.1, how would the resistor ranking change if the YMAX (rather than MAX) function were used?

8. Referring to the special note of Table 28.1, does the following calculation, based on the first run (for resistor RL), verify the correction?

$$\text{Nominal} + \quad .04801\% \ (.0004801) \text{ increase} \ = \text{change}$$

$$2.8341 + (2.8341 \times .0004801) = \ 2.8354$$

CHAPTER 29

Performance Analysis
Histograms

OBJECTIVES

- To use *performance analysis* to graph special functions.
- To generate a *histogram* from the results of a Monte Carlo analysis.

DISCUSSION

In Chapter 9, we designed an automotive suspension system using the RCL analog computer of Figure 29.1(a) to generate the parametric family of railroad-tie response curves of Figure 29.1(b).

Looking over the curves, we selected an *Rshock* value of 300Ω. Our primary reason for choosing this value is the size of the negative bounce shown in Figure 29.2 (−1.0769V). It seemed at the time to be just right: large enough to absorb the shock, but small enough to prevent significant oscillations.

However, since then, extensive laboratory and field testing now tells us that the ride is too stiff. The system does not bounce enough. We find that the ideal negative bounce is −1.2265V. The question is, what value of *Rshock* will give a bounce voltage of exactly −1.2265V?

We could interpolate the answer from Figure 29.1(b), or perform a number of trial-and-error runs—but *performance analysis* provides a better way. With performance analysis, we can directly generate a plot of bounce voltage versus *Rshock*. The value of *Rshock* that corresponds to −1.2265V will be picked right off the graph!

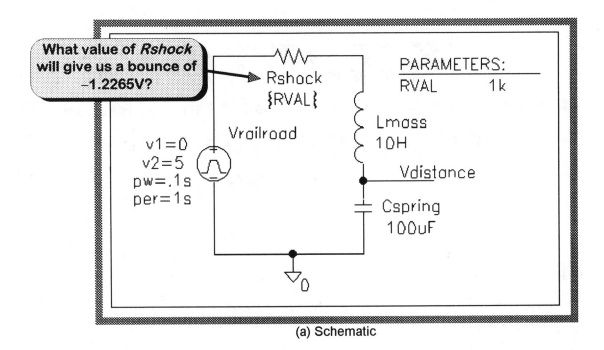

(a) Schematic

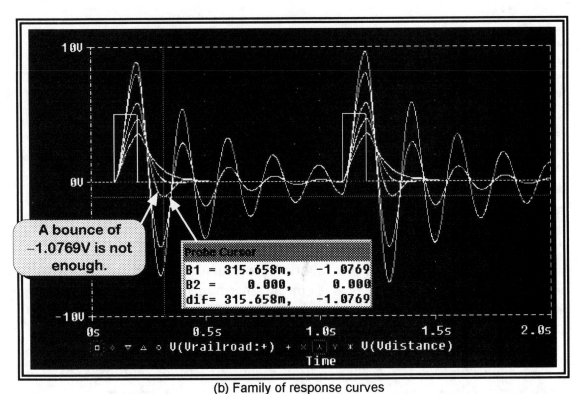

(b) Family of response curves

FIGURE 29.1

The analog computer
(a) Schematic
(b) Family of response curves

THE GOAL FUNCTION

At the heart of performance analysis is the *goal function*. A goal function will scan each curve of our suspension-response family of curves, and return the bounce voltage—which is then plotted against the parameter value (*Rshock*).

The question now becomes, what goal function will serve our needs? Looking at Figure 29.1(b), it is clear that the bounce voltage is also the *minimum* voltage! So—how do we create a goal function that will return the minimum voltage of each curve?

Fortunately, MicroSim provides a number of built-in goal functions that we are free to use. These are listed in Appendix H under three categories: *general*, *AC*, and *transient*. Turning to the *general use* section, we quickly locate goal function *Min* (reproduced in Figure 29.2). *Min* will search each response curve and return the corresponding minimum Y-axis value for storage. This value is, of course, the bounce value we are seeking.

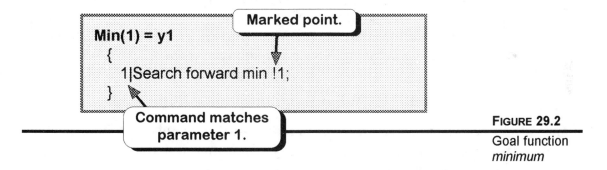

FIGURE 29.2

Goal function
minimum

Referring to Figure 29.2, the major sections of the goal function are as follows:

- *Min* is the goal function name.

- *1* represents a parameter, in which specific values are entered when the curves are plotted. For us, "1" will be *V(distance:+)*.

- *y1* specifies the returned value to be stored and plotted against the parameter variable. These are called *marked point expressions*.

- *search forward min !1* scans each curve from left to right and issues a marked point (!1) when each minimum value is found.

During simulation, goal function *min* searches each transient curve corresponding to parameter 1 [*V(distance:+)*] for the minimum value. When found, it issues a marked point (*!1*) specifying the corresponding *x* and *y* coordinates (*x1* and *y1*).   Coordinate *y1* (the desired minimum value) is returned and stored for later use in generating the plot of minimum values versus *Rshock*.

HISTOGRAMS

Once the correct value of *Rshock* is determined, the next logical step is to assign it a tolerance and note its statistical effect on the response curve. After all, we can't expect all shock absorbers coming off the assembly line to have exactly the same damping characteristics.

To accomplish this, we generate a *histogram*—a performance analysis done by varying *Rshock* randomly about its nominal value according to the multiple runs of a Monte Carlo analysis.

With a histogram, the X-axis takes on the returned values of the goal function (the bounce voltage) and the Y-axis takes on units of percent. Using histograms, we will determine the percentage probability that the suspension system will lie in various X-axis (bounce voltage) slots due to the random tolerance variations of *Rshock*.

GLOBAL GOAL FUNCTIONS

As we learned earlier, MicroSim provides a number of built-in goal functions (Appendix H). These *global* goal functions are provided within file *msim.prb*. Should we require a goal function that is not found within *msim.prb*, we are free to write our own and add it to *msim.prb*.

SIMULATION PRACTICE

1.   Draw (or obtain from Chapter 9) the resonant RCL circuit of Figure 29.1(a).

2.   Be sure the main sweep is a transient sweep from 0 to 2s, and the nested (parametric) sweep is *Rshock*, having global values (RVAL) from 275 to 300 in linear increments of 1.

3. Run PSpice, leave **All** available sections selected by default, **OK**, and generate the initial graph.

4. Switch to performance analysis (*Turn Performance Analysis On/Off* toolbar button), and note that *the X-axis switches from frequency to Rshock* (RVAL) with values from 275Ω to 300Ω.

Performance analysis

5. To display the available goal functions, *Add trace(s) to the selected plot* toolbar button. When the *Add traces* dialog box comes up, note that the list of available goal functions (Appendix H) is automatically displayed in the *Functions or Macros* box.

> The *Functions or Macros* box is actually three boxes in one: *Analog operators and functions*, *Macros*, and *Goal functions*. To switch among the three, open the *Functions or Macros* menu and **CLICKL**. When entering a trace variable expression, you may wish to switch back and forth between these menu categories.

6. We are now ready to solve our problem: to plot *bounce* versus *Rshock* and select the value that corresponds to −1.2265V. To accomplish this: **Min(1)**, **V(Vdistance)** (to create trace variable *Min(V(Vdistance))*), **OK**. The resulting performance analysis plot is shown in Figure 29.3.

7. Based on the results of Figure 29.3, what value of *Rshock* comes closest to giving our suspension system a bounce of −1.2265V?

    ***Rshock* (at bounce of −1.2265) = _____**

8. To test the result, assign *Rshock* the value determined in step 7, disable the parametric analysis, and generate the response curve of Figure 29.4. Is the bounce voltage equal to −1.2265V (within ±.0005)?

    Yes   **No**

9. If you wish, select any other value of *Rshock* from Figure 29.3 and verify the results. Did the performance analysis graph correctly predict the actual response?

    Yes   **No**

PSpice for Windows

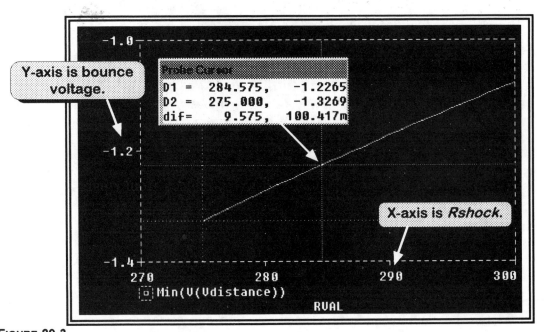

FIGURE 29.3

Plot of bandwidth
versus Rtank

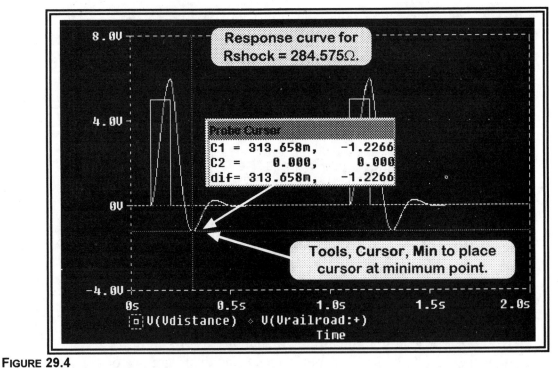

FIGURE 29.4

Response curve test
showing mission
accomplished

Histogram

> We now know that an *Rshock* value of ≈285Ω gives us the desired
> bounce response. However, because we don't live in a perfect world,
> we find that the shock absorbers coming off the assembly line actually
> have a uniform distribution of *Rshock* values about a 10% tolerance.
> What we need is a way of showing how the statistical distribution of
> *Rshock* values affects the bounce voltages. The *histogram* is such a
> device.

10. To prepare for a Monte Carlo analysis, assign *Rshock* a 10%
     tolerance. (**DCLICKL** on *Rshock's* symbol, etc.)

11. Enable the *Monte Carlo/Worst Case* analysis.   Within the *Monte
     Carlo* dialog box, set *Analysis* to **Monte Carlo**, choose 25 MC
     runs, set *Analysis Type* to transient, and *Output* to **All** (under
     MC Options).   [Because we will not be accessing the output file,
     set *Output Var* and *Function* to any convenient terms, such as
     I(Vsource) and YMAX.]

12. Run PSpice and wait for the *Available sections box* to appear.
     Note that ALL (all runs) is selected by default. **OK** to bring up the
     default probe graph.

13. Switch to performance analysis and note the initial histogram chart.

14. Enter the same trace expression as before (*Min(V(Vdistance))*) and
     generate the bounce response histogram of Figure 29.5.

15. Based on the random (Monte Carlo) tolerance variations of *Rshock*
     about its base value, the histogram shows the percentage
     probability that the bounce response voltage will fall into one of 10
     bounce voltage slots. Considering the results of Figure 29.5:

     (a) What is the range of probabilities?   (What is the highest
         probability minus the lowest probability?)

         Probability range = _____

**Performance
analysis**

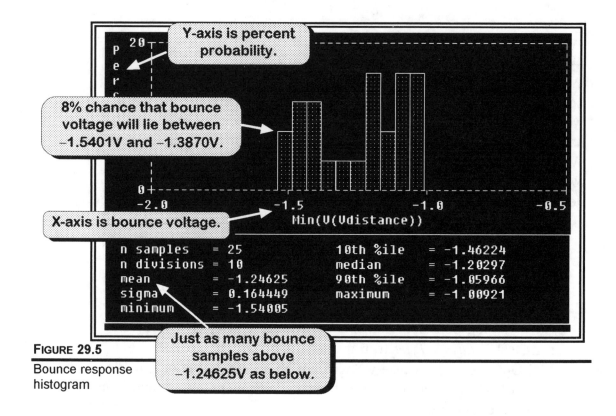

FIGURE 29.5

Bounce response
histogram

(b) What is the average (median) bounce voltage?

   Average = _____

(c) What is the standard deviation (sigma)?

   Standard deviation = _____

Advanced Activities

> The bounce response histogram of Figure 29.5 seems unrealistic.
> Shouldn't the responses be clustered about the center (have a bell-
> shaped distribution)?

16. To change the histogram from the default *uniform* case to the more
     realistic *Gaussian* distribution: **Analysis, Setup, Options** (from
     schematics) to bring up the *Options* dialog box. Set
     DISTRIBUTION to GAUSS, **Accept, OK, Close**, and generate the
     histogram of Figure 29.6.   (When done, return to UNIFORM
     case.)

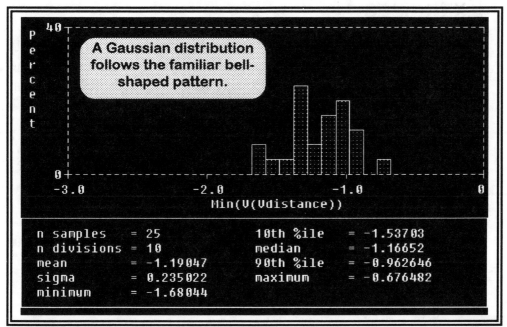

FIGURE 29.6

Histogram using
Gaussian tolerance
distribution

17. Does the histogram of Figure 29.6 seem more realistic, and is the range of bounce voltages (maximum – minimum) greater?

    Yes   **No**

18. If you wish, repeat the histogram generation using various *seed* values. (The seed value box within the Monte Carlo analysis box sets the random number generator. That is, each seed value generates a unique random number sequence.)

19. Using the equations below, calculate the *mean* and *sigma* (standard deviation) for either of the histograms of Figures 29.5 or 29.6. Do your answers agree with those calculated by Probe?

$$\text{mean} = \frac{1}{N}\sum_{0}^{N}X_N \qquad \text{sigma} = \frac{1}{N-1}\sqrt{\sum_{0}^{N}(X_N - \text{mean})^2}$$

PSpice for Windows

EXERCISES

- Referring to the swamped amplifier of Figure 29.7 (from Chapter 16), use performance analysis to determine the value of RS that will yield a voltage gain of exactly 10. Be sure to test your result. Then assign the correct value of RS a 10% tolerance and generate a Gaussian histogram showing the resulting statistical distribution of gain.

- Referring to Chapter 13 (Figure 13.3), use performance analysis to plot the relationship between the maximum crash force and *Rbag*.

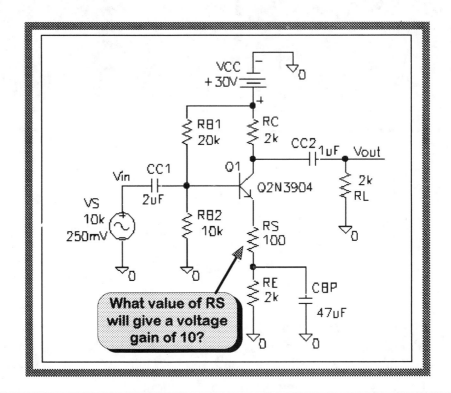

FIGURE 29.7

Swamped small-signal amplifier

QUESTIONS AND PROBLEMS

1. Does performance analysis require multiple runs of a waveform?

        Yes   **No**

2.   When using performance analysis, the X-axis is

(a) the single returned value from the goal function.
(b) the varying parameter value.

3.   A goal function returns how many values when it analyzes a single waveform?

4.   When a performance analysis is run on a family of curves generated by the random tolerance variation of a Monte Carlo analysis, we generate a:

_____.

5.   Analyze goal function *centerfrequency()* and explain how it works.

```
CenterFreq(1, db_level) = (x1+x2)/2
{
    1|Search forward level(max-db_level,p) !1
      Search forward level(max-db_level,n) !2;
}
```

6.   The X-axis of a histogram is

(a) the returned goal function values.
(b) percentage.
(c) time or frequency.

7.   How can we change the number of histogram slots (presently ten)?   (Hint: **Tools**, **Options** under *Probe*.)

8. Why is a Gaussian-based histogram (Figure 29.6) usually more realistic than a conventional histogram (Figure 29.5)?

9. To save time, our histograms were generated with only 25 Monte Carlo runs. What do you think either curve (uniform and Gaussian) would look like if the number of runs approached infinity?

CHAPTER 30

Controlled Sources
Analog Behavioral Modeling

OBJECTIVES

- To use *controlled sources* to model a circuit element.
- To add *behavioral modeling* to simulate more complex circuit components.

DISCUSSION

CONTROLLED SOURCES

To simplify initial circuit design and to model customized components, PSpice offers the four types of *controlled sources* listed below:

Device	Description
E	VCVS (Voltage-Controlled Voltage Source)
F	ICIS (Current-Controlled Current Source)
G	VCIS (Voltage-Controlled Current Source)
H	ICVS (Current-Controlled Voltage Source)

These devices have ideal input/output characteristics and simple transfer functions. For example, Figure 30.1 shows an E device (a VCVS) used as a simple voltage amplifier with a gain of 10.

By generating various time- and frequency-domain test curves, such as those in Figure 30.2, we find that the E device is a perfect voltage amplifier, with a gain of exactly 10, infinite Z_{IN}, zero Z_{OUT}, infinite bandwidth, and zero harmonic distortion, and it is totally noiseless.

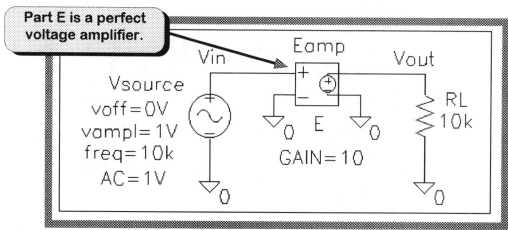

FIGURE 30.1

The E device as a
voltage amplifier

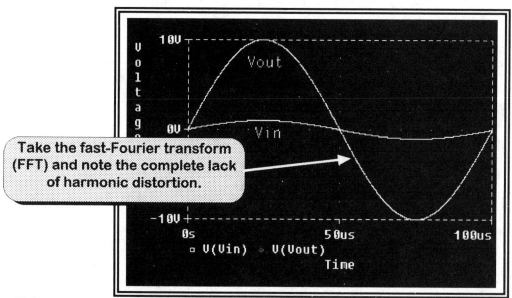

FIGURE 30.2

E device V$_{IN}$ and
V$_{OUT}$ waveforms

BEHAVIORAL MODELING EXTENSIONS

Because the simple E, F, G, and H devices are so perfect, they are not always appropriate in a real-world environment. For this reason, PSpice also offers special extended versions of the E and G devices that provide *analog behavioral modeling.*

Analog behavioral modeling allows the designer to specify complex transfer functions that more closely represent actual circuit components and systems. For each of these special E and G type controlled sources, we can select from among the following mathematical relationships:

- **Sum (SUM)**
- **Multiply (MULT)**
- **Table (TABLE)**
- **Value (VALUE)**
- **Frequency (FREQ)**
- **Laplace (LAPLACE)**
- **Chebyshev Filters (CHEBYSHEV)**

As an example of the use of these extensions, let's model a single JFET for use in a voltage amplifier. Since a JFET (when properly biased) is a VCIS with a parabolic transfer function, we select the GVALUE model. We specify the transfer function, add a load resistor and bias voltage, and generate the amplifier circuit of Figure 30.3.

When we test the amplifier, it does give the expected results (Figure 30.4).   (Be aware that the JFET's other characteristics, such as Z_{IN}, Z_{OUT}, bandwidth, and noise, are still perfect. However, as expected, it does show a total harmonic distortion of approximately 6%.)

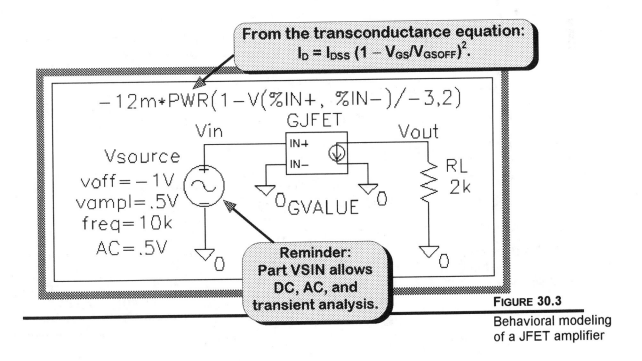

FIGURE 30.3

Behavioral modeling
of a JFET amplifier

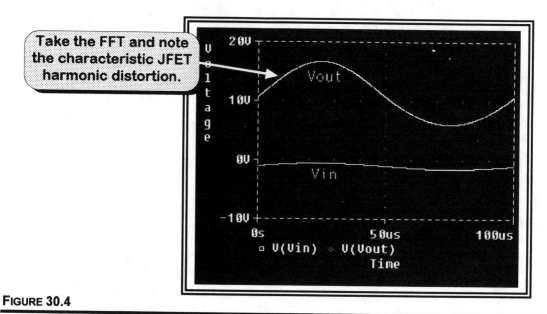

FIGURE 30.4

JFET model
waveforms

FREQUENCY-DOMAIN MODELING

The frequency-domain models (FREQ and LAPLACE) are considerably more complex because the output is not instantaneous with each input value, but depends on the input characteristics over time (such as its frequency).

To model a filter, such as the simple passive low-pass filter of Figure 30.5, we first calculate several of its characteristics:

- **Fbreak = 1/(2πRC) = 159.15Hz ≈ 160Hz**

- **A(low frequency) = 0dB   Rolloff = 20dB/dec**

- **Phase = atan(X_C/R)**

We then use these characteristics to form a look-up table to describe the frequency response and to program the device.

Frequency	A(dB)	Phase
100	0	0
160	–3	–45
1.6k	–20	–84
16k	–40	–89
160k	–60	–90

This means 0Hz to 100Hz.

More values can be used when greater resolution is desired.

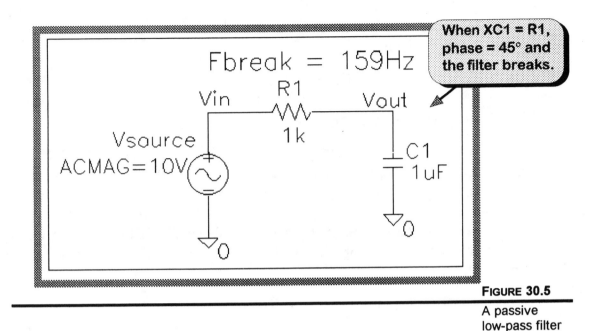

FIGURE 30.5

A passive
low-pass filter

During our *simulation practice*, we re-create the circuits of Figures 30.1, 30.3, and 30.5 and verify that they have the expected properties.

SIMULATION PRACTICE

The VCVS Device

1. Draw the VCVS amplifier of Figure 30.1 and set the attributes as shown.   (Note: The E, F, G, and H controlled source devices are found in library *analog.slb*.   **DCLICKL** on the E device to set gain.)

2. Using conventional techniques from this and previous chapters, generate the curves of Figure 30.2. By examining the results of these curves, *and others as needed*, determine each of the following:

A = _____	BW = _____
Z_{IN} = _____	HD = _____
Z_{OUT} = _____	ONOISE = _____

3. Based on the results of step 2, does the E device have perfect VCVS characteristics?

    Yes   **No**

Behavioral Modeling

4. Draw the amplifier circuit of Figure 30.3 and set all the attributes as shown—except the transfer function. (The GVALUE VCIS device is in library *abm.slb*.)

5. To set the VCIS characteristics of device GJFET, we review Chapter 20 and obtain the transconductance characteristics for a JFET.

    $$I_D = I_{DSS}(1 - V_{GS}/V_{GSoff})^2$$

    Also from Chapter 20, we find that device J2N3819 has the characteristics: $I_{DSS} = 12mA$ and $V_{GSoff} = -3V$.

    $$I_D = 12mA(1 - V_{GS}/-3)^2$$

6. **DCLICKL** on the GJFET device to bring up its *Part Name* dialog box and enter the following in the *value* box for name EXPR (expression):

    $-12m*PWR(1 - V(\%IN+,\%IN-)/-3,2)$.

    where *V(%IN+,%IN−)* refers to the voltage between the two input nodes. (The minus sign is required to simulate the $180°$ phase shift.)

7. Set up the system for transient and DFT Fourier analysis (10k center frequency, 3 harmonics, and output *V(Vout)*). Run PSpice and generate the input/output curves of Figure 30.4. What is the approximate (average) gain of the amplifier?

    A = _____

8. Locate the Fourier section of the output file and record the total harmonic distortion.

    HD = _____

9. Using the DC sweep mode, generate the transconductance curve of Figure 30.6 and compare it to those of Chapter 20. Does the curve match the equations of step 5?

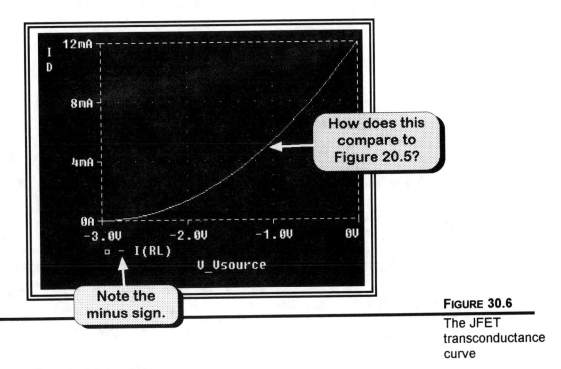

FIGURE 30.6

The JFET transconductance curve

Advanced Activities

10. To model the low-pass filter of Figure 30.5, draw the circuit of Figure 30.7—which uses the EFREQ device (from library *abm.slb*).

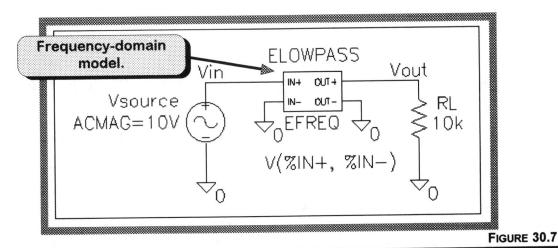

FIGURE 30.7

Modeling a low-pass filter

PSpice for Windows

11. Bring up the *Part Name* dialog box for part EFREQ (**DCLICKL** on part), **CLICKL** on *TABLE*, and enter the following in the *Value* box (see the discussion for an explanation of these values):

(100,0,0)(160,–3, –45)(1.6k, –20, –84)(16k, –40, –89)(160k, –60, –90)

12. Perform an AC sweep and generate the Bode and phase plots of Figure 30.8. Does the device reasonably model a low-pass filter?

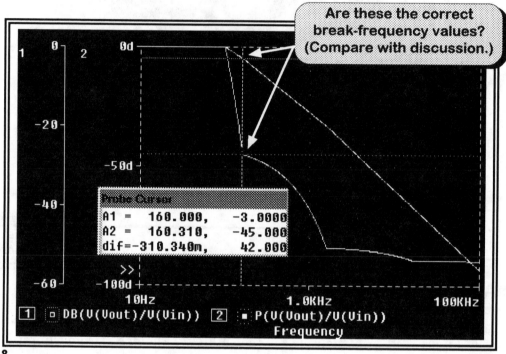

FIGURE 30.8

Bode plot of modeled
low-pass filter

13. Using part VPULSE, enter a square wave of approximately 100Hz (PER = 10ms) into the low-pass filter model of Figure 30.7 and perform a transient analysis. Are the results as expected?

> Because the circuit of Figure 30.7 includes no storage devices (such as capacitors), the time steps are determined by *Print Step*. Set *Print Step* to *Final Time*/100.

Generate an FFT for both the input and output waveforms. Does the filter greatly reduce the harmonic content of the input waveform?

EXERCISES

- Design and test a behavioral model for the tank circuit of Chapter 5. (<u>Hint</u>: Use a table.)

- Design and test a behavioral model that converts a graph of distance versus time to velocity. (<u>Hint</u>: Use part DIFFER.)

- Design and test a *compander* (a logarithmic amplifier found in telephone circuits). (<u>Hint</u>: Use part LOG10.)

QUESTIONS AND PROBLEMS

1. What are the major characteristics of a VCVS controlled source (E device)? Of an ICIS controlled source (F device)?

2. What is the relationship between input and output of the GMULT device?

3. Why should the output JFET waveform of Figure 30.4 show harmonic distortion?

4. Why is frequency-domain analysis (using a FREQ device) referred to as *noninstantaneous*?

5. Based on the E- and G Value devices studied in this chapter, would you expect the EFREQ device of Figure 30.7 to also have perfect Z_{IN} and Z_{OUT} characteristics (infinity and zero)?

CHAPTER 31

Modular Design
Hierarchy

OBJECTIVES

- To demonstrate the concept of *top-down* design.
- To create a circuit composed of levels of hierarchy.

DISCUSSION

The one word that separates today's circuits from those of the past is *complexity*. Clearly, new techniques must be used when we move from a small-scale circuit of 20 components to a large-scale circuit of thousands of components.

The solution to working in any complex environment is *top-down* design. The key element in top-down design is *modularization*, in which a large-scale, complex task is broken down into a hierarchy of modules, from the general and conceptual at the top, to the specific and detailed at the bottom.

Modularizing a program into a hierarchy of modules yields a number of benefits:

- We can focus our attention on one module at a time, without being hindered by the complexities of the entire circuit.

- Our initial design is from a high-level perspective, in which concepts are important and low-level details can be ignored.

- We are encouraged to create customized low-level tools that can be stored in a library and used over and over (so we don't spend our time "reinventing the wheel").

The major components of top-down design are *blocks, hierarchical parts, view*s, and *primitive parts.* A block is a rectangular "black box" that represents a collection of circuitry, a hierarchical part is a nested block within another block, a view allows a block to have more than one solution, and a primitive part is at the lowest nesting level and contains only circuit elements.

In this chapter, we design an amplifier using the techniques of top-down design.

SIMULATION PRACTICE

1. Beginning at the top, draw the design of Figure 31.1, and save the circuit to the suggested file name *top*. As shown, all we know at this time is that there is a source, a load, and a DC power supply—the amplifier itself is just a block.

Draw block

> The block is created by **CLICKL** on the *Draws a new block* toolbar button (or **Draw Block**). To change the size of the block, hold the shift key down, **CLICKRH** (click right and hold), and drag the sides of the block to the desired shape. When wires are drawn to the edges of the block, the pin numbers appear automatically *in the numerical order in which they are drawn*.

2. Because pin numbers (P1, P2, etc.) are not very descriptive, **CLICKL** on P1 to bring up the *Change pin* dialog box and enter *VIN* in the *Pin name* box (overwriting P1), **OK**. Repeat for P2, P3, and P4 to generate the new top-level design of Figure 31.2.

3. Next, we must *push* inside the top-level block to create the middle-level design. To accomplish this: **CLICKL** to select the block, **Navigate, Push** (or **DCLICKL** within the block) to bring up the *Setup Block* dialog box, enter the suggested file name *middle*, **OK**.

> Note the automatic appearance of the four *interface ports*, whose names correspond to the *top* block. Those corresponding to the right-hand side of a block are output ports (IF_OUT); those corresponding to the left, bottom, and top are input ports (IF_IN).

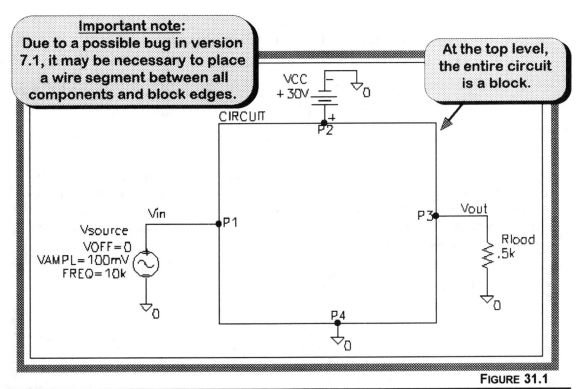

FIGURE 31.1

The top-level design

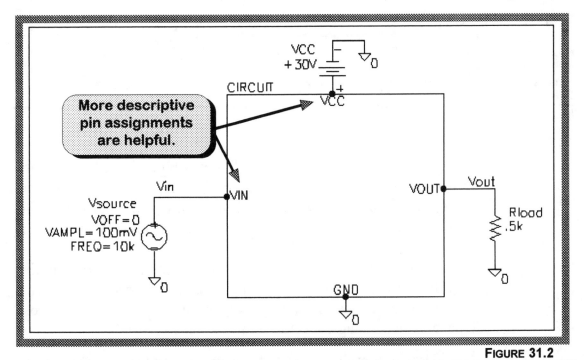

FIGURE 31.2

More descriptive pin assignments

4. We are now faced with a crucial design question: What overall circuitry do we need to create an amplifier? Because of the small value of the load (500Ω), we select a two-stage amplifier/buffer.

Using the interface ports, create the midlevel design of Figure 31.3. (Remember, **DCLICKL** on any attribute to change.)

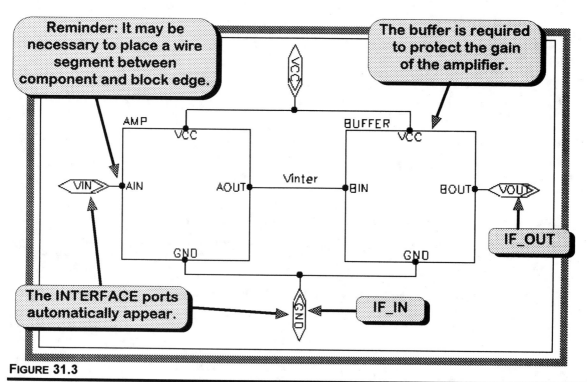

FIGURE 31.3

Midlevel design

5. Next, we must *push* into each middle-level block in order to create low-level circuitry. We start with the amplifier block: select, **Navigate**, **Push** (or **DCLICKL** within block *AMP*), and enter the suggested file name *lowamp* in the *Setup* dialog box, **OK**.

6. We are now at the lowest level, and it is time to design the amplifier. Because we require high gain, and because we can tolerate some degree of harmonic distortion, we choose a low-cost bipolar design, using collector-feedback biasing.

Draw the *primitive part* of Figure 31.4, again being careful to place the interface ports at the correct locations.

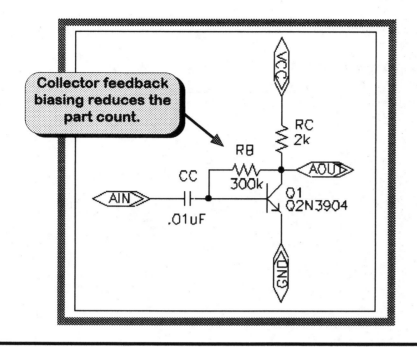

FIGURE 31.4

Primitive part:
Lowamp

7. Return to the middle-level design (**Navigate, Pop,** if necessary Save Changes). (*Navigate pop* returns to the next highest level; *navigate top* returns to the highest level.)

8. The last step is to design the buffer stage. This time, to avoid "reinventing the wheel," we will place a circuit we have already designed into block *BUFFER*. Because our circuit is battery-powered, we choose the highly efficient Class B buffer of Figure 31.5, first introduced in Chapter 19.

9. Select the BUFFER block, **Navigate, Push** to open the *Setup Block* dialog box, and enter the full file name (including directory, if different) of the Class B buffer of Figure 31.5.

    Note: If the Class B buffer of Figure 31.5 is not available, leave the present design, draw the circuit under file name *lowbuf.sch*, and repeat as necessary steps 1 to 9.

10. Modify the circuit to match the single power supply and interface ports—as shown by Figure 31.6. (Obtain *INTERFACE* ports IF_IN and IF_OUT from library *port.slb*.)

PSpice for Windows

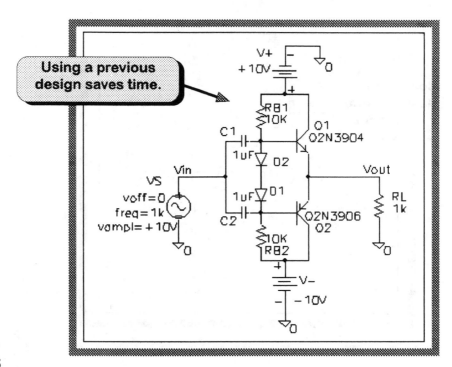

FIGURE 31.5

Previously designed
class B buffer

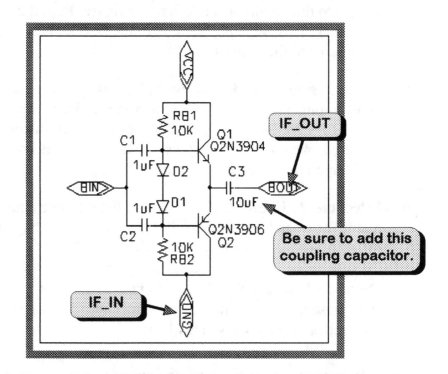

FIGURE 31.6

Previous design
modified for
hierarchical placement

PSpice for Windows

11. Our design is now finished. To test the system, return to the top level (**Navigate**, **Top**), and set up PSpice for a transient analysis from 0 to .2ms (2μs step ceiling).

12. Generate the input/output curves of Figure 31.7. What is the gain of the overall circuit? (Is this reasonable?)

    A = _____

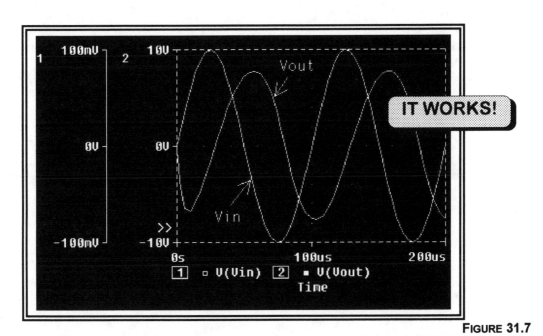

FIGURE 31.7

Circuit waveforms

13. To view any waveform at any hierarchical level, we string together a hierarchical list of block and variable names separated by dots. For example, display the following:

    (a) Voltage node *Vinter* from the middle-level block. (Use trace variable *V(CIRCUIT.Vinter)*).

    (b) The low-level buffer voltage at the emitter of Q2. (Use trace variable *V(CIRCUIT.BUFFER.Q2:e)*).

14. Perform a FFT (fast Fourier transform) on the output waveform. Is the harmonic distortion reasonably low?

    Yes   **No**

Fast Fourier transform

Navigation Path

15. Using PSpice, we have the ability to determine at any time exactly where we are in the hierarchy of modules.

    For example, push into block *BUFFER*, **Navigate**, **Where** to open up the *Where* dialog box. *Current Schematic* shows the current file name level, *Hierarchy Path* lists the sequence of block names that we pushed into, and *Levels Pushed Into* lists the same path in terms of file names.

Advanced Activities (Views)

16. During the design of a complex circuit, it is often desirable to give certain blocks alternative solutions, called *views*.

    For example, we may wish to assign block *BUFFER* a temporary solution while we complete the rest of the design. An ideal temporary solution is a *controlled source* from Chapter 30.

    To create this second view, navigate to the middle-level circuit (Figure 31.3).

17. Select block *BUFFER,* **Edit**, **Views** to bring up the Block *BUFFER* dialog box, enter any desired *View Name* (such as *alternate*) and *Schematic Name* (such as *VCVS*), **Save View**, **OK**.

18. Block *BUFFER* now has two views (*alternate* and *default*). To create the schematic circuit for view *alternate*, select *BUFFER*, **Navigate**, **Push** to bring up the *Select View* dialog box, **CLICKL** on *alternate=VCVS* to select this view, **OK**, and bring up the schematic block with the expected four interface ports.

19. Draw the circuit of Figure 31.8 and set the attributes as shown. Controlled source *E* is from library *analog.slb*. (Note that interface port VCC must be grounded through a resistor.)

20. The second view for *BUFFER* is finished, so we return to the middle level (**Navigate**, **Pop** and save current changes).

> To see the views available within any block, select the block, **Edit**, **Views**, note the listed views, **Cancel** when done.

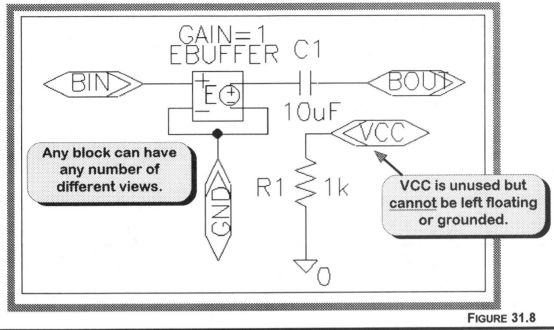

FIGURE 31.8

Alternative
view (VCVS)

21. To show how the circuit designer can bring up either view of block *BUFFER* during schematic design, push into *BUFFER* and select either *lowbuf* (the default view) or *VCVS* (the alternate name).

22. To command PSpice to select view *alternate* <u>during netlisting</u>: **Options**, **Translators**, select PSpice (under *Translator*), enter *alternate* (under *View*), **Apply**, **OK**.

23. Return to the top level (**Navigate**, **Top**) and Run PSpice.

24. Display the input and output of block *BUFFER* (*V(CIRCUIT.BUFFER:BIN)* and *V(CIRCUIT.BUFFER:BOUT)*). Are these the waveforms you would expect from a perfect buffer? (<u>Hint</u>: Except for any offset difference, are the two waveforms the same amplitude and shape?)

      Yes   **No**

> Remember, if you wish to include a particular view <u>during netlisting</u>, be sure to perform step 22. For example, to return to the default view of module BUFFER, enter *default* under *View*.

EXERCISES

- Design the power supply of Chapter 11 using the techniques of hierarchy.

- Design a three-stage audio amplifier (FET input, bipolar middle, Class B output) using the techniques of hierarchy. (Hint: See Figure 22.5.)

QUESTIONS AND PROBLEMS

1. When using top-down design, what kinds of modules are at the top and what kind are at the bottom?

2. What are the advantages of modularization?

3. What is the difference between a *hierarchical part* and a *primitive part*?

4. With PSpice, how many levels of hierarchy are possible?

5. To go from a higher level module to a lower level module, we

    (a) push.
    (b) pop.

6. What is displayed by **Navigate**, **Where**?

7. Can more that one circuit belong to a given module?   (<u>Hint</u>: What is a view?)

CHAPTER 32

Optimization
Goals, Parameters, and Constraints

OBJECTIVE

- To use optimization in the design of various circuits.

DISCUSSION

Suppose you set out to design a house. Chances are you would have various *goals* in mind (such as the size of the house), *parameters* that you can vary to help meet your goals (such as the choice of materials), and *constraints* that limit your options (such as cost).

The same is true when designing an electronic circuit; we have goals to set, parameters to vary, and constraints to meet.

To ease us into the optimization process, our first circuit will be one we have seen before: the class A amplifier of Figure 32.1. Our design objective is to select the value of RE that will give us a voltage gain of exactly 3.1, but with an input impedance of at least 425Ω.

Using official optimization language, this reduces to:

Goal	Gain = 3.1
Parameter	RE
Constraint	$Z_{IN} > 425\Omega$

Normally, a typical circuit design project would involve <u>numerous</u> goals, parameters, and constraints. However, as listed above, the evaluation version allows only a single instance of each.

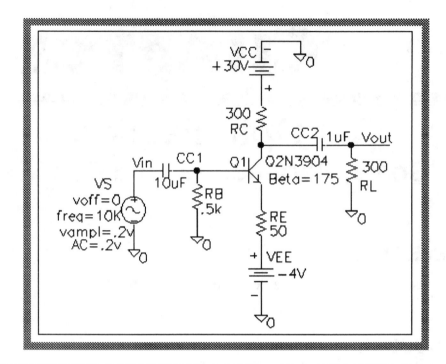

FIGURE 32.1

Class A amplifier

SIMULATION PRACTICE

1. Draw the amplifier circuit of Figure 32.1, set the attributes as shown, and store in suggested file name *amp.sch*.

Step 1: Identify a parameter to vary

We begin by identifying variable *RE* as the component that the optimizer will vary in order to meet the goal. We carry out this step first because it is performed from *Schematics*.

2. To make *RE* a variable, change *50* (ohms) to *{RVAL}*.

3. To define *RE* as a parameter, place special component *OPTPARAM* (from *special.slb*) at any convenient location on the schematic. **DCLICKL** on *OPTIMIZER PARAMETERS* to bring up the *Optimizer Parameters* dialog box of Figure 32.2, and fill in as shown, **Add Param**, **OK**.

   After steps 2 and 3 your schematic should look like Figure 32.3.

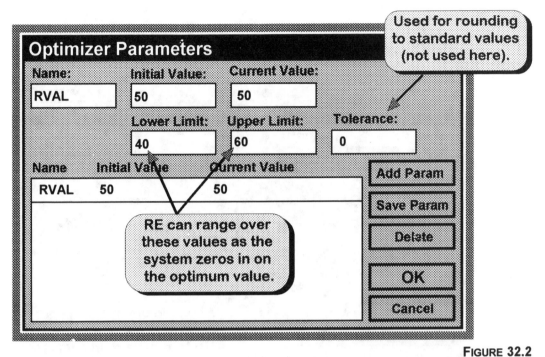

FIGURE 32.2

The *Optimizer Parameters* dialog box

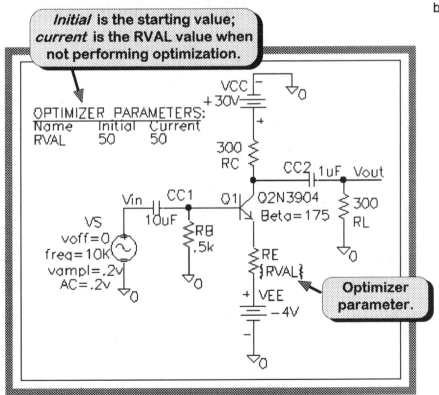

FIGURE 32.3

Defining *RE*

4. Enter the optimizer process with **Tools**, **Run optimizer** to bring up the *Optimizer* window of Figure 32.4.

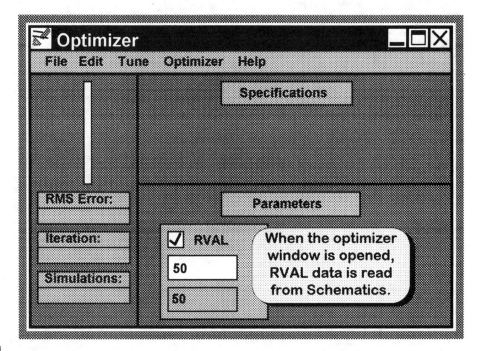

FIGURE 32.4
The optimizer window

Step 2: Identify a goal

As shown in Figure 32.4, the parameter (*RVAL*) is now fully specified. We next set the *goal* specification for a voltage gain of 3.1.

5. To set our goal, **Edit**, **Specifications** to bring up the *Specifications* dialog box. **Add**, to bring up the *Edit Specification* dialog box of Figure 32.5, and fill in as shown.

    *   *Name* is the name of the specification.

    *   *Enabled* is checked to enable the process.

    *   *Internal* means the target value and range are defined in this dialog box. (*External* means these values are defined in an external file, and the *External* boxes would be filled in.)

    *   *Weight* assigns relative weight values when using multiple specifications. (Since we are allowed only one goal specification, we always default to 1.)

- *Target* is the desired design goal (a gain of 3.1).

- *Range* tells us how close we can come to target and still meet the goal. (A range of .001 means the gain can be 3.1 ± .001.)

- *Circuit file* is the name Schematics file. (We choose *amp.sch.*)

- *Probe File* is not required when using global goal functions.

- *Evaluate* tells the optimizer how to compute the goal values. (*max(V(vout))/.2* will return the voltage gain.)

- *AC, DC,* or *Tran* defines the type of analysis to be performed during optimization. (We will perform a transient analysis.)

- Constraint is not used by a goal specification and is left disabled.

OK, **Close** and note the *Gain* block in the *specifications* section. (Leave the *Optimizer* window open.)

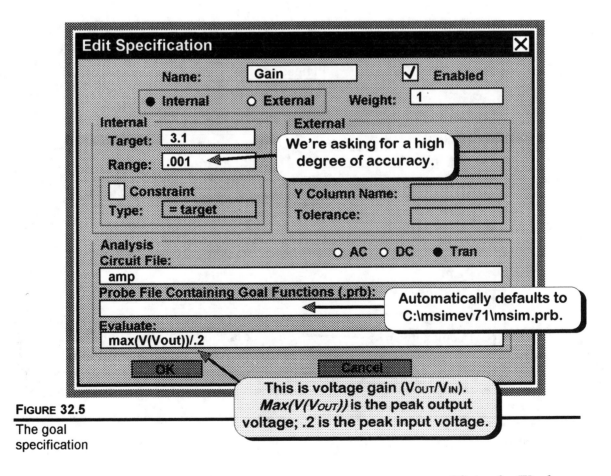

FIGURE 32.5

The goal specification

Step 3: Identify a constraint

The parameter and goal are now set (*RE* and *gain*). The third and final step is to identify a *constraint*. In our case, we wish to have the maximum input impedance greater than or equal to 425Ω.

6. To set this constraint: **Edit**, **Specifications** to again bring up the *Specifications* dialog box. **Add**, to bring up the *Edit Specification* dialog box of Figure 32.6, and fill in as shown.

        To fill in the *Constraint* box:

- **CLICKL** to enable constraint.

- **CLICKL** within the *Type* dialog box to open. Since our constraint is 425Ω or greater, we select *>=target*.

        OK, **Close** and note the *Impedance* box in the *specifications* section of the *Optimizer* window. The constraint ($Z_{IN} >= 425-1\Omega$) is now set. (Be sure to leave the *Optimizer* window open.)

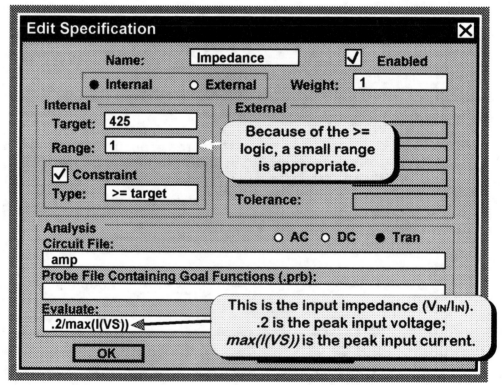

FIGURE 32.6

The constraint
specification

Specify the optimization type

7. We have now set our parameter, goal, and constraint (RE, *gain*, and Z_{IN}). Next, we specify the optimization type by: **Options**, **Defaults** to bring up the *Options* dialog box of Figure 32.7 and fill in as shown, **OK**.

   - *Delta* tells the optimizer the size of the incremental steps when varying RE.

   - *Max Iterations* tells the optimizer the maximum number of calculations to make as it zeros in on the target value.

   - *Probe File* and *Display* are typically left blank. (These are used only if we wish to load a saved display.) *Advanced Options* are also not used.

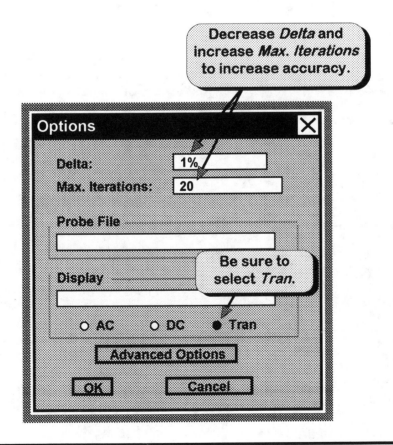

FIGURE 32.7

Options dialog box

Set up the analysis mode

8. The goals and constraints of this example require a series of Transient sweeps while the system varies resistor *RE*. Therefore, leaving the *Optimizer* window open, bring back the *Schematics* window (Alt/Tab) and enable a transient *sweep* to .2ms with a *Step Ceiling* of .001ms.

    > Note: Do not set up a parametric sweep of *RE*; the optimizer will do that automatically.

Performing the optimization

9. To start the optimization process, re-enter the *Optimizer* window, **Tune**, **Auto**, **Start**.

10. If there are no errors, the system will zero in on the goal value and generate the results of Figure 32.8.

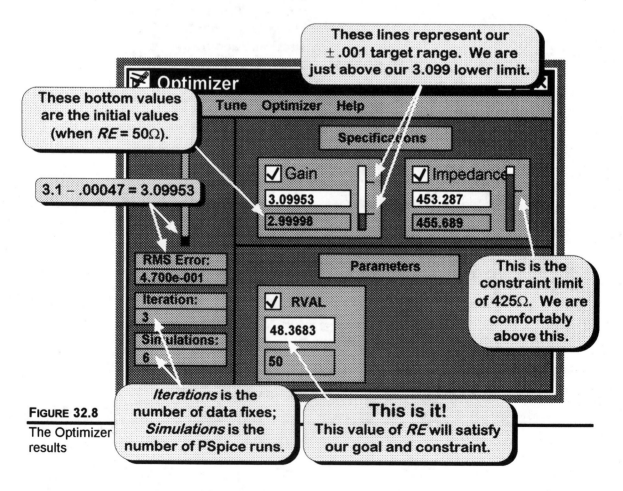

FIGURE 32.8

The Optimizer results

11. Refer to the result:

(a) What value of *RE* did the system compute? _____

(b) What value of Z_{IN} resulted? _____ Was it above the constraint of 425Ω?

      Yes   **No**

(c) What was the RMS error between the goal and the optimized voltage gain? _____

(d) Did we achieve our goal in fewer than 20 iterations?

      Yes   **No**

12. Exit the *optimizer* window, assign the value of *RE* generated by the optimizer (step 11a) to the amplifier circuit of Figure 32.1, and run a transient analysis.

(a) Is the voltage gain very close to 3.09953?

      Yes   **No**

(b) Is Z_{IN} very close to 453.287Ω?

      Yes   **No**

Advanced Activities

13. Increase the Z_{IN} constraint value from 425Ω to 500Ω, re-optimize the circuit, and explain the results.

EXERCISES

- In Chapter 29, we used performance analysis to determine the value of *Rshock* that would give a negative bounce of -1.2265. Repeat the process using optimization.

- Use optimization to design the tank circuit of Chapter 5 to have a bandwidth of exactly 4k. The peak impedance must also be greater than 60dB.

QUESTIONS AND PROBLEMS

1. If our goal is to climb K2 (the second highest mountain in the world), name a possible parameter to vary and a constraint to obey.

2. What is a parameter?

3. What does it mean when the impedance *target* of this chapter is 425Ω and the *range* is 1Ω?

4. Does an unreacheable constraint prevent the system from reaching its goal? (Hint: See step 13.)

5. During the optimization process, the system makes use of derivatives—such as those shown below. Why does the system use such derivatives?

    d(gain)/d(RE)   **d(max Z)/d(RE)**

PART VII
Analog Communications

In the single chapter of Part VII, we concentrate on analog communications.

Historically, the first form of analog communications was called *amplitude modulation*—the subject of Chapter 33. We will find that the processes of *modulation* and *detection* can be performed by the quite ordinary components and circuits introduced in previous chapters.

CHAPTER 33

Amplitude Modulation
Detection

OBJECTIVES

- To generate an amplitude-modulated (AM) signal.
- To detect an AM signal.

DISCUSSION

An electromagnetic wave is generated whenever an electron is accelerated. However, transmission of electromagnetic waves through the atmosphere is efficient only at frequencies well above audio. This fact led to the concept of a low-frequency information-carrying signal *modulating* a high-frequency *carrier*. The first form of modulation was *amplitude modulation*.

AMPLITUDE MODULATION

A signal is amplitude modulated when a low-frequency information signal controls the amplitude of a high-frequency carrier. A bipolar transistor can be used to modulate a signal because its gain depends on bias current (A = rl/re' and re' $\cong$ 25mV/I_{EQ}).

The term *percent modulation* is a measure of the strength of the modulating signal. It is defined as follows:

$$\% \text{ Modulation} = \frac{\text{Maximum gain - Minimum gain}}{\text{Nominal gain (no modulation signal)}} \times 100$$

Linear versus nonlinear

When the modulation circuit is nonlinear, the resulting modulated signal contains *sidebands* equal to all multiples of the sum and difference of the carrier and modulation signals. A Fourier analysis of the output signal will reveal these information-carrying frequency components.

When the modulated signal is received, it must be *demodulated* (the information signal must be extracted from the carrier). The simplest demodulator (detector) is a peak rectifier. The RC time constant must be short compared with the modulating period, but long compared to the carrier period.

SIMULATION PRACTICE

1. Draw the modulation circuit of Figure 33.1. (<u>Note</u>: A lower-than-normal 100kHz carrier frequency is used to shorten computation times.)

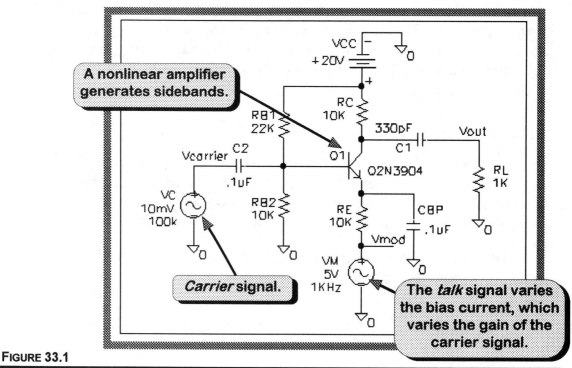

FIGURE 33.1

Amplitude modulation
circuit

2. Generate the output waveforms of Figure 33.2 for the modulation and no-modulation modes. For the modulated case, what is the percent modulation?

    Percent modulation = _____

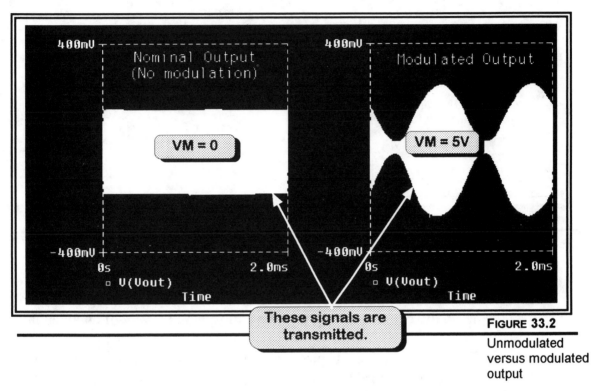

FIGURE 33.2

Unmodulated versus modulated output

3. Reduce the audio input amplitude (V_M) to 2V, generate V_{OUT}, and determine the reduced percent modulation. (When done, return V_M to 5V.)

    Percent modulation ($V_M = 2V$) = _____

Demodulation (Detection)

4. Add the amplifier/detector to your modulation circuit (Figure 33.3).

5. If the circuit works as expected, what should be the shape and frequency of the output signal ($V_{RECEIVE}$)?

    Expected shape (sine wave?) = _____

    Expected frequency = _____

PSpice for Windows

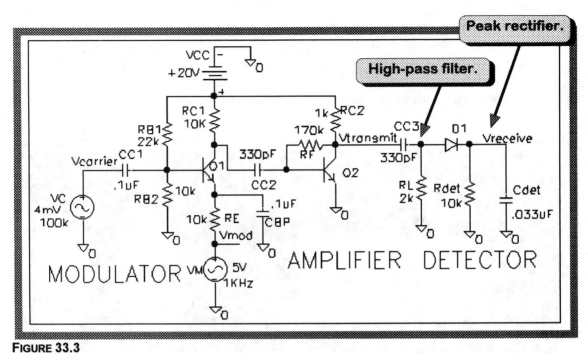

FIGURE 33.3

Adding AM detection

6. Place an arrow at the point in the circuit where the signal would normally be transmitting into the atmosphere by way of an antenna.

7. Create the transient plots of Figure 33.4, which compare the modulation, carrier, transmit, and receive waveforms. Does $V_{RECEIVE}$ have approximately the expected shape and frequency?

   Yes   No

Fourier Analysis

Fast Fourier

8. Use FFT (fast Fourier transform) analysis on the time-domain curves of Figure 33.4 (and expand the X-axis) to generate the frequency spectrum plots of Figure 33.5.

9. The default frequency spectrum waveforms of Figure 33.5 are hard to see because X-axis ranges are inconsistent. To solve the problem, generate the plots of Figure 33.6, which use a combination of multiple Y-axes, multiple plots, unsynced X-axes, and user-defined X- and Y-axes settings.

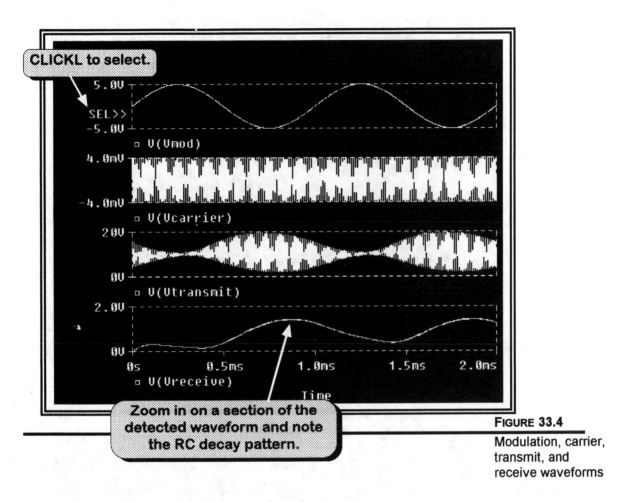

FIGURE 33.4

Modulation, carrier, transmit, and receive waveforms

10. Based on Figure 33.6, list here the <u>significant</u> transmitted sideband frequencies. How do the frequencies relate to the modulation frequency?

f (lower sidebands) = _____

f (upper sidebands) = _____

11. Is the only <u>major</u> difference between V_{MOD} and $V_{RECEIVE}$ the presence of a DC component in $V_{receive}$?

Yes   No

Advanced Activities

12. By examining waveforms before and after capacitor CC2 (Figure 33.3), what is the purpose of CC2? (<u>Hint</u>: What happened to the 1kHz modulation signal?)

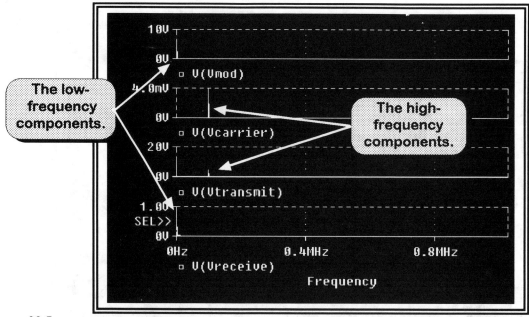

FIGURE 33.5

Frequency spectrum
waveforms

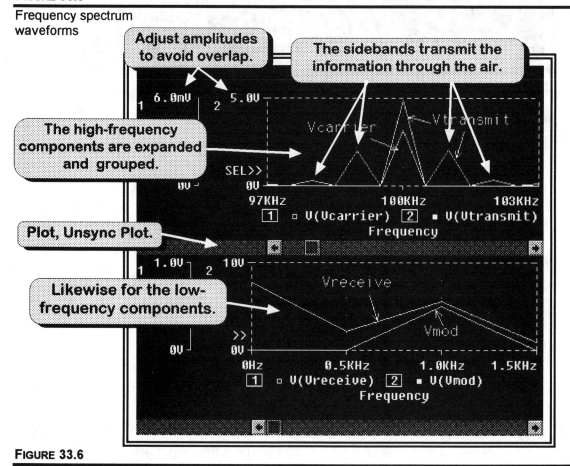

FIGURE 33.6

Reformatted waveforms

PSpice for Windows

13. Reduce the percent modulation (Figure 33.3) and compare the resulting frequency spectrum waveform set with Figure 33.6. Explain the difference.

14. Modulate the system with a square wave and compare the frequency spectrum of the input and output. What does the result say about the harmonic content of a square wave and the ability of the circuit to process high modulation frequencies?

15. Modulate the system with a *damped* sine wave and view the results in the time domain.

EXERCISE

- Design an AM modulation and detection system that matches a specific station within the AM band (such as 740kHz).

QUESTIONS AND PROBLEMS

1. Which of the following circuit elements is responsible for the gain variation during amplitude modulation?

   (a) RL
   (b) C1
   (c) re'
   (d) VCC

2. Capacitor CBP is designed to short which of the following signals to ground?

   (a) Vcarrier
   (b) Vmodulation

3. Why must the key element of a modulation circuit (such as the bipolar transistor of Figure 33.1) be a *nonlinear* device?

4.   What is the purpose of the *carrier* signal?

5.   What is the difference between a *detector* and a *peak rectifier*?

6.   For a real broadcast, why would the Fourier spectrum of the transmitted signal likely be a continuum?

APPENDIX A

Notes

Schematics

PSpice

Probe

2.1   How do I enter custom Y-axis variables?
2.2   How do I print my circuit, graph, or output file?
3.1   How do I use the cursor?
3.2   How do I create multiple Y-axes?
4.1   What special markers are available to plot advanced waveforms?
4.2   How do I open up multiple windows under Probe?
5.1   How do I place legend symbols on the curves?
6.1   How do I expand or compress waveforms?
7.1   How do I mark coordinate values on my graphs?
7.2   How do I generate multiple plots within a single Probe window?
7.3   How do I label the Y-axis?
9.1   How do I single out individual curves from a family of curves?
10.1   How do I change the X-axis variable?

APPENDIX B
Probe

Probe Function	Description
( )	Grouping
-	Logical complement
*/	Multiply/divide
+−	Add/subtract
&^|	AND, Exclusive OR, OR
AVGX(x,d)	Average (x to d)
RMS(x)	RMS average
DB(x)	x in dB
MIN(x)	Minimum real part of x
MAX(x)	Maximum real part of x
ABS(x)	Absolute value of x
SGN(x)	+1 if x > 0, 0 if x = 0, -1 if x < 0
SQRT(x)	$x^{1/2}$
EXP(x)	e^x
LOG(x)	Ln(x)
LOG10(x)	log(x)
M(x)	Magnitude of x
P(x)	Phase of x (degrees)
R(x)	Real part of x
IMG(x)	Imaginary part of x
G(x)	Group delay of x (sec)
PWR(x,y)	$(x)^y$
SIN(x)	sin(x)
COS(x)	cos(x)
TAN(x)	tan(x)
ATAN(x)	$\tan^{-1}(x)$
d(x)	Derivative of x with X-axis
s(x)	Integral of x with X-axis
AVG(x)	Average of x

Probe Setup

To set up Probe, **Analysis**, **Probe Setup** from *Schematics* to bring up the *Probe Setup* dialog box shown below. The settings shown are the recommended settings for most of the operations in this text.

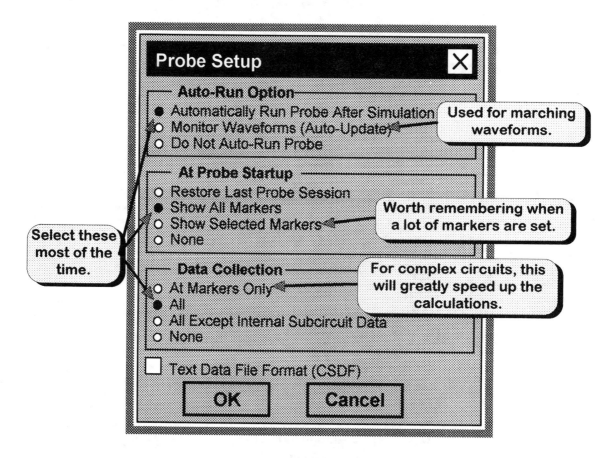

Regarding markers:

- They can be placed on the schematic before analysis, and the curves will automatically appear (providing "show all markers" is set as shown above).

- They can be placed on the schematic after analysis and the Probe graph is initially displayed. **DCLICKL** on any marker to cause its corresponding waveform to be displayed. Move the marker, and the Probe waveform will change accordingly.

To document a Probe graph

If more than one Probe window is open, first **CLICKL** to select the desired window. From the main menu bar on the Probe graph: **Tools**, **Label** to pull down the label menu. Each of the items listed can be used to document your graph:

- **Text** to bring up the *Text Label* dialog box, enter the desired statement, **OK**, **DRAG** to desired location, **CLICKL** to place.

- **Line** to create pencil, **CLICKL** to anchor an endpoint, **DRAG** pencil to draw line, **CLICKL** to anchor second endpoint.

- **PolyLine** to create pencil and use a series of **CLICKL/DRAG** steps to draw a line. **CLICKR** when done.

- **Arrow** to create pencil, **CLICKL** to anchor end of arrow, **DRAG** arrow tip to desired location, **CLICKL** to place.

- **Box** to create pencil, **CLICKL** to anchor corner of box, **DRAG** to create box, **CLICK** to place box.

- **Circle** to create pencil, **CLICKL** to anchor center of circle, **DRAG** to create size of circle, **CLICKL** to place circle.

- **Ellipse** to open up "Ellipse Label" dialog box, enter inclination angle (0 or 90 for up/down inclination; 45 for 45-degree tilt to ellipse), **CLICKL** to anchor center of ellipse, **DRAG** to create ellipse size and shape, **CLICKL** to place ellipse.

- **Mark** to display coordinates of last cursor positioned. (Cursor must first be enabled.)

     Edit, **Delete** to remove any selected (red) labels.

APPENDIX C

Scale Suffixes

Case insensitive; use upper or lower case.

Symbol	Scale	Name
F	10E−15	*femto-*
P	10E−12	*pico-*
N	10E−9	*nano-*
U	10E−6	*micro-*
M	10E−3	*milli-*
K	10E+3	*kilo-*
MEG	10E+6	*mega-*
G	10E+9	*giga-*
T	10E+12	*tera-*

Caution!
Don't confuse
M with MEG.

APPENDIX D

Spec Sheets

D1N750
ZENER DIODE

Rating	Symbol	Value	Unit
DC Power Dissipation at TA <= 50 $^{\circ}$C Derate > 50°C	PD	500 3.3	mW mW/$^{\circ}$C
Operating and Storage Junction Temperature Range	TJ, Tstj	-65 to +200	$^{\circ}$C

Type Number	Nominal Zener Voltage Vz at IZT Volts	Test Current IZT mA	Maximum Zener Z Zzt at Izt Ohms	Maximum Zener Current IZM mA	TA = 25°C IR at VR = 1V uA	TA = 150°C Ir at VR = 1V uA
D1N750	4.7	20	19	75 95	2	30

2N3904/3906
NPN/PNP SILICON SWITCHING AND AMPLIFIER TRANSISTORS

Rating	Symbol	Value	Unit
Collector-Base Voltage	VCB	60	Vdc
Collector-Emitter Voltage	VCEO	40	Vdc
Emitter-Base Voltage	VEB	6.0	Vdc
Collector current	IC	200	mAdc
Total Power Dissipation at TA = 60°C	PD	250	mW
Total Power Dissipation at TA = 25°C	PD	350	mW
Derate above 25°C		2.8	mW/$^{\circ}$C
Total Power Dissipation at TC = 25°C	PD	1.0	mW
Derate above 25°C	PD	8.0	mW/$^{\circ}$C
Junction Operating Temperature	TJ	150	$^{\circ}$C
Storage Temperature Range	Tstg	-55 to +150	$^{\circ}$C
Characteristic	**Symbol**	**Max**	**Unit**
Thermal Resistance, Junction to Ambient	R0jA	357	$^{\circ}$C/W
Thermal Resistance, Junction to Case	R0jC	125	$^{\circ}$C/W

Characteristic	Symbol	Min	Max	Unit
Collector-Base Breakdown Voltage (IC = 10uAdc, IE = 0)	BVcbo	60		Vdc
Collector-Emitter Breakdown Voltage (IC = 1mAdc, IB = 0)	BVceo	60		Vdc
Emitter-Base Breakdown Voltage (IE = 10uAdc, IC = 0)	BVebo	6.0		Vdc
Collector Cutoff Current (VCE = 30 Vdc, VEB(off) = 3.0 Vdc)	Icex		50	nAdc
Base Cutoff Current (VCE = 30 Vdc, VEB(off) = 3.0 Vdc)	Ibl		50	nAdc
DC Current Gain (IC = 0.1 mAdc, VCE = 1.0 Vdc) (IC = 1.0 mAdc, VCE = 1.0 Vdc) (IC = 10 mAdc, VCE = 1.0 Vdc) (IC = 50 mAdc, VCE = 1.0 Vdc) (IC = 100 mAdc, VCE = 1.0 Vdc)	Hfe	40 70 100 60 30	300	
Collector-Emitter Saturation Voltage (IC = 10 mAdc, IB = 1.0 mAdc) (IC = 50 mAdc, IB = 5.0 mAdc)	VCE(sat)		.2 .3	Vdc
Base-Emitter Saturation Voltage (IC = 10 mAdc, IB = 1.0 mAdc) (IC = 50 mAdc, IB = 5.0 mAdc)	VBE(sat)	.65	.85 .95	Vdc

2N5484-5486 (Similar to 2N3819)
JFET
Maximum Ratings

Rating	Symbol	Value	Units
Drain-Gate Voltage	VDG	25	Vdc
Reverse Gate-Source Voltage	VGSR	25	Vdc
Drain Current	ID	30	mAdc
Forward Gate Current	IG(f)	10	mAdc
Total Device Dissipation at TC = 25°C Derate above 25°C	PD	310 2.82	mW mW/^{O}C
Operating and Storage Junction Temperature Range	Tj, Tstg	−65 to +150	^{O}C

ELECTRICAL CHARACTERISTICS

Characteristic	Symbol	Min	Typ	Max	Unit
Gate-Source Breakdown Voltage (IG = −1.0uAdc, VDS = 0)	V(BR)GSS	−25			Vdc
Gate Reverse Current (VGS = −20 Vdc, VDS = 0)	IGSS			−1.0	μAdc
Gate-Source Cutoff Voltage (VDS = 15Vdc, ID = 10nAdc)	VGS(off)	−.5		−4.0	Vdc
Zero-Gate-Voltage Drain Current (VDS = 15Vdc, ID = 10nAdc)	IDSS	4.0		10	mAdc
Forward Transfer Admittance (VDS = 15Vdc, VGS = 0, f = 1kHz)	Yfs	3500		7000	μmhos
Input Admittance (VDC = 15Vdc, VGS = 0, f = 100 MHz)	Re(Yis)			100	μmhos
Output Admittance (VDS = 15Vdc, VGS = 0, f = 1.0MHz)	Yos			60	μmhos
Output Conductance (VDS = 15Vdc, VGS = 0, f = 100MHz)	Re(Yos)			75	μmhos
Forward Transconductance (VDS = 15Vdc, VGS = 0, f = 100MHz)	Re(Yfs)	3000			μmhos

APPENDIX E

Windows Tutorial

The following conventions are used within the text and this tutorial.

CLICKL or **BOLD PRINT** (*click left once*) to select an item
DCLICKL (*double click left*) to end a mode or edit a selection.
CLICKR (*click right once*) to abort a mode.
DCLICKR (*double click right*) to repeat an action.
CLICKLH (*click left, hold down, and move mouse*) to drag a
selected item.   Release left button when placed.
DRAG (*no clicks, move mouse*) to move an item.

Follow the steps below to review the use of the mouse, and for changing the size
and location of windows, pull down menus, and dialog boxes.

For Windows 3.1 Users

1. Turn on the computer and bring up the *Program Manager* window of Figure
    E.1. (**DCLICKL** on the *Main* icon, if necessary.)

2. **DCLICKL** on the *Schematics* icon to open the *Schematics* window (similar to
    Figure 1.2).

Changing the size and location of a window

All windows are in one of three size modes: *full screen, intermediate variable*, and *icon*.

3. To change the size of the window, **CLICKL** on the size *buttons* at the upper
    right of the window. Experiment with all combinations and possibilities until
    you understand their use.

4. When in the intermediate variable mode, the size of the window can be
    changed. To accomplish this, move the cursor to any corner or edge and
    CLICKLH and **DRAG** to the desired size.

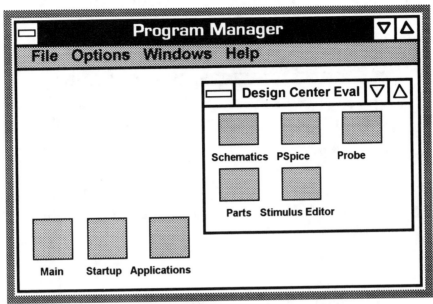

Figure E.1
The Program Manager Window

5. To change the location of the window, **CLICKLH** on the color bar at the top of the window and **DRAG** to desired location.

Entering data into the dialog box

When entering data into any dialog box, follow standard word processing techniques.

6. For example, **CLICKL** on the *Selects a part to draw* toolbar button (or **Draw**, **Get New Part**) to open up the *Part Browser Basic* dialog box.   Enter "r" from the keyboard, **OK**, **CLICKL**, **CLICKR** to place the resistor symbol.

Special Note: When more than one window is open, it is easy for windows to be covered up by other windows.   To bring each window to the forefront in sequence, press ALT-TAB continuously.

For Windows 95 Users

1. Turn on the computer and bring up the initial window of Figure E.2.

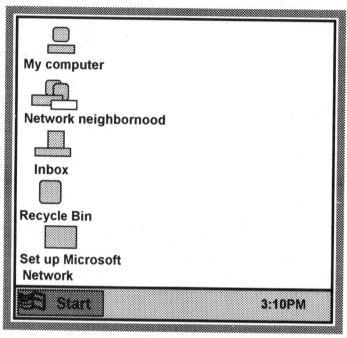

Figure E.2
The Initial Windows 95 Window

2. **CLICKL** on *Start* to bring up the main menu.

3. **DRAG** cursor to *Programs* to bring up the Programs submenu.

4. **DRAG** cursor to the MicroSim71 (or other) to bring up the PSpice menu.

5. **CLICKL** on *Schematics* to bring up the Schematics Window of Figure 1.2.

Changing the size and location of a window

As with Windows 3.1, all windows are in one of three size modes: *full screen, intermediate variable,* and *icon.*

6. To enter these modes, look to the upper right of the Schematics window and note the three boxes (as shown by Figure E.3.)

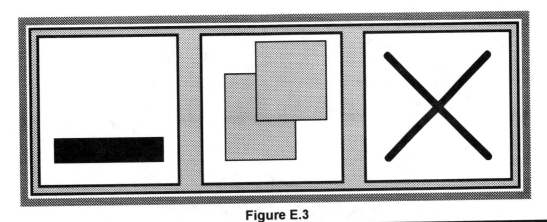

Figure E.3

The Windows 95 Icons

7.   To shrink the window down to icon size mode, **CLICKL** on the left icon. To enter the intermediate changeable mode, **CLICKL** on the middle icon. To exit the window, **CLICKL** on the right icon.

8.   In all other respects, Windows 95 operation is the same as Windows 3.1 operation. (See steps 5 and 6 of the Windows 3.1 section.)

APPENDIX F
Part Search Techniques

Technique 1
We can copy an existing part.

To place a copy of a part that <u>already exists</u> on the schematic: Select the part to copy, **CLICKL** on the *Copies selected item(s) to paste buffer* toolbar button (or **Edit, Copy**), **CLICKL** on the *Pastes item(s) to paste buffer* toolbar button (or **Edit, Paste**), **DRAG** to desired location, **CLICKL, CLICKR**.

Technique 2
We can use the *Previous Part* box

Turn to Figure 1.2 in the text and find the "previous part" box. It contains a list of up to 10 of the last parts placed.

To select one of the parts, **CLICKL** on the arrow box, **CLICKL** on the desired part, **DRAG** to the desired location, **CLICKL** to place, and **CLICKR** to abort.

Technique 3
We can use advanced search techniques

Finally, when techniques 1 and 2 don't apply, we **CLICKL** on the *"Selects a Part to Draw"* toolbar button to open one of the two dialog boxes shown in Figures F.1 and F.2 on the following page (*Part Browser Basic* or *Part Browser Advanced*). <u>Which one opens depends on which one was last used to place a part</u>.

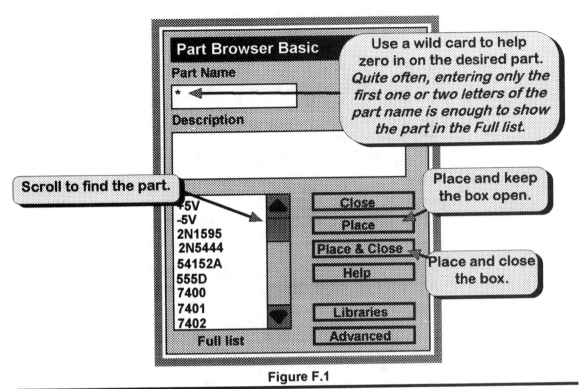

Figure F.1

The *Part Browser Basic* dialog box

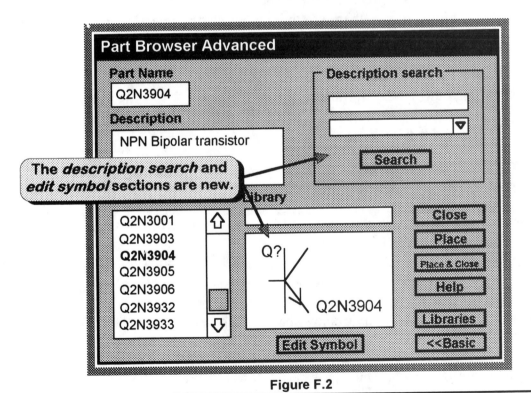

Figure F.2

The *Part Browser Advanced* dialog box

From either one of these dialog boxes, we can open the *Library Browser* dialog box shown in Figure F.3 to further streamline our part search.

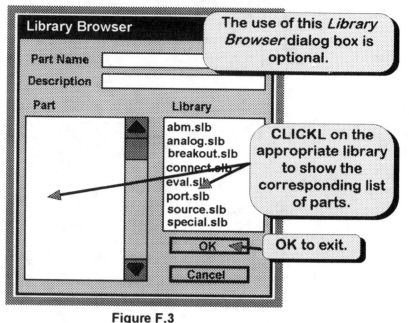

Figure F.3

The *Library Browser* dialog box

Using these three dialog boxes, there are three methods for selecting parts.

- Search for the part by name.
- Search for the part by description.
- Browse through the symbol libraries.

Search for the part by name

1. **CLICKL** on the *Selects a part to draw* toolbar button to display a Part Browser (either *Basic* or *Advanced*).

2. Enter the name directly in the *Part Name* text box, or scroll through the part list and **CLICKL** on the part name.

> Note the "*" (wildcard) symbol in the box. It works like this: Suppose you are seeking a certain bipolar transistor, but you cannot remember its part number. However, you do know that all such devices begin with Q2N. So, you enter Q2N*, press Enter, and all devices that begin with Q2N appear in the list box. The process can be continued any number of times. For example, if you next enter Q2N3* and press Enter, you will further narrow down the list to all devices that begin with Q2N3.

3. **Place** or **Place & Close**, **Drag** to desired location, **CLICKL**, **CLICKR**. (**Close** if necessary.)

Search for the part by description

1. **CLICKL** on the *Selects a part to draw* toolbar button to display a Part Browser (either *Basic* or *Advanced*). If *Basic*, **Advanced**. (It is necessary to be in *Part Browser Advanced* to select a part by description.)

2. Type a description of the part in the *Description Search* text box.

3. Select one of the three available options: *Create New Part List*, *Add to Part List*, or *Search Within Part List*. We recommend *Create New Part List*, which creates a new list consisting of only parts that match the description.

4. **Search**. When done, all parts matching the description are listed in the dialog box.

5. **CLICKL** on the desired part to preview the part symbol.

6. **Place** or **Place & Close**, **Drag** to desired location, **CLICKL**, **CLICKR**. (**Close** if necessary.)

Browse through the symbol libraries

1. **CLICKL** on the *Selects a part to draw* toolbar button to display a Part Browser (either *Basic* or *Advanced*).

2. **Libraries** to display the *Library Browser* dialog box.

3. **CLICKL** on the desired library to display all corresponding parts. Scroll the corresponding list of parts, **CLICKL** on the desired part when found, **OK**, **Drag** to desired location, **CLICKL**, **CLICKR**. (**Close** if necessary.)

APPENDIX G

Schematic Display Options

The Schematics program offers a number of options related to the display and movement of components on the screen.   In most cases, we will accept the default settings, and only occasionally will it be desirable to change them.

To access the *Display Options* dialog box shown in Figure G.1, **Options**, **Display Options** from the *Schematics* window.   The default status is shown.

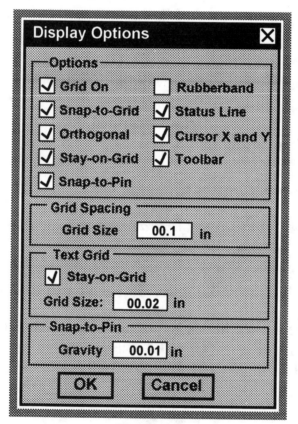

Figure G.1

The *Display Options* dialog box

- *Grid On* displays the background grid on the schematics screen.

- *Snap-to-Grid* causes components to snap to the nearest grid point when placed.

- *Orthogonal* causes the wire and bus lines to be drawn only at right angles.

- *Stay-on-Grid* causes components to stay on the grid lines when moved.

- *Snap-to-Pin* causes the endpoint of a wire or bus to snap to the nearest pin (if inside the radius defined by the Gravity setting).

- *Rubberband* causes wires and bus lines to stretch and remain attached when a component is moved.

- *Status Line* enables the display of the status line at the bottom of the *Schematics* screen.

- *Cursor X and Y* enables the display of the cursor position at the lower left of the schematics display.

- *Toolbar* enables the display of the toolbar buttons at the top of the *Schematics* screen.

- *Grid Spacing* defines the horizontal and vertical grid spacing on the drawing area. Default is .1 inches.

- *Text Grid* sets the grid spacing for text separately from the normal grid spacing.

- *Gravity* specifies how close an object must be to a pin to snap to it.

APPENDIX H
Built-In Goal Functions

The following goal functions are found in global file *msim.prb* in directory *msimeval71,* and are available for instant use when the goal function feature is activated.

*** Goal functions for general use ***

```
Max(1) = y1
*#Desc#* Find the maximum value of the trace.
*#Arg1#* Name of trace to search
   {
     1|Search forward max !1;
   }
```

```
MAXr(1,begin_x,end_x)=y1
*#Desc#* Find the maximum value of the trace within the specified X range.
*#Arg1#* Name of trace to search
*#Arg2#* X range begin value
*#Arg3#* X range end value
   {
     1| search forward (begin_x,end_x) max !1 ;
   }
```

```
Min(1) = y1
*#Desc#* Find the minimum value of the trace.
*#Arg1#* Name of trace to search
   {
     1| search forward min !1;
   }
```

```
MINr(1,begin_x,end_x)=y1
*#Desc#* Find the minimum value of the trace within the specified X range.
*#Arg1#* Name of trace to search
*#Arg2#* X range begin value
*#Arg3#* X range end value
   { .
     1| search forward (begin_x,end_x) min !1 ;
   }
```

```
XatNthY(1,Y_value,n_occur)=x1
*#Desc#* Find the value of X corresponding to the nth occurrence of the
*#Desc#* given Y_value, for the specified trace.
*#Arg1#* Name of trace to search
*#Arg2#* Y value
*#Arg3#* nth occurrence
   {
     1| search forward for n_occur:level (Y_value) !1 ;
   }
```

```
XatNthYn(1,Y_value,n_occur)=x1
*#Desc#* Find the value of X corresponding to the nth negative slope
*#Desc#* crossing of the given Y_value, for the specified trace.
*#Arg1#* Name of trace to search
*#Arg2#* Y value
*#Arg3#* nth occurrence
   {
     1| search forward for n_occur:level (Y_value,negative) !1 ;
   }
```

```
XatNthYp(1,Y_value,n_occur)=x1
*#Desc#* Find the value of X corresponding to the nth positive slope
*#Desc#* crossing of the given Y_value, for the specified trace.
*#Arg1#* Name of trace to search
*#Arg2#* Y value
*#Arg3#* nth occurrence
   {
     1| search forward for n_occur:level (Y_value,positive) !1 ;
   }
```

```
XatNthYpct(1,Y_pct,n_occur)=x1
*#Desc#* Find the value of X corresponding to the nth occurrence of
*#Desc#* the trace crossing the given percentage of its full Y-axis
*#Desc#* range; i.e., nth occurrence of Y=Ymin+(Ymax-Ymin)*Y_pct/100
*#Arg1#* Name of trace to search
*#Arg2#* Y percentage
*#Arg3#* nth occurrence
*
   {
     1| search forward for n_occur:level (Y_pct%) !1 ;
   }
```

```
YatX(1,X_value)=y1
*#Desc#* Find the value of the trace at the given X_value.
*#Arg1#* Name of trace to search
*#Arg2#* X value to get Y value at
* Usage:
*          YatX(<trace name>,<X_value>)
   {
      1| search forward Xvalue (X_value) !1 ;
   }
```

```
YatXpct(1,X_pct)=y1
*#Desc#* Find the value of the trace at the given percentage of the
*#Desc#* X axis range.
*#Arg1#* Name of trace to search
*#Arg2#* X percentage to get Y value at
* Usage:
*          YatXpct(<trace name>,<X_pct>)
   {
      1| search forward Xvalue (X_pct%) !1 ;
   }
```

****
*** Goal Functions for AC Analyses ***
****

```
Bandwidth(1,db_level) = x2-x1
*#Desc#* Find the difference between the X values where the trace
*#Desc#* first crosses its maximum value minus db_level (Ymax-db_level)
*#Desc#* with a positive slope, and then with a negative slope.
*#Desc#* (i.e., find the <db_level> bandwidth of a signal.)
*#Arg1#* Name of trace to search
*#Arg2#* db level down for bandwidth calc
*#ForceDBArg1#*
   {
      1|Search forward level(max-db_level,p) !1
        Search forward level(max-db_level,n) !2;
   }
```

```
LPBW(1,db_level) = x1
*#Desc#* LowPass Cutoff.
*#Desc#* Find the X value at which the trace first crosses its maximum
*#Desc#* value minus db_level with a negative slope.
*#Arg1#* Name of trace to search
*#Arg2#* db level down for measurement
*#ForceDBArg1#*
   {
      1|Search forward level(max-db_level,n) !1;
   }
```

BPBW(1,db_level) = x2-x1
#Desc# BandPass BandWidth. Same as Bandwidth.
#Desc# Find the difference between the X values where the trace
#Desc# first crosses its maximum value minus db_level (Ymax-db_level)
#Desc# with a positive slope, and then with a negative slope.
#Desc# (i.e., find the <db_level> bandwidth of a signal.)
#Arg1# Name of trace to search
#Arg2# db level down for bandwidth calc
#ForceDBArg1#
  {
    1|Search forward level(max-db_level,p) !1
      Search forward level(max-db_level,n) !2;
  }

HPBW(1,db_level) = x1
#Desc# HighPass Cutoff.
#Desc# Find the X value at which the trace first crosses its maximum
#Desc# value minus db_level with a positive slope.
#Arg1# Name of trace to search
#Arg2# db level down for measurement
#ForceDBArg1#
  {
    1|Search forward level(max-db_level,p) !1;
  }

CenterFreq(1, db_level) = (x1+x2)/2
#Desc# Find the midpoint between the X values where the trace first
#Desc# crosses its maximum value minus db_level (Ymax-db_level) with
#Desc# a positive slope, and then with a negative slope.
#Desc# (i.e., find the <db_level> center frequency of a signal.)
#Arg1# Name of trace to search
#Arg2# db level down for measurement
#ForceDBArg1#
  {
    1|Search forward level(max-db_level,p) !1
      Search forward level(max-db_level,n) !2;
  }

GainMargin(1,2) = 0-y2
#Desc# Find the value of the dB magnitude (second) trace at the same
#Desc# X value where the phase (first) trace crosses −180.
#Arg1# phase trace
#Arg2# magnitude trace in dB
* Usage:
*   GainMargin(<phase trace>, <dB magnitude trace>)
  {
* Search for where the phase is −180 degrees
    1|Search forward level (-180) !1;
* Find the magnitude where the phase is −180 degrees
    2|Search forward xval (x1) !2;
  }

PhaseMargin(1,2) = y2+180
#Desc# Find the value of the phase (second) trace at the same X value
#Desc# where the dB magnitude (first) trace crosses 0.
#Arg1# magnitude trace in dB
#Arg2# phase trace
* Usage:
*   PhaseMargin(<dB magnitude trace>, <phase trace>)
  {
* Search for where the magnitude is 0 dB
     1|Search forward level (0) !1;
* Find the phase where the magnitude is 0 dB
     2|Search forward xval (x1) !2;
  }

****
*** Goal Functions for Transient Analyses ***
****

Risetime(1) = x2-x1
#Desc# Find the difference between the X values where the trace first
#Desc# crosses 10% and then 90% of its maximum value with a positive
#Desc# slope.
#Desc# (i.e., find the risetime of a step response curve with no
#Desc# overshoot. If the signal has overshoot, use GenRise().)
#Arg1# Name of trace to search
* Usage:
*   Risetime(<trace name>)
  {
     1|Search forward level(10%, p) !1
       Search forward level(90%, p) !2;
  }

GenRise(1)=x4-x3
#Desc# Find the first and final Y values of the trace. Then find the
#Desc# difference between the X values of the points where the trace
#Desc# first crosses 10% then 90% of the range between its
#Desc# starting and final values with a positive slope.
#Desc# (Find the risetime of a step response curve.)
#Arg1# Name of trace to search
* Usage:
*   GenRise(<trace name>)
  {
     1|Search forward x value (0%) !1
       Search forward x value (100%) !2
       Search forward /Begin/ level (y1+0.1*(y2-y1),p) !3
       Search forward level (y1+0.9*(y2-y1),p) !4;
  }

Falltime(1) = x2-x1
#Desc# Find the difference between the X values where the trace first
#Desc# crosses 90% and then 10% of its maximum value with a negative
#Desc# slope.
#Desc# (i.e., find the falltime of a signal with no overshoot.
#Desc# If the signal has overshoot, use GenFall)
* Usage:
*   Risetime(<trace name>)
  {
    1|Search forward level(90%, n) !1
     Search forward level(10%, n) !2;
  }

GenFall(1)=x4-x3
#Desc# Find the first and final Y values of the trace. Then find the
#Desc# difference between the X values of the points where the trace
#Desc# first crosses 10% then 90% of the range between its starting and
#Desc# final values with a negative slope.
#Desc# (i.e., find the falltime of a negative going step response curve.)
#Arg1# Name of trace to search
* Usage:
*   GenFall(<trace name>)
  {
    1|Search forward x value (0%) !1
        Search forward x value (100%) !2
        Search forward /Begin/ level (y1+0.1*(y2-y1),n) !3
        Search forward level (y1+0.9*(y2-y1),n) !4;
  }

Overshoot(1) = (y1-y2)/y2*100
#Desc# Find the difference between the maximum and final Y values of
#Desc# the trace.
#Desc# (i.e., find the overshoot of a step response curve.)
#Arg1# Name of trace to search
* Usage:
*   Overshoot(<trace name>)
  {
    1|Search forward max !1
     Search forward xval(100%) !2;
  }

Peak(1, n_occur) = y1
#Desc# Find the value of the trace at its nth peak.
#Desc# (A peak is only recognized if 3 data points before it, and 3
#Desc# data points after it have smaller Y values.)
#Arg1# Name of trace to search
#Arg2# Number of peak to find
* Usage:
*   Peak(<trace name>, <n_occur>)
  {
    1|Search forward #3# n_occur:peak !1;
  }

Period(1) = x2-x1
#Desc# Find the difference between the first and second X values at
#Desc# which the trace crosses the midpoint of its Y range with a
#Desc# positive slope.
#Desc# (i.e., find the period of a time domain signal.)
#Arg1# Name of trace to search
* Usage:
*   Period(<trace name>)
  {
    1|Search forward level (50%, p) !1
      Search forward level (50%, p) !2;
  }

Pulsewidth(1) = x2-x1
#Desc# Find the difference between the X values where the trace first
#Desc# crosses the midpoint of its Y range with a positive, then with a
#Desc# negative slope.
#Desc# (i.e., find the width of the first pulse.)
#Arg1# Name of trace to search
  {
    1|Search forward level (50%, p) !1
      Search forward level (50%, n) !2;
  }

SWINGr(1,begin_x,end_x)=y2-y1
#Desc# Find the difference between the maximum and minimum values of
#Desc# the trace within the specified range.
#Arg1# Name of trace to search
#Arg2# Beginning of X range
#Arg3# End of X range
* Usage:
*   SWINGr(<trace name>,<X_range_begin_value>,<X_range_end_value>)
  {
    1| search forward (begin_x,end_x) min !1
       search forward (begin_x,end_x) max !2 ;
  }

TPmW2(1, Period) = (y1-y2)*1000/(x1-x2)
#Desc# Total power dissipation in mW during the final 'Period' of time.
#Desc# Find the difference between the final Y value of the trace and
#Desc# the Y value one period before that.
#Desc# (Can be used to calculate total power dissipation in mW, if the
#Desc# first trace is the integral of V(load)*I(load).)
#Arg1# s(load_voltage * load_current)
#Arg2# Period
* Usage:
*   TPmW2(s(<load_voltage>*<load_current>), <period>)
  {
    1|Search forward xvalue(100%) !1
      Search backward /x1/ xvalue(.-Period) !2;
  }

PSpice for Windows

Index